COMMISSION OF THE EUROPEAN COMMUNITIES

A STUDY OF THE CONCENTRATION, PRICES AND MARK-UPS IN THE DISTRIBUTION OF FOOD PRODUCTS:

VOLUME 1:
General approach and methodology for the analysis of price structures

by Remo LINDA

COLLECTION STUDIES
Evolution of concentration
and Competition Series — no. A24
Brussels, June 1978

A bibliographical slip can be found at the end of this volume

ISBN 92-825-0899-4   Catalogue number: CB-NU-78-A24-EN-C

CONTENTS

THE RESEARCH PROGRAMME: ITS AIMS AND STAGES

CHAPTER ONE

THE FIRST STAGE

INQUIRY INTO PRICES AND MARK-UPS

The aim of the research

There is one introductory question which obviously demands an immediate answer: why set up this extensive and costly research programme?

We might begin by recalling the general objective of the studies the Commission has undertaken since 1970, namely to inform Parliament as well as public opinion, the interests concerned and the Commission itself of the various patterns of development of concentration, competition and prices in the various industries, markets and countries covered by the research.

But is it really necessary to set up such a far-reaching research programme simply to disseminate some fairly straightforward, albeit important economic (and economo-political) information?

The studies clearly have a deeper purpose. We must not lose sight of the instrumental and operative nature of the research programme as it relates to the tasks conferred on the Commission by Articles 85 (restrictive practices) and 86 (abuse of dominant positions) of the Treaty establishing the European Economic Community.

Article 85

1. The following shall be prohibited as incompatible with the common market: all agreements between undertakings, decisions by associations of undertakings and concerted practices which may affect trade between Member States and which have as their object or effect the prevention, restriction or distortion of competition within the common market, and in particular those which:

(a) directly or indirectly fix purchase or selling prices or any other trading conditions;

(b) limit or control production, markets, technical development, or investment;

(c) share markets or sources of supply;

(d) apply dissimilar conditions to equivalent transactions with other trading parties, thereby placing them at a competitive disadvantage;

(e) make the conclusion of contracts subject to acceptance by the other parties of supplementary obligations which, by their nature or according to commercial usage, have no connection with the subject of such contracts.

2. Any agreements or decisions prohibited pursuant to this Article shall be automatically void.

3.   The provisions of paragraph 1 may, however, be declared
inapplicable in the case of:

-     any agreement or category of agreements between under-
      takings;

-     any decision or category of decisions by associations
      of undertakings;

-     any concerned practice or category of concerned practices;

which contributed to improving the production or distribution of
goods or to promoting technical or economic progress, while
allowing consumers a fair share of the resulting benefit, and
      which does not:

(a)   impose on the undertakings concerned restrictions which are
      not indispensable to the attainment of these objectives;

(b)   afford such undertakings the possibility of eliminating
      competition in respect of a substantial part of the products
      in question.

Article 86

Any abuse by one or more undertakings of a dominant position within
the common market or in a substantial part of it shall be prohibited
as incompatible with the common market in so far as it may affect
trade between Member States.

Such abuse may in particular, consist in:

(a)   directly or indirectly imposing unfair purchase or selling
      prices or other unfair trading conditions;

(b)   limiting production, markets or technical development to
      the prejudice of consumers;

(c)   applying dissimilar conditions to equivalent transactions
      with other trading parties, thereby placing them at a
      competitive disadvantage;

(d)   making the conclusion of contracts subject to acceptance
      by the other parties of supplementary obligations which,
      by their nature or according to commercial usage, have
      no connection with the subject of such contracts.

The fundamental importance of prices - both as a market-regulating mechanism and as a basic indicator of the degree of competition actually prevalent on the market - to Europe's economy, is beyond dispute. It follows, then, that the system embodied in Articles 85 and 86 rests heavily on the principle of familiarity with and studies of prices; without this familiarity and without these studies the possibility of giving practical effect to Article 85, and more especially to Article 86, would be seriously compromised from the outset.

Let us at this point quote an important passage from the Introduction to the Commission's Seventh Report of Competition Policy (Brussels/Luxembourg, April 1978, p.10 in the English version):

"Market structure have been a priority concern of competition policy during the year 1977. The work of analysing degree of concentration, competition and price formation has been extended, the object being to highlight the underlying causes of the poor functioning of competition. About a hundred markets have been identified in which the most important undertaking holds more than a half-share. It has also been possible to establish that there is a strong tendency towards concentration in the distribution field and that there are some important price differences for the same product at all levels even on the purely local level.

The Commission has the firm intention of systematically applying Article 86 against undertakings in a dominant position which directly or indirectly impose discriminatory or unfair prices. It is not the Commission's object- ive to set itself up as a price control organization, nor to put an end to price variations which are an essential part of the competitive process, but solely to attack practices which become illegal when they are carried out by undertakings in a dominant position; the reason is the injury which these practices can cause to the user and the consumer.

The Commission considers that the recent Decision in the United Brands case is of great importance for the development of an effective policy regarding the control of abuse of dominant position. The considerations expounded by the Court of Justice have given concrete form to the question of the applicability of Article 86 to abnormal price situations. Though it may remain very difficult to specify in general terms the criteria which enable one to define an unfair price, nevertheless the Court has provided highly valuable pointers which will guide the Commission's work."

This passage highlights the aims of the competition policy and the reasons and criteria underlying our research programme, namely to provide the Commission with a coherent set of economic studies covering an increasingly wide range of industries and markets and bringing out the aims, the salient features, and the effects of any industrial strategies or actual practices which might affect trade between Member States to the detriment of the Community consumer.

For this very purpose - to bring out the aims, the salient features and above all the effects of such strategies and practices - the programme includes a set of dynamic and international comparative studies of price structures covering a precise and clearly defined series of products and markets in all Community countries.

Final consumer prices provide the critical "thermometer" for determining the form and structure of each study. The studies should not be seen as an "inquisition", since they require only the voluntary collaboration of the undertakings themselves. It is in the best interest of every economic operator (consumers as well as undertakings) living and working in the Community to have a more transparent picture of market structures.

The conclusion to this report (Section 2.10 - "The crucial points of the research") demonstrate point by point the extent to which the programme really does attain its objectives.

Stages of the survey

The Sixth Report on Competition Policy[1] stated that the provisional and partial results of the pilot surveys on the structure and evolution of prices and mark-ups in the distribution of processed food products indicated that:

a.   these surveys are of the greatest interest both for assessing the actual working of the competition mechanism and for the information and guidance of consumers and households;

b.   detailed basic data are available which can reasonably be considered indispensable for the continuation and extension of the prices mark-ups surveys;

c.   both the immediate and ultimate targets of the long-term research programme should be expanded and clearly defined as a matter of urgency by incorporating them into a more systematic and complete methodological framework. For a further in-depth extension of the multiple analyses, a distinction should be made between two fundamental stages and aspects of the research:

   1)   First stage (Chapter One): survey on prices and mark-ups: aims and criteria of the research programme - computer programming requirements;

   11)   Second stage (Chapter Two): thepower interplay between retailers and producers.

Generally speaking, the first stage aims to collect a much greater quantity of detailed information on specific, actual prices and mark-ups, in order to build up a fairly representative picture of "price galaxies" at different levels (final retail prices, buying prices for retailers, etc.,) and of their variations (according to sales point, country, products brand and size).

In this context, implementation of the first stage calls for an extension of the sample of shops (or sales points) covered by the survey and also a very substantial extension of the sample of products to include more brands and more sizes(packages).

---

1. Third part, paragraph 4, No.319

The second stage of research aims at identifying and analysing the forms and effects of interplay between the laws and factors governing variations of the price galaxies mentioned above.

In concrete terms , therefore, the aim will be to analyse the evolution of competition as regards relationships:

(a)   Between retailers and consumers;

(b)   Between retailers and producers;

by describing:

-       the salient features of the power relationships underlying the negotiating powers and actual behaviour of the selected major retailers and manufacturers, and

-       the immediate and ultimate effects of the retail prices paid by the consumer on his freedom of choice and decision.

Clearly, the first stage is the prerequisite basis for the second stage of research, which is based on <u>selection</u>, from among the large quantity of atoms of information provided by the first stage, of those elements which are of the greatest significance and value for a more advanced and concentrated analysis.

In fact, the <u>selection</u> operated during the second stage of research has the effects of focusing attention on a <u>more restricted sample</u> of:

(a)   products;

(b)   retailers;

(c)   manufacturers.

During the second stage, to be described in Chapter Two, account will have to be taken not only of the quantitative data resulting from computer elaborations but also of all financial, economic and legal information which may be ascertainable.

*

*   *

The present chapter deals more particularly with the following:

(a)   the tables

(b)   the various operational criteria for the collection, processing, i.e. regrouping and classification of the thousands (or millions) of atoms of information required to achieve the targets and goals in relation to our basic problem of <u>identifying</u> firstly the relationships existing between structures and behaviour and secondly the practical consequences for the practical working of competition;

(c)   the more technical and specific commentaries explaining each of the tables covered by the present chapter.

The layout of the chapter is, therefore, as follows:

I   Series of detailed tables: "Prices mark-ups".

II   Criteria for regrouping and reclassifying data - Relationships between concentration and price.

III   Commentaries on tables.

1.1 CRITERIA FOR REGROUPING AND CLASSIFYING DATA - RELATIONSHIPS BETWEEN CONCENTRATION AND PRICES

1.1.1. The criteria

The new programme lays down a number of criteria for regrouping and therefore comparing and analysing the data collected, which are mainly the selling prices but also include the buying prices for each specific item covered by the survey.

The 18 criteria adopted are listed below, but it has not yet been possible to apply many of them.

1.1.2. Criterion No.1.: Unit Price

Products are classified according to unit price. This operation assumes prior standardization of brands, sizes and packages for any given product, to enable unit prices comparison of different brands and sizes of the same product. The determination of unit price is fundamental because there are large numbers of own labels and commercial brands, as well as several sizes and packages, not only in each country considered but also at every sales point. In practice, the quality and content of these numerous items are frequently the same and this is why they have to be compared on the basis of unit price. See Tables 1, 8 and 10 compiled from the computer print outs.

1.1.3. Total Price and Unit Price

Labels on packages offered for sale on the shelves of big stores often show:

(a)   Total Price;

(b)   Weight;

(c)   Unit Price;

For other products, the exact quantity sold is sometimes fixed at the express request of the consumer; this applies to fresh meat, vegetables and fresh fish.

Here. two principles will be applied:

I)   when the unit price is displayed, it will be used and not the total price of a given size of weight;

II)   A total quantity of 1 will then be shown, i.e. total price and unit price will coincide;

III)   if the price differs substantially according to weight or package
         (e.g. a 240 gramme piece of Finnish Emmenthaler cheese costs Bf.25
         per 100 grammes while a 3 kg. block costs Bf.180 per kilo), two
         different units of measurement (100 grammes and 1 kg) will have to be
         used to show this fact;

IV)   in describing the items considered, therefore, the particular size and
         form will be stated(in our example, blocks of Finnish Emmenthaler
         cheese in packages of 100 grammes and multiples of 100 grammes or in
         packages of 1 kg and multiples of 1 kg).

1.1.4.   Criterion No.2 : the 22 groups of food products, beverages and tobacco

The mass of data obtained by enquiry are classified by "groups of related products", i.e. we consider a number of products which are related either by similar manufacturing processes or by their final use by consumers. On this basis all the products considered - food products, beverages and tobacco - are classified into 22 main groups.

The aim is to measure and identify:

- differences in price between the shops included in the sample, for each group
  of products so defined and, in particular,

- differences in price movements between surveys, for each of the above mentioned
  groups of products, as between the shops included in the sample.

This is a very difficult operation, from which it is intended to compile at a
later stage:

A)   Several specific price indices for each of the 22 groups of food products,
         beverages and tobacco, programmed into the computer, as follows:

I)   "CON" (canned fish, meat, vegetables and fruit);
II)   "ENF" (baby foods);
III)   "SOU" (soups);
IV)   "LEG" (packet vegetables);
V)   "EPI" (meat extracts and seasonings);
VI)   "GRA" (edible oils and fats, margarine);
VII)   "BIS" (biscuits, cakes, "bakery products", confectionery and
                 chocolates);
VIII)   "FAR" (crispbreads, crackers, cake mixes, flour, salt, sugar and
                 jellies);
IX)   "CER" (cereals);
X)   "MAR" (jams and marmalades);

XI)	"BOI"	(beverages, coffee, tea, soft drinks, mineral waters);
XII)	"LAI"	(dairy and related products, milk, eggs, butter and various kinds of cheese);
XIII)	"FRO"	(frozen foods, including ice cream);
XIV)	"SPA"	(pasta, spaghetti, macaroni, etc., ready-cooked dishes, pizza, ravioli, spaghetti in sauce and so on);
XV)	"BIE"	(beer);
XVI)	"ALC"	(alcoholic beverages: whisky, brandy, Martini, wine etc.,);
XVII)	"CHA"	(ham, delicatessen meats, cured meats);
XVIII)	"PAI"	(bread);
XIX)	"FRU"	(bananas, pineapples, grapefruit, lemons, oranges, apples, peaches, pears etc.,), i.e. fresh fruit traded internationally on a large scale;
XX)	"VIA"	(meat, poultry, game);
XXI)	"POI"	(fresh fish, shellfish (crustaceans, molluscs,etc));[1]
XXII)	"TAB"	(various brands and types of cigarettes and tobacco).

Criterion No. 2a, setting the storage limit, (shelf life) for each group of products is very closely linked with the above classification. At the present stage, however, no return on this point will be required. Later on, it will be covered by the following gradings:

1= no set storage limit;

2= over three years,

3= over one year,

4= over six months, etc.,

B)   A general food price index recording changes in the price of a set "basket" made up of items included and analysed in the 22 groups of products enumerated above. See Tables 4, 6, 7 and 9 compiled from the computer print outs.

It should be noted that provision has also been made for the alphabetical coding of groups of products which are not food products but are fairly often sold at supermarkets and hypermarkets selling food products: examples are detergents and household cleaning materials.

1.1.5.   Calculation of Price Indices

Two alternative criteria can be applied for the computation of price indices:

---

1. It should be noted that deep frozen fruit(e.g. strawberries),meat and fish come under the heading of frozen products (Group XIII:"FRO").On the other hand, meat and fish which are frozen for long storage and are imported in large quantity, will be included in the appropriate group (XX or XXI). In any case, the Institutes which carry out the survey will have to give full explanations, in a detailed note attached to the coding sheets so that the correct quality and characteristics of the products can be accurately assessed.

<u>Either</u>:

a)   Start with the unit price for each item (brand and size) of each product (e.g. all varieties, brands and package sizes of "salmon"), then compute the arithmetic mean for the product concerned on the basis of the unit price (taken from Table 8);

b)   then calculate the overall price for each of the 22 groups of products (e.g. one for group "CON", one for group "ENF", and so on), on the basis of the unit price for each product computed as described under ('a');

c)   calculate the arithmetic mean of the 22 price price indices, corresponding to the overall price for each group of products;

d)   finally, compute the above-mentioned overall and mean prices for two different periods, in order to establish the price index.

<u>Or</u>:

a)   calculate directly the overall price for each of the 22 groups of products on the basis of the single items taken separately, i.e. on the basis of the total price at each time and, therefore, <u>ignoring</u> the unit prices computed for the various products;

b)   compare the above overall prices at two different times in order to establish the corresponding index.

        At this stage of the enquiry it is preferable to adopt the <u>second method</u>. Overall and mean prices , and the price variations to appear in Tables 1,2,3,4, 7 and 9 will, therefore, be calculated directly from the data for <u>each</u> item (<u>each</u> brand and size).

        However, for Table 8 which has a special purpose, the first method will be used for stage (a) because the groups covered by this table are not the 22 "groups of related products" but "single products" only (e.g. "salmon" only and not "CON").

1.1.6.   <u>Criterion No.3 : type of brand</u>

        The data are classified by <u>type of brand</u> sold to the consumer, namely;

        1= manufacturer brand
        2= commercial brand
        3= own label (i.e. exclusive marketing brand)

        In Table 3, the <u>type of brand</u> will be entered just below the "number and name of product". Table 4 will show more particularly the share of each type of brand in the overall cost of the basket as well as percentage price variations for the whole basket, by type of brand. Lastly, the last part of Table 9 also gives useful information classified by type of brand.

1.1.7.   Criterion No.4 : Origin of Product (imported, home produced, etc.,)

This is defined according to the geographical origin of the product, namely;

1= national product (home-produced goods);
2= imported products;
3= mixed products (the final manufacturing price is made up partly of value added in the country and partly of value added abroad);
4= product of undefined origin.

Tables 3, 4 and 9 contain information classified according to this criterion, together with similar information on the type of brand (see Criterion No.7).

1.1.8.   Criterion No. 5:Pricing

The code number allocated indicates whether the price for a given brand is a special or a promotional price,namely;

1= normal price of product;
2= special offer as part of an advertising campaign;
3= non-defined methods of pricing.

The information given under "Pricing" in Tables 1,2,5 and 10, indicates the strategy adopted for any given item (normal price, specialoffer or non-defined method of pricing). In practice it should be noted that:

a)   It is not always possible to determine whether the price charged is a special price or not;

b)   As a rule,some big retailing groups use "special offers" for a limited period, on a planned basis, so that a number of items are at all times offered to the consumer as special offers.

1.1.9.   Criterion No 6: Importance of a Product in the Family Budget

The code number allocated indicates whether the product in question is an essential item of consumption or not, namely:

1= product which is an essential item in the pattern of household consumption;
2= product which is a non-essential, or little used item in household consumption.
3= product with variable interest.

This approach should allow a new typical price index to be worked out, which would

18

be roughly homogenous for all Member States. Table 1 contains a column for tbis entry.

1.1.10.   Criterion No. 7. : Nationality of Manufacturer or Producer

The code number allocated indicates the nationality of the manufacturer which is that of the country where the decision centre of the group is located.

        1= Federal Republic of Germany
        2= France
        3= Italy
        4= Netherlands
        5= Belgium
        6= United Kingdom
        7= Ireland
        8= Denmark
        9= Greece
        10=Spain
        11=Portugal
        12=Switzerland
        13=Austria
        14=Sweden
        15=United States

In the case of an unprocessed product (e.g. fresh fruit: bananas, lemons, etc.,) the nationality of the producer will be entered, i.e. not the place of origin of the product but the country where the decision centre of the group is located.

The note to the coding sheet (Annex 1) will give full explanatory details for:

a)   identifying the quality and characteristics of the various products;

b)   giving a full picture of the structure of the producing group and its subsidiaries, as well as of import and export flows generated by the group's activities;

c)   showing the place of origin on production of the product, so that the overall policy of the producing group can be assessed.

There may be cases where the name and location of the manufacturer are not known but the country of origin or production of the product is known (e.g. Hong Kong). The name of the country concerned will be given in the explanatory note referred to above and annexed to the coding sheet, in which no country name will then be entered.[1]

---

1. The information in this explanatory note will be particularly valuable during the second stage of the survey which is dealt with in Chapter II.

1.1.11.   Criterion No. 8: Manufacturing (or producing) Group

The code number allocated identifies the name of the group which manufacturers or distributes (if the manufacturer is not known) the product in question. Code numbers are allocated according to nationality (criterion No.7). One hundred code numbers are available for each nationality, except for the United States for which there are 500 numbers. Thus, numbers from 101 to 200 indicate German firms, from 201 to 300 French firms and from 1501 to 2000 American firms. The names of big retailers using own labels will be followed by the initials "O.L." and will be numbered from 8000 onwards on the coding sheet.

In the case of a product which is not processed (fresh fruit such as bananas and lemons, etc.,) the name of the producing group will be entered. A detailed note, like that described under the previous point ("10. Criterion No. 7")will be attached to the coding sheet.

1.1.12.   Criteria Nos.9, 10 and 11 : Degrees of Concentration

Three different criteria are applied according to the degree of concentration. Taking for example, the index $*C_4$ ("standard" concentration ratio), we shall have four types of structure according to the value of the index, as follows:

- 1 = red zone   (of the overall national structure)
- 2 = orange zone
- 3 = yellow zone
- 4 = green zone

It will be possible for apply the index $*C_4$ to at least three different definitions of the "structure" to be considered:

I)   at "specific product market" level (e.g. tinned salmon);

II)   at the level of "combined markets for related products"(e.g. tinned fish);

III)   at "sub-sector" level (e.g. "tinned food").

The "standard ration"$*C_4$ will, as a rule, be higher at the first level and lower at the third.

However, the drop in the cumulative percentage represented by the concentration ration (following the elimination of one or more firms) partially offsets the rise of the index through the application of the standardizing mechanism (in accordance with the different hypothesis : (a), (b) and (c)).

Consequently, although fairly sensitive, the standard index maintains a fairly regular trend.

1.1.13.   Concentration of Manufacturers (or producers) and Working of Competition

Even if the leading firm has a very large share of a particular market or sector (index C1), e.g. over 40%, it should not be concluded that:

a)   the firm in question has an oligopolistic or even a monopolistic market power;

b)   the firm in question uses this situation to impose excessive prices and thereby earn monopoly profits.

In practice, the manufacturer or producer cannot deal direct with final consumers but has to sell his products to retailers or even wholesalers (importers or exporters in some cases).

His selling price will therefore be determined by his bargaining power in relation to his purchasers. However, as already noted:

I)   there are purchasing groups and large distributing firms (large stores) which have very substantial bargaining power;

II)   this bargaining power cannot be simply measured at the level of national concentration because the strength of these major retailers lies in:

a) the dominant position which they hold over retail sales in certain regions and cities;
b) the substantial extent of their centralised cumulative demand, which no manufacturer or producer can ignore;
c) their consequent ability to buy enormous quantities from anybody and anywhere.

1.1.14.   Relationships between Degree of Concentration and Price Movements

It follows from what has been said that the following information must be available in order to assess the working of competition:

a)   not only the degree of market power held by any one manufacturer or producer;
b)   but also selling prices to retailers, i.e. the actual buying prices negotiated by retailers;
c)   a significant and objective "parameter" for assessing the relevance of those prices, i.e. a basis for affirming that these prices demonstrate that either the supplier (manufacturer or producer) or the buyer (large retailer or importing or exporting wholesaler) has strong bargaining power.

Clearly, the problem of assessing the <u>relevance of a price</u> comes back to that of determining <u>a fair price for each market</u> from which any divergence or deviation would constitute abuse. While the solution to this problem is no easier that the discovery of the "philosophers' stone", there is nevertheless a "magic key" which can be used (key no.2: international - and interregional - comparison of <u>price movements</u> and of the other magnitudes analysed). This will be discussed in Chapter II.

In practice, by making an international - and interregional - comparison of all the available data, i.e.:

a)   comparison of the degrees of concentration for a particular industry in the various countries and, in particular, comparison of the market share of each major manufacturer or producer in each country;

b)   comparison of levels of buying prices (producer-manufacturer price) negotiated between the supplier and the buying retailer, in each country and region;

c)   comparison of retail price levels;

d)   comparison of the trend of all the above data;

it is at least possible to deduce the regions, countries and products for which positions of dominance or bargaining strength exist, in favour either of certain manufacturers (or producers) or more particularly for certain big retailers.

In this respect, it would appear obvious that:

a)   even if there is no automatic relationship between the degree and trend of concentration on the one hand, and the fixing of "<u>domination prices</u>" and the acquisition of "<u>domination profits</u>" on the other;

b)   it must be known whether or not dominant or even monopoly positions exist before being able to conclude that such <u>domination prices and profits also exist;</u>

c)   consequently, the degree of concentration of manufacturers or producers must be analysed before the results of <u>analyses of the movements of the different prices</u> can be interpreted (producers' prices, i.e. buying price for retailers and retail prices);

d)   in particular, this knowledge (and measurement) is essential in order to explain and understand the pricing policy:
-        of the principal manufacturers or producers;
-        of the principal retailers.

1.1.15.   <u>Price Variations and Concentration of Markets : Frequency, Extent and Speed of Price Adjustments</u>

The modern theory of oligopolies has frequently emphasised the <u>rigidity of prices</u> in <u>highly concentrated</u> structures, characterised by confrontation between or, better, the "peaceful co-existence " of what is in fact a very small number of large firms.[1]

The current theory is that, for fear of starting a competitive price war (described as "ruinous") these oligopolistic units tend:

a)   to link price levels with the level of a given set of variable costs (full cost principle)[2];

b)   to hold their prices relatively stable and hence to <u>raise or lower their prices as infrequently as possible</u> (Hitch, Hall and Sweezy's hypothesis of the "bent demand curve")[2].

One of the aims of the price and mark up analyses forming the subject of this research programme should be to determine the actual behaviour of big oligopolistic units operatingin highly concentrated markets.

In other words, price policy has to be described and analysed:

a)   in the present period of inflationary pressures;

b)   in periods of <u>price controls</u> which are imposed more or less regularly by the countries worst hit by inflation;

In order to assess and measure the impact of such <u>price policies</u> - and of action taken by governments - on the growth and spread of inflation.

In the last analysis, a three sided reciprocal causal relationship has to be established between:

- market power;
- domination prices and profits
- inflation;

distinguishing clearly the respective <u>shares</u> of manufacturers (or producers) and large retailers in market power, domination profits and responsibility for the triggering and growth of inflation. In particular, more than one hundred questions put to the Research Institutes in ChapterII of the research programme seek to determine and define all the facts of the

---

1. See: P.Sylos-Labini, "Oligopolio e progresso tecnico"(Oligopoly and technical progress), Giuffre, Milan 1957 and in particular:Part One,Chapter 1: "L'oligopolio"(The oligopoly) and Einaudi, Turin 1961.

    R. Linda, "Concurrence oligopolistique et planification concurrentielle internationale". (Oligopolistique, competition and international competition planning)in "Economie Appliquée, Archives of the ISEA 1972, Nos.2-3, Librairie Droz,Geneva, pages 325 et seq. and in particular pages 357 to 369.

2. See P.Sylos-Labini, op.cit.Chapter 1, sections 1-6; R.L.Hall-C.J.Hitch,"Price Theory and Business Behaviour" in "Oxford Studies in the Price Mechanism",Oxford 1951,pp.106-138; P.M.Sweezy,"Demand under conditions of oligopoly" in "Readings in Price Theory", Allen and Unwin,London,1953, pp.404-409. These works are quoted in note (6)on page 27 of the cited works by P.Sylos-Labini.

problem with which we are concerned.

For a better understanding of the practical importance of this set of problems, it may be helpful to adopt the following working hypothesis, which of course, is not necessarily related in any way to real cases and situations.

Strict price controls are imposed for one year in a country suffering from galloping inflation. The effects of this action might be as follows:

a)   Working on the premise that two extreme types of structure exist in the country concerned:

  (a) competitive and more or less atomistic;

  (b) unbalanced oligopolistic, because one or two firms have dominant power.

b)   The first effect of government price controls is to discourage new investment by firms operating in both the competitive structure (a) and the unbalanced oligopolistic structure (b). This is not necessarily a positive effect. Quite the reverse !

c)   The other effects depend on the form and application of price controls: freeze, increases requiring government approval, limitation of the frequency of price changes:

  I) Price freeze.

  II) Increases subject to prior approval by the relevant government department.

  III) Limitation by government of the frequency of increases.

1.1.16.   First Hypothesis : Price Freeze and its Effects

A price freeze can only be temporary; it penalizes competitive firms and structures which by definition tend to keep prices and costs as low as possible. If such firms can no longer adjust their prices to demand conditions and to the constraints imposed by their cost curves, some will go bankrupt and will leave the market, thus increasing the degree of concentration. Against this, a freeze will "upset" the dominant firms much less because their market power has already enabled them to fix their prices at a comfortable, relatively high level. Here again, a price freeze will lead to a greater concentration by favouring the dominant firms and the more concentrated structures.

But this is not sufficient.

However paradoxical it may seem, a price freeze triggers off a whole series of consequences which all have the perverse but systematic effect of prolonging, stimulating and accentuating inflation. There is nothing better than a price freeze for unleashing and perpetuating the vicious circle of inflation.

First effect of a price freeze: no firm will reduce its prices and this applies particularly to dominant firms, which, in order to hide their profits from the government and the public, will prefer to take on unnecessary administrative and managerial staff with nothing to do and to grant excessive bonuses and rise to their managers, foremen, office staff and wage earners. Wage increases will in particular start a general "follow-my-leader" reaction, which will trigger off wage increases even in sectors and firms where they can scarcely be justified on grounds of productivity. This will have two consequences, incompatible with (a) their production pattern and (b) market conditions; and consequently, a further fresh increase in concentration; a fresh impetus is given to the spread of inflation by the artificial and forced increase in labour and production costs: these are known as "cost-push pressures."

This is a vital point which must be strongly emphasised.

The effective, normal working of market mechanisms implies as a "natural and continuing consequence" that prices can fall.

One look around is enough. Competition leads to big price reductions. What else are special offers (Section 8: Criterion No.5) and the other promotional measures adopted by the big firms when they can operate in a "competitive environment"? And it would be wrong to ignore the extent and the impact - on the trend of prices and the cost of living - of these special offers and price reductions even when they are only temporary.

However, the most disastrous effect of a price freeze is that it specifically discourages any possibility of price reductions because it must be appreciated that the unhealthiest aspect of inflation is not the rise in prices but the irreversibility of the trend.

In the dialectics of the market economy, prices must vary but the changes should be "reversible" sometimes upwards and sometimes downwards. Inflation appears when price reductions no longer take place because of a perverse factor such as a price freeze.

It has, however, just been stated that the most disastrous consequence of a price freeze is that it rules out any chance of price reductions. Why? And how?

The answer is simple. We must go back to the main, specific causes of inflation[1],

---

1. The four "classical" causes are:
   a) demand pressures;
   b) cost-push pressures, set up mainly by trade union wage claims;
   c) the expectation cause (anticipating future inflation);
   d) international causes, linked with international prices and exchange rates.

   On inflation problems and the role of a Price Commission, reference may be made to the excellent report by Stephen Lofthouse (of Capel-Cure Myers Ltd.)" The New Price Commission: A Microeconomic approach to price control", London 1977.

which include the "expectation cause".This means that operators in the economy expect and anticipate the future growth of inflation and, therefore, put up their prices in advance even if such an increase is in no way justified by the existing structure of costs and the market.

There is no practical difference between:

a)   increasing a price without economic justification;

b)   not reducing the same price when existing conditions suggest that there should be a reduction.

When price controls are imposed no firm will reduce its prices precisely because of this expectation cause. Moreover, what more damaging admission can there be of inability to check inflation than the adoption of the desperate measure of a price freeze? When a government makes this admission, firms and economic operators know only too well what to do: they hold their selling prices at the highest possible level (or even raise them) so that, whatever happens, they lose nothing and are absolutely sure of not being overtaken by rising inflation, without thought for the fact that by acting in this way they generate and increase inflation.

But price freezes have an even worse and more disastrous inflationary effect because they trigger off inflationary demand pressures.

Indeed, everyone is very well aware of two essential facts concerning price freezes and this awareness is the knell of doom which condemns such a policy in advance:

1)   The price freeze will be lifted one day;

2)   The price freeze will be re-introduced some day.

Let us take the first "fact": a measure which is so anti-economic in character it can only be temporary and when the freeze is lifted, prices which have been artificially frozen too long, so that they are squeezed and held down, will leap upwards causing an inflationary explosion.

Hence:

1) large quantities of products which are expected to rise in price must be purchased and held in stock. This means that purchases must cover not only products subject to the price freeze but also others which may be affected by a similar measure and yet others which can be expected to be carried along on the wave of rising inflation.

2) Money, therefore, has to be borrowed to finance these speculative purchases and, consequently, money not used for productive investment will be used to fuel speculation and inflation. Money will become dearer thus further dis-

couraging demand for productive investment which has already been weakened and hit by the measures taken in connection with the price freeze. Any obstacle to productive investment of course constitutes an autonomous, indirect factor which helps to prolong and spread inflation.

3) Even if price reductions were theoretically possible in a highly competitive sector for very special reasons inherent in the workings of the market, it will no longer take place precisely because of the general, inflationary pressure of demand. In the short run, prices are not cut when demand is high. This applies in both competitive and monopoly conditions.

1.1.17.   <u>Effects of the Anticipation of a Price Freeze</u>

Everyone is aware of the second essential "fact": once a government has added the price freeze to its arsenal of economic measures, the freeze will be reimposed some day, even after it has first been lifted, whenever the authorities are faced with public anxiety at the growth of inflation and are left with no other escape hatch.

In these circumstances, a price freeze has a further effect. Even when there is no freeze, firms tend to set their selling prices artificially high. How do they do this? By applying the full cost principle, that is, by adding to a set of variable or direct costs, a fixed margin (q) to cover the firm's overheads and profits. Here the modern theory of oligopolies (propounded by P. Sylos-Labini and others) seems to be confirmed by experience during the present bout of inflation and price controls. But the perverse mechanism intervenes in the fixing of prices at the stage of calculating direct costs, i.e. <u>the whole set of variable costs</u>. In practice, if the firm has the power to do so, it will not take account of current variable costs but will seek to anticipate the imposition of a new price freeze for a certain time. From this it automatically follows that:

a)   the selling price will have to be high enough to withstand a price freeze of varying length without loss of money;

b)   the probable increase in variable costs, and of wages in particular, will have to be estimated to allow for the foreseeable rise in the rate of inflation and in particular for the inflationary explosion which will precede, accompany and fol-low the imposition of a price freeze, in accordance with the example we have just described.

But an even more perverse feature of this perverse mechanism is that this opportunity of setting excessively and artificially high prices is offered gratis to big firms in particular (manufacturing, distributing or both) with a strong enough market power to impose their prices.

This fixing of prices at an artificially high level will inevitably help:

a)   to add still further to inflation;

b)   to penalize yet again and as always, firms operating within competitive
           structures and under competitive conditions, which, as purchasers, will have to
           suffer the artificially high prices set by the dominant undertakings and will also
           be exposed to pressure from trade unions (for higher wages and salaries), but will
           not themselves be able to charge artificially high prices (as a hedge against
           the future growth of inflation) because the machinery of competition in the
           markets where they operate does not allow them to charge such prices (by defin-
           ition of the concept of competition itself).

           The final result is the disappearance of a number of competing firms and a higher
degree of concentration. In other words, the perverse mechanism underlying this perverse
process is simple: concentration stimulates inflation and inflation helps to increase concentration.
           The following hypothesis must be checked:

a)   Is not inflation highest in countries with a high degree of concentration?
b)   Are not inflation and concentration highest in countries which are currently
           applying price controls?

           In our research programme and more particularly in the set of 140 plus questions
listed in Chapter 11, an attempt will be made to test these and other working hypotheses
empirically.

1.1.18.   Second Hypothesis : Increases Subject to Prior Authorization

           When a price freeze is lifted, there is generally a price explosion for products
to which the freeze applied:

a)   the rate of increase is increased by the fact that everyone knows that he must
           hurry to make money as much as possible before the next freeze (see Section 19);
b)   it is also increased in proportion to the market power of firms to impose such
           high prices;
c)   it is also increased in proportion to the degree of concentration and non compet-
           itivity of the sector.

           Then, faced with such a catastrophe, which is easily foreseen but no less
disastrous for that, the government has no option but to:

i)   introduce a system of prior authorization of price increases;
ii)   limit by law the frequency with which prices can be changed.

           Let us first consider the system of prior authorization which is accompanied by
two countervailing factors in one:

<u>First perversity of the system</u>: immediately a price increase is sanctioned, i.e. in practice a maximum price, this becomes a sole price, which is also by definition the maximum price possible because:

a) firms able to sell only at a higher price will be forced out of the market thus increasing the degree of concentration of the structure, with all the perverse effects already enumerated;

b) the most efficient and profitable firms, which could sell at a lower price, are quite happy to align themselves on this maximum price and to increase their profits with government blessing; this of itself will be a co-factor in inflation (see Section 21, however).

In any event, firms with market power - and therefore operating in concentrated structures - will consistently apply the maximum price which will therefore, tend to become the sole price.

In conclusion: the mechanism of competition will no longer be able to fulfil its role of establishing a system of multiple, differentiated equilibrium prices, fixed at the lowest level possible in the specific individual conditions of the various markets and structures.

<u>Second perversity of the system</u>: in order to obtain prior sanction for price increases, it is clearly in the interests of firms to inflate total variable costs artificially, because this is the total figure that the authorities will consider in granting price increases, in accordance with the full cost principle.

The reasoning is even simpler than its statement: if the authorities approve a rate (q) of 30% on total variable costs, the selling price will be 130 if the original total is over 100 and there will be a gain (gross margin) of 30; but if the total is inflated to 200, permission to sell at 260 will be given and the gain (gross margin) will be 60. And Mr. Palisse would say that it is better to gain 60 than 30.

It is obvious that managers controlling big firms with market power will find it in their interest:

a) to grant all trade union claims for wage increases, resulting in the common but paradoxical situation that a workman (steelworker, electrician or engineer) gains twice as much as a teacher;

b) to profit themselves from such increases in two ways:
     . directly, insofar as their salaries are increased;
     . indirectly, insofar as they are entitled to bonuses and shares based on company profits.

1.1.19.   Structural prerequisites for competition to operate

The perverse mechanism described above is triggered by the joint action of concentrated (and dominant) oligopolies and price controls imposed by government. In any analysis of modern structures, however, care must be taken to avoid the axiomatic generalisations and traps of economic determinism.

Thus, even in this "perverse mechanism" there are "stops" and competition can emerge even with price controls, if certain basic conditions are fulfilled.

In this context, the expression "effective and efficient working of competition" is used simply to describe its most salient and significant effect (and result) namely, the possibility that prices lower than the maximum prices fixed by the authorities may be recorded in certain sectors and markets.

If this is to happen, the heads of certain firms operating in certain markets must of course have the will to compete.

If this spirit of competition is lacking - and it sometimes does not enter the thoughts of managers of certain dominant firms (both public and private) - very little can be done, but it is still of interest to know:

a)   the conditions which generally tend to inspire this "spirit of competition";

b)   the instruments available to the government to activate and stimulate these competitive factors which will induce firms to compete.

We shall consider exclusively objective structural conditions in which competition can work. They are:

a)   the presence of numbers of independent economic operators;

b)   the existence of a certain balance of power between economic operators;

c)   the existence of highly elastic demand, to bring down prices;

d)   the existence of major economies of scale, both technological and commercial (arising therefore from the structure of the distribution system), and/or of excess production and/or distribution capacity, i.e. unused capacities;

e)   the existence of a compatible, clear and definite legal framework (legal certainty) in relation to the working of the market economy.

Brief consideration must be given to these conditions:

a)   plurality of economic operators, and,

b)   balance of power

are the linchpin of any competitive mechanism, in the sense that:

i)   there is no possibility of competition where there is absolute monopoly or where a dominant position is held by a firm which is so powerful that any spirit of competition in other firms is discouraged from the start. It then becomes necessary to determine the critical ceiling of disequilibrium, as measured by the various Linda indices[1], because as the degree of concentration (and imbalance) approaches this ceiling, competition tends to be snuffed out;

ii)   the independence of these economic operators must also be ensured and kept under scrutiny, because the conclusion of various types of agreement (specialisation, market-sharing, etc.,) can lead to at least the temporary elimination of the plurality of operators which is obviously the essential pre-condition for competition to work.

It is clear that the other two conditions -
c)   elasticity of demand, and,
d)   economies of scale -
can act as an extremely powerful stimulus to price competition even when prices are controlled, always provided the first two conditions (a) and (b) are fulfilled.

The example of special offers by big stores and retail groups speaks for itself. It must again be stressed that government price controls, particularly the fixing of maximum prices, is liable to divert such competitive action, which should naturally be directed to selling prices, towards more modern forms of competition of much less benefit to consumers and to the economy in general, namely;

        - advertising;
        - very frequent changes in products (brands, packaging, weight, etc.,)

The heartbreaking fact is that even when imposed on a competitive structure, maximum prices fixed by the government by their nature constitute a barrier to price competition.

Conversely, they are an incentive to modern forms of competition which, as we have stressed, can be a source of inflation and waste, as in the case of advertising and constant product changes[2].

More accurately, the government assumes the role of price leadership or delegates this role tacitly to the biggest firm in each market, the reference price then being the maximun price fixed by the government.

1. "Methodologie", op.cit. Chapters II and VII, section 56 et.seq.and our report "Domination, Concurrence et concentration des marchés dans la structure industrielle de la Communauté" published in "La réglementation du comportement des monopoles et des entreprises dominantes en droit communautaire", De Tempel, Tempelhof, Bruges 1977, pages 29-109.

2. For comments on the sterility of certain strategies and certain weapons of competition-which are a pure waste of resources for the community at large- see R.Linda "Concurrence oligopolistique et planification concurrentielle internationale", op.cit.pp.443 to 449. See also the paper, read at the Bruges Symposium ("Domination,concurrence et concentration des marchés dans la structure industrielle de la Communauté"),pp.67 to 71.

Lastly, as regards the last condition,

e)   legal framework,

it is quite clear that the fixing of maximum prices introduces an element of uncertainty into that framework. What could be more arbitrary and discretionary than a maximum price - more or less fiscal in nature - which can be fixed or changed at any time by a simple government order?

In these circumstances, it becomes impossible to make any economic forecast for the conditions governing the working of the market or for the formation of the different equilibrium prices.

The normal market machinery gives way to arbitrary government intervention - and this new form of taxation. This is serious, because the workings of the market can be analysed, and interpreted and can, therefore, be evaluated and managed to some extent, whereas the striking power of the authorities is unknown and cannot be evaluated; it cannot be anticipated, is formidable and is (too often) affected by pressures from certain dominant pressure groups (economic, financial, social, political, etc.,) whose role is even more difficult to evaluate.

It may therefore, be wondered whether the fixing of maximum prices does not amount to an admission that competition does not work and that the government can do nothing about it.

Is this a question of "power" or of "imagination"?

In answer to the second question, we believe that the government in fact has at its disposal many means of activating and stimulating the factors of competition without taking direct action on prices[1]:

a)   the systematic provision of full information to consumers and all economic operators so that they have equal access to knowledge of structures, markets and products;

b)   the liberalisation of international trade in sectors and markets where dominant (or even monopolistic) positions exist at national level;

c)   in general, all measures designed to break down barriers to entry preventing any extension of the oligopolistic arena(e.g. permission to set up new "independent" large stores, liberalisation of patent laws, banning of exclusive sales contracts, etc....);

---

1. On these points see paper to the Bruges Symposium 1977, mentioned earlier: "Domination, concurrence et concentration des marchés dans la structure industrielle de la Communauté", pages 71 to 85.

d) prohibition or penalisation of the systematic, excessive or abusive use of certain competitive weapons and strategies, such as advertising or constant product changes, because the introduction of what are represented to be new products and/or models is designed solely to deceive the consumer by preventing him from comparing qualities and prices;

e) the prohibition or penalisation of the abusive use of patent rights;

f) the banning of certain agreements and practices;

g) the scrutiny of all mergers, concentrations and acquisitions of holdings;

h) a series of special provisions ("rules and regulations") for all large firms, dominant firms, diversified and multinational groups, requiring the regular supply of information (covering financial and economic data, wages and salaries, investments and prices) to the authorities.[1,2]

These are only examples.

Another possible measure, applied directly to prices but with some justification in the theory of competition, is government limitation of the frequency of price increases.

1.1.20.   Third Hypothesis : Government Limitation of the Frequency of Price Increases

In our view, this is the only form of price intervention which in certain circumstances may have more advantages than disadvantages from the point of view of competition policy.

It is easy to apply: an order is made under the terms of which every undertaking, operating in a given sector of market, or of a specified size[2] is only allowed to raise its prices every three (or six or nine) months. But every undertaking can:

a) lower its prices as and when it wishes;

b) fix the rate of price increase without restriction.

A fixed interval may be ordered for price reductions in the same way as for increases.

As a result the machinery of competition tends to become much more rigid but at the same time much more transparent because:

both government and consumers can assess price increases more accurately because

---

1. On these points see the paper read at the Bruges Symposium 1977 already referred to "Domination, concurrence et concentration des marchés dans la structure industrielle de la Communauté", pages 71 to 85.

2. For example, these rules could apply to the first 900 manufacturing and service firms and to the first 500 distributing firms in any given country.

they take place at pre-determined dates, and

a "red warning signal" flashes, particularly for governments when:

a)   increases are particularly high;

b)   increases are made by big firms holding a dominant position on certain markets.

In this context, the most recent experience would appear to contradict the theory of the rigidity of oligopoly prices[1].

In any country where a special formula is used to restrict the frequency of price increases by law, the following conditions are observed:

a)   the big firms, which dominate certain markets, miss no opportunity of raising prices and if the interval between increases is set at, for example, three months, they will therefore raise their prices regularly every three months;

b)   the increases charged by these big firms are particularly high because they are in a position to exploit their market power, whereas smaller firms are compelled to follow, being fully aware that they would not be able to oppose the dominant power of the big firms or to compete with them;

c)   consequently, the dominant big firms act as price leaders; and

d)   by using their market, big firms tend to increase their profit-earning capacity because they benefit from economies of scale and are not handicapped by dis-economies of scale;

e)   conversely, the profit-earning capacity of firms operating within competitive structures and markets is limited by the existence of this machinery which by its nature tends to stabilise prices at the lowest possible level.

The purpose of the foregoing argument is to demonstrate that:

i)   the relationship between concentration and price level is very close;

ii)   consequently, an active competition policy, aimed at checking excessive concentration, is an essential prerequisite for checking the growth and spread of inflation.

Once again, we have confirmation of the practical value of our programme of research which seeks to link the findings of studies on the trend of concentration with those of studies on the trend of prices and mark-ups.

---

1. Thus, P.Sylos-Labini quoting the observations of Hitch and Hall, in Italian, affirms that "il prezzo sara mantenuto sul livello segnato dal costo pieno e non portato piu alto per timore dei possibili rivali potenziali"(the price will be held at the level set by the full cost and will not be raised further for fear of potential rivals) (1957 edition,p.33) and again "se esso (il prezzo) e fissato in un punto di un ampio tratto,esso avra la tend-enza a restare li"(if the price is set at one point in a broad range, it will tend to remain there).

1.1.21.   Concentration of the Machinery of Distribution and Barriers to Entry:
           Recapitulation

The power of domination is not limited to production or manufacture, but also extends to distribution; in the latter case, however, its effects on competition can be much more serious for the following reasons:

a)   the appropriate geographical dimension for the machinery of retail distribution is local not national;

b)   consequently, any excessive growth of concentration and of dominant power in a city or a region is liable to create a barrier to entry.

The barrier to entry will be greater and more formidable if the big retailer who dominates the market in a city or region also operates in other cities and regions in the same Member State, because he is then in a position to exert very heavy power on producers, manufacturers or wholesalers who are, or wish to become, his suppliers.

The bargaining power considerably increases domination over market outlets (retail sales) by discouraging the entry of potential competitors, who would not be able to buy on such favourable terms.

The combination of all these factors shows clearly that the perverse dialectic of domination and inflation described in the foregoing pages finds very fertile soil in the field of distribution.

The social cost of these barriers to entry can be measured by analysing the actual mark-ups applied by big retailers and for this purpose the real buying price paid by such retailers will obviously have to be determined (Chapter II, Section VII).

It has already been noted that the role of governments is to try and break down all barriers to entry (Section 21) which, by their nature, interfere with the workings of competition. Criteria for analysing distribution structures - with particular reference to big retailers - will be considered later (Chapter II, Section IX).

1.1.22.   Criterion No 15: Regrouping and Classification of Sales Points

Data are classified according to type of sales point. A large number of categories of sales point based on size, location and function (totalling 96) are reclassified into six broad groups based exclusively on size. Using, for example, the coding system proposed by Development Analysts Limited the classification will be as follows, overleaf:

Broad Group of Sales Points	Detailed Categories of Sales Points
1	HYPERMARKET :50,000sq.ft. or over
	06 – 12 – 18 – 24 – 30 – 36 – 42 – 48 – 54 – 60 – 66 – 72 – 78 – 84 – 90 – 96 .
2	SUPERSTORE : 25,000 sq.ft. to 49,000 sq.ft.
	05 – 11 – 17 – 23 – 29 – 35 – 41 – 47 – 53 – 59 – 65 – 71 – 77 – 83 – 89 – 95 .
3	LARGE SUPERMARKET: 8,000 to 25,000 sq.ft.
	04 – 10 – 16 – 22 – 28 – 34 – 40 – 46 – 52 – 58 – 64 – 70 – 76 – 82 – 88 – 94 .
4	SUPERMARKET : 4,000 sq.ft. to 7,999 sq.ft.
	03 – 09 – 15 – 21 – 27 – 33 – 39 – 45 – 51 – 57 – 63 – 69 – 75 – 81 – 87 – 93 .
5	LARGE SELF-SERVICE:2,000 to 3,999 sq.ft.
	02 – 08 – 14 – 20 – 26 – 32 – 38 – 44 – 50 – 56 – 62 – 68 – 74 – 80 – 86 – 92 .
6	SMALL SELF-SERVICE:less than 1,999 sq.ft.
	01 – 07 – 13 – 19 – 25 – 31 – 37 – 43 – 49 – 55 – 61 – 67 – 73 – 79 – 85 – 91 .

1.1.23.   Criterion No. 16 : Absolute or Total Price Variations

The increase (or decrease) of the total price of the specific items during the reference period is taken into account. We refer to the following tables:

Table 3 is of particular interest. It shows the following types of variation:

a)   maximum variation (or increase), i.e. the rate of mark-up applied by that sales point which, of all the sales points in the sample, has raised its total selling price the most over the period in question;

b)   minimum variation (increase or reduction), i.e. the rate applied by that sales point which, of all the sales points in the sample, has increased its prices the least (or cut its prices the most) over the period in question;

c)   the difference between these two variations giving:

.   the absolute deviation as a percentage (ƐAs).

The table also shows the sales point with the maximum and minimum variation. The products are ranked according to the difference in the price variations (ƐAs) between sales points over the period in question.

1.1.24.   Criterion No. 17: Variations of Unit Prices

This refers to the increase (or decrease) of the unit price of products, re-grouped on the basis on standardisation of different brands and size/weights (see Criterion No.1).

The unit price is entered in a column of the right hand side of Table 1. All price variations covered by Tables 2, 3, 4 and 9 relate to total prices and not unit prices.

Conversely, Tables 8 and 9 give variations of unit prices.

Clearly, there is no problem when total and unit prices coincide.

1.1.25.   "Pathological" and "Concerted" Price Variations

A systematic study of price variations brings to light valuable information on the actual working of competition.

Here a distinction must be made between two kinds of variations which have to be considered:

a)   pathological variations;
b)   concerted variations.

It will be recalled that in Table 4, price variations over the reference period are classified in decreasing order for each item and sales point (the total number of lines in the table is, therefore, the number of different items multiplied by the number of sales points at which they are offered).

Pathological variations appear at the top of the table: these are the biggest price increases recorded during the period covered. The table also gives prices at the start of the period (time t) and at the end of the period (time t + i) as well as the sales point involved. If these pathological price increases are charged by sales points which already had the highest retail prices, it may be concluded that these outlets have dominant power in the area or district where they are located. It will then be essential to analyse their buying prices and mark-ups. In any event, the causes of these pathological variations will have to be explored by the method described in Chapter II.

But Table 4 also switches on another "red warning light" for concerted variations.

Any "identical" price variation, i.e.an identical percentage for the same product at several points not owned by the same purchasing group or organisation (operator group) is always suspect: it is suspect even if the percentage rise is small or a price is reduced.

It is the fact that the rate of variation is identical for several shops which renders such a variation suspect, i.e. the result of concerted action. The degree of suspicion will be increased if prices at the start (time t) and the price at the end of the period (time t + i) are very different before the change and therefore remain so afterwards, as between the different sales points. And yet the shops concerned vary their prices by exactly the same amount. This would be impossible without prior concerted action.

Table 3a shows clearly, not only price variations but also the price before and after, together with the sales points concerned.

Table 3a, therefore, brings to light restrictions on competition and concerted practices affecting not only price levels at a given time but also levels of price variations.

Retailers who engage in such concerted practices have probably concluded an informal agreement to base their price policy on a specified rate (or increase of decrease) which is either fixed case by case, or, is automatically determined on the basis of a special formula of which it would be interesting to have details.

Quite obviously, a practice of this kind is a very powerful and destructive factor in the spread and growth of inflation.

This would seem to be further confirmation of the view that the findings of this research programme can make an effective contribution to the fight against inflation.

Two practical examples will help to illustrate the circumstances described above.

FIST EXAMPLE : One product, one brand (I)

We will take a single product (rice) costing respectively Lit.500, 600, 700, 800, 900 or 1000 at six different sales points (A, B, C, D, E, F,) on 15th January 1977.

We then assume that six months later, the unit price for the same product of the same type, brand and size are as follows:

Sales Point	Unit price in lire.		Price increase
	15.1.77	15.6.77	(%)
A	500	550	+ 10 %
B	600	660	+ 10 %
C	700	770	+ 10 %
D	800	880	+ 10 %
E	900	990	+ 10 %
F	1000	1100	+ 10 %

Without prior agreement between the six retailers involved, is it possible that variations should be identical for such widely differing selling prices? The question answers itself.

Price can therefore differ, even to a very considerable extent, even when their movements are the result of a retailers' price agreement; at first sight this may appear something of a paradox.

SECOND EXAMPLE : One product, three brands (I, II, III)

Instead of a single brand, let us next take the case of three different brands of the same product, made and marketed by three different producers. The position as at 15th January 1977 and 15th July 1977 is summarised in the table below:

Sales Point	Unit price in lire						Price increase (%)		
	15.1.77			15.6.77					
	Brand			Brand			Brand		
	I	II	III	I	II	III	I	II	III
A	500	520	600	550	572	660	+10%	+10%	+10%
B	600	600	560	660	660	616	+10%	+10%	+10%
C	700	650	600	770	715	660	+10%	+10%	+10%
D	800	800	700	880	880	770	+10%	+10%	+10%
E	900	850	750	990	935	825	+10%	+10%	+10%
F	1000	1000	800	1000	1100	880	+10%	+10%	+10%

A table like this suggests the existence of a network of agreements and concerted practices, quite certainly involving the six retailers (A,B,C,D,E,F) and also most probably the three "independent" producers of the three different brands (I, II, III). Otherwise,what explanation is there for the perfect synchronisation of the changes in retail prices, all fixed at the absolutely identical rate of 10% despite the substantial differences between the prices charged at the six sales points?

To sum up, Table 3a can act as a "red warning" giving the signal for thorough and promising investigations of restraints on competition.

1.1.26   Criterion No.18: Classification of Sales Points on the Basis of Mark-Ups

The mark-up ($q_j x$) on each specific item covered by each survey is calculated.

A column in Table 1 gives:

a)   selling price;

b)   buying price[1];

c)   mark-up expressed as the percentage of the buying price which has to be added to that price in order to arrive at the selling price.

However, differences in the mark-ups for each item and for each type of business are to be found in Table 5, in which the items are listed in decreasing order according to percentage mark-up. The same table also gives the sales points with the maximum and minimum mark-up for each item in the sample.

In a period of inflation and steep price increase, a very high mark-up rate is to be expected and the mark-up then includes the retailer's speculative profit.

Mention should also be made of Table 5a which acts as a "red warning" in the same way as Table 3a (see comments in Section 27). This table will classify in decreasing order real, actual mark-ups for each item and each sales point (the total number of lines in this table will be the total number of items multiplied by the number of sales points at which they are offered).

The products, i.e. the specific items and sales points at which the mark-up ("marge beneficiare brute") is greatest will appear at the top of the table while the items and sales points where the mark-up is lowest or is even a mark-down (actual selling price less than the actual price paid for a given item) will appear at the bottom.

1.1.27.   Scrutiny of Trends and Concept of "Combined" Tables:"Linda zones"(Tables 11 & 12)

The combined tables (11/A and 11/B) will be particularly helpful in tracking down the "critical" products which will have to be chosen for in-depth analysis during the second stage of research (Chapter II). These tables have three essential features:

---

1. Buying price is the seller's invoiced price for each specific item covered, for delivery to a retailer's shop or warehouse. It is therefore the "real" price paid by the retailer to buy - at some date which obviously precedes the time of the survey - each specific item on display in his shop. Clearly therefore, it is not the current buying price at the time of the price survey which has to be considered.

I.   They deal only with "critical" products and sales points which raise questions and doubts regarding the effectiveness of competition to which such products and sales points are exposed.

II.   They are concerned not with absolute values but with "relative" magnitudes expressed as percentages. For example:

   (a) $t + i_{s_j}$: percentage variation of retail price over a given period;

   (b) $t + i_{q_j}$: percentage mark-up;

   (c) $*C_4$: degree of concentration of the market for the product in question, at national level in the country concerned. Only Table 11/A gives this figure.

III. In this way, each combined table sets out, side by side, strictly comparable magnitudes in the form of percentages relating to several countries and/or regions.

These tables should reveal not only restrictions at national or local level but also restrictions which may result from agreements or concerted practices between manufacturers and/or retailers in different countries and/or regions.

In the case of Tables 11/A and 11/B, the "flashing light" which sets off the alarm signal is the rate of price increase (t + i sj) over the period under consideration and, to a lesser extent, the percentage mark-up (t + i qj), because a higher figure for even one of these percentages is always a disturbing symptom as regards the health of the machinery of competition for the product or sales point involved.

Consequently, the classification criterion for these tables is the "degree of danger" to the working of competition in the market for each product (Table 11/A) and at each sales point (Table 11/B) in the national and/or regional samples analysed. The tables are based on the colours of the four "Linda zones"[1]:

   a)   red   : serious, probable danger;
   b)   orange   : serious or possible danger;
   c)   yellow   : situation to be kept under scrutiny;
   d)   green   : probably no danger.

How is the appropriate colour zone for a given product or sales point decided? There are two basic criteria:

---

1. See: R.Linda "Domination, concurrence et concentration des marchés dans la structure industrielle de la Communauté", op.cit. pp. 71 - 85.

a)   the "absolute" criterion of relative size;

b)   the "relative" criterion of relative size (or criterion of the
           "quartile" in the statistical series).

Relative size can in fact be expressed as a percentage.

The absolute criterion has already been applied to the degree concentration (see Section 12 above) in stating, for example, that all products with a standard concentration ratio ($*C_4$) exceeding 80% belong to the "red zone" by definition. This absolute criterion has been worked out from great practical experience of research into the evolution of concentration and competition in all sectors and markets in the EEC Member States.[1]

This criterion is, therefore, also applied to the third section of Table 10/A ($*C_4$: concentration of the product at national level).

This criterion cannot, however, be applied to the other two sections of Table 10/A (variation of prices and mark-ups) because of the very complex and irregular nature of the phenomenon of inflation in the case of price variations and because of the equally irregular and complex effect of inflation on the rate of mark-up.

Some other criterion must therefore be sought because it is absolutely essential to be able to rank both products and sales points in relation to each other as regards danger to competition.

A relative criterion is therefore introduced by sub-dividing the statistical series (assuming 2400 terms)[2] in Table 4 (price variations in decreasing order) into four "zones":

a)   the first (red zone) from the maximum value (maximum price increase) down to the first quartile (in our example, the 600 terms showing the biggest increase);

b)   the second (orange zone) between the value of the first quartile and the median value;

c)   the third (yellow zone) between the median and the last quartile;

d)   the fourth (green zone) between the last quartile and the minimum value

---

1. A list of concentration studies can be found in Annex 2 of the "Methodology".

2. The example is based on an "average" hypothesis of 80 items (on average) sold by 30 sales points. This gives a total of 2400 terms or lines in Table 3a. However, as products for which no price variation falls within the red or orange zones are not included, the total number of terms or lines which will be ranked and used to produce Table 11/A will be somewhere between 1200 and 2400. If all three sections of the table (price variations and mark ups, and concentration) show that any product (item) always comes within the yellow or the green zone, the product (item) in question is not included. In the extreme case, therefore, the same products (items) could be eliminated from each section, so that the total number of products (items) to be considered and ranked would automatically drop to half 2400.

(in our example, the 600 terms showing the lowest increase, or even a price reduction).

Terms below the median and hence the last two zones will not be included in Table 10/A[1].

The procedure is the same for mark-ups, using the statistical series in Table 6.

On this basis it will be possible to count and regroup all the products coming within each zone and to enter the number of cases in Table 11/A which deals with products. Naturally, each product (item) is taken separately for each country, even though it is classified and entered in the same table.

Table 11/B for sales points in compiled in much the same way but is much smaller than Table 11/A because in our specimen sample of 30 sales points, there will be only 15 to 30 lines. For example only 15 sales points will be included when the same sales points fall in the red and orange zones for both price variations and mark-ups.

Table 11/B has only two sections instead of three as in Table 11/A because it does not cover either the national concentration of products or - as might have been anticipated because of the enormous technical obstacles - the inclusion of degrees of local concentration of sales points in the "classification into zones".

Nevertheless, when the second stage of the survey has been completed (Chapter II) it may prove possible to add the third section to Table 11/B.

Finally, it should be noted that:

a)   it will not be easy to complete Tables 11/A and 11/B in full and the total number of cases coming within each zone will not be entered for products and sales points for which it has not been possible to complete all sections of each table;

b)   Nevertheless, even if they are completed only partially and incompletely, these tables have very considerable practical value[2] because they reveal significant relationships.

---

1.   The example is based on an "average" hypothesis of 80 items (on average) sold by 30 sales points. This gives a total of 2400 terms or lines in Table 3a. However, as products for which no price variation falls within the red or orange zones are not included, the total number of terms or lines will be ranked and used to produce Table 11/A will be somewhere between 1200 and 2400. If all three sections of the table (price variations, mark-ups, concentration) show that any product (item) always comes within the yellow or the green zone, the product (item) in question is not included. In the extreme case, therefore, the same products (items) could be eliminated from each section, so that the total number of products (items) to be considered and ranked would automatically drop to half 2400.

2.   This is why, for the correct interpretation of the tables, a detailed note will have to be appended setting out criteria and reservations concerning the collection and processing of the data for certain products and sales points. In particular, the concept of mark up adopted and the basis of evaluation used will have to be explained in detail.

a)   As regards products:

I)   between price increases and rates of mark-up;

II)   between price increases and degrees of concentration of products at national level;

III)   between rates of mark-ups and degrees of concentration of products at national level.

b)   As regards sales points:

i)   between price increase for all products sold at each sales point;
                                and
ii)   general level of mark-ups applied (at the end of the period) at each sales point considered.

This gives very valuable guidance on any increase in the market power of the sales points in the sample.

1.1.28   "Identical data" (either absolute or relative) as a sign of concerted practices

Another "flashing light" which sets off the alarm system is to be found in identical price variations or mark-ups.

It was noted earlier in the discussion of concerted price variations (Section 27 above) that producers and/or retailers can very easily agree always to vary their prices by exactly the same percentage. They do not fix an absolute price but they do fix price variations. This is very simple, but the effect on inflation can be decisive.

Tables 12/A and 12/B will include only products and sales points affected by such concerted variations.

Three comments have to be made, however, concerning the concept of "relative identity" and its interpretation, the special position of price controls and the computation and interpretation of the mark-up.

I)   Concept of relative identity and its interpretation

It may be assumed that when producers and/or retailers reach agreement on fixing price variations or rates of mark-ups, the parties to the agreement are allowed a certain latitude.

The concept of "identical" (in the absolute sense) has, therefore, been somewhat extended and adapted to actual conditions by including deviations of not more than 4% from the reference percentage. Thus, if an "identical" 10% variation of price is found to have been applied by a number of sales points, Tables 12/A and 12/B will also include other sales points applying a price increase of between 10 and 10.4% (the actual percentage will be shown in brackets beside the name of the sales point).

This will be referred to as "relative identity".

There remains the problem of interpreting the significance of such "relatively identical variations".

Reference is made here to our earlier remarks concerning pathological and concerted price variations (Section 27 above). But these are identical variations in the absolute sense: exactly 10% (or 20% or 50%) and nothing more or less !

On the other hand, when the variation is 10.4% instead of 10%, how can we exclude the possibility that the rates of variation may have been brought closer by the stabalising effect of competition?

It should be borne in mind, that surveys are carried out at six monthly intervals. It is also possible, therefore, that a given retailer increases prices and that, under the influence of the type of competition and market pattern typical of oligopolistic structures, other retailers align on the price charged by the first who, in that case, would play the role of price leader.

These circumstances would automatically lead to uniform prices. But three points have to be noted:

First Point

Uniform prices are the result of the working of a certain kind of competition, but do not in any way presuppose that a genuinely competitive market mechanism will operate subsequently. Far from it. The existence of uniform prices is an obstacle to the working of competition.

Second Point

If, starting from a differential price system, alignments result in a system of uniform prices, this amounts to saying that price variations have not been uniform but differential. This situation is not,therefore, covered by our hypothesis (on which Tables 11/A and 11/B are based) which is founded on the existence of identical price variations.

Third Point

Lastly, if we have a combination of two hypotheses:

a)   uniform prices to start with;
b)   identical price variations;

the result will be the establishment of a new balance based on uniform prices.

All these aspects will be clearly demonstrated by Tables 11/A and 11/B and enable us to conclude that, in this case, there are very severe restraints on competition. The combination of agreement, price leadership and concerted practices results in uniform prices and identical variations which are concerted in one way or another.

Moreover, these are not identical variations in the relative sense but identical variations in the absolute sense, because, starting from uniform (initial) prices they result in new and equally uniform prices.

To go further into the problem of relative identity, therefore, we must take up again the hypothesis of Section 27 of this chapter, which is based on differential prices; it is, therefore, a question not of the alignment of prices, but something quite different, the alignment of variations of prices which continue to differ between sales point.

It is clear, however, that when variations are relatively identical (deviations from 1 to 4% above the identical reference rate) there are few grounds for automatically concluding that concerted practices exist (as was possible for identical variations in the absolute sense); stage two of the research will then have to be initiated and the frequency of surveys will have to be stepped up to one a month instead of one every six months, as is made quite clear in Section 5 of Chapter II (2.5.19; 2.5.20; 2.5.21).

II)   Special position of price controls

The foregoing arguments once again show clearly how disastrous the fixing of maximum prices by governments is for any clear insight into the actual working of competitive mechanisms.

The fixing of maximum prices has the effect of setting up a screen or throwing a blanket of fog over the activities and more especially the aims and motives of oligopolists. No-one can know whether they are bound by practices which limit competition or whether they simply align themselves on the maximum prices fixed by the government.

The final outcome is uniform initial prices + identical variations = new uniform prices = stifling of competition, with no chance for governments to intervene effectively.

These conclusions confirm those of Sections 18 to 21 above and those of the Sixth Report on Competition Policy (Brussels- Luxembourg, April 1977) of the Commission of the European Communities.

This report quite rightly stressed the very serious danger which any government price-fixing policy carries for the spread of inflation.

Indeed, the alternative for any such policy is either to fix uniform prices, aligned on the most efficient sales points and thus to eliminate from the market all marginal sales points with higher distribution costs and prices, or to fix uniform prices aligned in the highest prices charged at the dearest sales points, thus causing great economic hardship for consumers and creating huge "rents of position" for the most efficient and cheapest sales points, which is hardly likely to check inflationary trends.

These conclusions reached by the Commission of the European Communities are backed by the following arguments. On the basis of some provisional results of surveys now in progress, it is reasonable to assume that the size and location of sales points have a decisive effect on the distribution costs and profit-earning capacity of each sales point. Taking the extreme case, it becomes possible to state the following simpler hypothesis; a small supermarket or a small independent shop in a city centre may have a cost structure forcing it to charge prices 40% higher than those of a huge supermarket located on the edge of the country where land is cheap, near to the interchange of several fast motorways so that goods are delivered more easily and are easier to store.

On the basis of this simplified hypothesis, a relative difference of 10 to 40% over minimum prices can be regarded as almost a normal hypothesis linked with the very different cost structure of each sales point.

This gives three hypotheses for price differences:

a)   normal hypothesis: the difference between maximum and minimum price is 10% or over but less than 40%;

b)   hypothesis of divergence: the difference is 40% or over;

c)   hypothesis of uniformity: the difference is less than 10%.

III)   Computation and Interpretation

Measurement of mark-up depends not only on conditions of competition both upstream (bargaining power of the retailer in relation to the supplier) and downstream (pressure of competition from other retailers on consumer markets), but also on the nature of the product, shelf life, storage time and costs, cost of transport between a retailer's warehouses and shops, total quantity sold by the retailer concerned etc,.

As was quite correctly noted in the Fifth Annual Report of Competition Policy, these conditions vary considerably as between sales points (see preceding page).

Consequently:

a)   a very high mark-up is no more than a disturbing symptom of restrictions on competition and even then it has to be interpreted with caution and all kinds of reservations;

b)   the existence of identical mark-ups - even if only "relatively identical" - applied at different sales points is a much more disturbing symptom of such restrictions on competition because sales points operating in different conditions would naturally be expected to apply different mark-ups.

The practical value of Tables 11/A and 11/B is thus further confirmed but there remains the crucial problem of computing the real mark-up at each sales point. This involves the whole problem of real purchase price and real date of purchase.

This problem is so complex that it can only be dealt with exhaustively and systematically in the second stage (see Section VII of Chapter II).

It is therefore, quite possible that the mark-up section of Tables 11/A and 11/B cannot be completed until the results of the second stage of the surveys are available. Meanwhile, however, it may be possible to work on the basis of mark-up _ranges_, at least for certain products and sales points, so as to reveal any signs of concerted action by some sales points in the way they set and/or vary their mark-ups.

1.1.29   General Points

At this stage it should be noted that:

a)   the purpose of this section has been to provide a general survey of the background to the research, and in particular to identify the general idea, behind Tables 1-11:

b)   the next step is to enumerate all the technical considerations required for the computer processing of these tables, and to explain the specific scope and purpose of each table.

1.2.   SERIES OF DETAILED TABLES : PRICES - MARK-UPS

1.2.1.   Overall survey of the tables

        During the fist stage (Chapter I) of the survey, a series of tables must be
produced to indicate the reference points needed for setting up the next stage (Chapter II).

        The first-stage tables cover all the products (items) and all the sales points
in the sample.

        We can sub-divide the tables as follows:

a)   Tables 1 - 8 , to be compiled for each country and/or region studied;
b)   Table 9, representing a first attempt at a country-by-country comp-
            arison of prices;
c)   Tables 10 and 11, representing a possible subsequent stage during
            which specific restrictions of competition will be tracked down and
            brought to light.

TABLE 1   Detailed results by sales point and product – new version suggested by Mr Allaya
            (Montpellier).

TABLE 2   Products ranked according to price differences (ϵRp) in per cent between sales
            points.

TABLE 3   Products ranked according to differences in price variations (ϵAs) between two
            given surveys.

TABLE 4   Ranking by decreasing order of price variations for all items and all sales points
            covered.

TABLE 5   Products ranked according to relative differences between mark-ups (ϵqj)

TABLE 6   Ranking by decreasing order of mark-ups for all articles and all sales points
            covered.

TABLE 7   Measurement of price differences by product group.

TABLE 8   Regrouping of products/brands (including own labels) according to unit price and
            variations on unit prices.

As noted, these tables will be compiled for each country (or region), on the basis of a very limited sample of sales points (on average 30 to 50 per country or region). Tables 4 and 6, however, may also be compiled for a specific group of countries and/or regions. The tables should be fairly easy to interpret.

Naturally, only part of these tables will be published in the final reports; the bulk of them will be used as raw material for summary tables.

TABLE 9   List of products comparable at international level on the basis of unit price.

This table illustrates price differences at Community level for certain specific products.

All the above tables will be prepared by computer.

1.2.2.   The "Combined Tables"

These tables consist of a combination of:

- data relating to separate but linked phenomena, for which it is important to determine any correlation;

- geographical coverage, since data for different countries and/or regions can be combined in the same table.

TABLE 10   Combined tables for the "zones".
            A.   Ranking of products;
            B.   Ranking of sales points.

TABLE 11   Combined tables for "identical data".
            A.   Ranking of products;
            B.   Ranking of sales points.

Tables 10 and 11 are already selective in that they cover only products and sales points of interest for the study of restrictions of competition, the"critical" products and sales points, as it were.

These tables cover a number of products, whereas those planned for Stage 2 (Chapter II) will cover only one "critical" product or one "critical" sales point at a time.

1.3. COMMENTS ON THE PRICE MARK-UPS TABLES

The following notes should be consulted before reading and interpreting Tables 1 - 11B.

1.3.1. Table 1

It should be noted that any future analysis or study must take Table 1 as its starting point. Generally speaking, it sets out the data as collected by the researcher, and indicates the mark-up, that is, the percentage added to the buying price by each retailer to give the retail price. The table also shows the type of business (e.g. suburban super-market) for each sales point in the sample and gives all the figures (overall prices, unit prices, mark-ups) not only for the most recent survey but also for an earlier survey, for comparison purposes.

Table 1 gives detailed figures for both the sales point and for each product, that is, for each item (brand/size). It should be noted that the table gives a number of important details for each product:

a) the product group : the product is placed in one of the 22 product groups according to Criterion No.2. (alphabetical code, i.e.: "CON", "ENF", "SOU", "LEG", etc.,)

This information is to be supplied by the Research Institute.

b) The importance of the item in question -(according to Criterion No.6):
   i.e. (1) essential item;
        (2) non-essential item;
        (3) item of varying importance.

c) The origin of the product, i.e. home-produced, imported or partly home-produced (see Criterion No.4)

d) The method of pricing: usual price of special offer, or other unspecified methods (see Criterion No.5).

e) The size of packaging, generally indicating the exact net weight, in grammes or kilos (drained net weight for certain types of preserved and tinned foods).

f) The brand name under which the product is marketed in the country in question.

g)   The type of brand, that is, the manufacturer's brand, trademark or distributor's own label (see Criterion No. 3).

h)   The name and nationality of the manufacturer, or, if the manufacturer is unknown, the name of the commercial group or sole distributor (own label) (see Criterion No.8).

i)   Selling price and buying price: this is the total price paid for a given article, i.e. for each brand, type, size and weight of the product in question. In the case of bulk buying and selling, the selling and buying prices must be those of the same item.

j)   Overall mark-up: this is the difference between the total selling price and total buying price.

k)   Coefficient: this is the clearly-defined quantity (e.g. kg) to which the overall price refers.

l)   Unit price: this is normally obtained by the computer by dividing the total selling (or buying) price by the quantity (= coefficient).

m)   Mark-up : this is the percentage which must be added to the unit buying price to obtain the unit selling price.

1.3.2.   Complex algebraic expansions and interdependent variables in the analysis

We can therefore ask questions along the following lines:

a)   Are differences in selling price greater:
        - for home-produced goods:
        - or for imported products?

b)   is there a price relationship between all the items produced by a large manufacturer, or between the items produced by all the manufacturers of a given nationality?

        For example, are differences in overall price more or less the same for the various items produced by a given manufacturer, or on the contrary, highly variable?

        Are mark-ups more or less the same for all (or nearly all) the goods produced by a given firm, or do they vary greatly according to the item and/or the sales point?

Do some manufacturers (and perhaps some sales points) consistently charge different prices according to the size or form of the packing?

c)   Are the unit prices of "own-label" items comparatively higher or lower than those bearing the manufacturer's label (sold everywhere else) at sales points where:

  - there is nor competition with similar products bearing the manufacturer's brand;

  - there is such competition since similar products bearing the manufacturer's brand are also available at the "sales points" in question?

These three points will be further considered in order to throw light on a number of basic questions:

a)   What role do imports and importers play in price movements, from the standpoint of analysing the process of inflation? To what extent can imports become a deflationary factor?

b)   What is the overall strategy applied by the largest manufacturers to fix the price of their various products, according to geographical area, type of retailer (buying these products) and certain characteristics of the goods in question?

c)   What use do the largest retailers make of their bargaining power in relation to manufacturers? To what extent does competition between retailers really exist, and what benefits does the consumer gain from the effects of retailers' bargaining power?

1.3.3.   Dynamic and international approaches

It is even more important that all these relationships, and other possible relationships, may be used:

a)   as the first step in working out a "dynamic framework", since Table 1 gives data not only for the survey in question, but also for any chosen, previous survey (six months, one year, five years etc.,) according to the aims and requirements of the research. The static comparative method, which analyses differences in price and mark-ups between two different points in time, allows significant conclusions to be drawn on the evolution of commercial structures and of industrial and commercial strategies.

b) internationally, to compare:

- prices and profits in the various EEC Member States;
- changes in these given structures over a period.

It should then ultimately be possible to identify two "long-term industrial strategies":

I) The pricing policies of the largest manufacturer in the international field and changes as regards products, countries, retailers and profitability;

II) the pricing policy of the largest retailers, their profitability and their tendency to retain commercial power by the use of own labels in order to offset the power of supply.

In this way the quantitative data obtained from a long series of surveys on prices and mark-ups would provide the basis for a full factual analysis of the interaction, at international level, of interdependent strategies practised by manufacturers and retailers, the aim of this analysis being to identify developing trends in the structure of competition.

1.3.4.   Breakdown of Table 1

There is clearly no single economic approach capable of interpreting all the data in Table 1, and in particular the salient features of the many facts it contains, because it is very wide in scope and includes all the raw data collected as well as some processed data.

Table 1 must, therefore, be processed as follows:

a) its contents must be logically sub-divided so that meaningful partial synthesis of the specific points to be brought out can be achieved; this is done here by means of Tables 2 to 10; see the following paragraphs.

b) by an "overall dynamic synthesis" which enables and compares in one or more tables all the data which seems particularly significant in the long term.

This second operation clearly depends on the results of the research project, as presented in concrete form in three or four years time. Only then will it be possible to attempt a new overall dynamic synthesis of this kind.

1.3.5.   Table 2

Table 2 contains the results of a series of computer calculations using the basic figures; it gives the difference between the maximum and minimum price of each product (right of table) and shows the corresponding sales points and the name of their owners, as well as the type of business (distinguishing at the same time between the broad group, based solely on size, and the detailed category based on size, location and purpose).

The products (that is the specific items according to brand and size of packing) are classified according to difference between maximum and minimum prices (£Rp in %: at the bottom of Column 3 of Table 2). We shall call this percentage difference "the relative percentage difference".

This index cannot be calculated unless:

- a comparison is made of all the prices recorded for an identical item (same product, same brand, same size) in all the shops covered, thereby ensuring that the number of observations (n*) coincides with the number of shops in which that identical item can be found and its price recorded;

- the two extreme prices (maximum and minimum)within the number n* of prices covered in the survey are isolated.

The next step is to visit the shop in question and check the accuracy of these two extreme prices so as to avoid factual errors wherever possible. These checks are all the more important when it turns out that the average price differs greatly from either the maximum price or the minimum price. When this happens (very wide price spread) it might be sensible to consider not only the highest prices - maximum price or "first maximum" - but also the next three prices down, i.e. second highest, third highest and fourth highest.

Where necessary these other maximum prices - and the sales points where they are found - will be entered in the last two columns 17 and 18 in Table 2. It will be useful to be able to compare the average price with the median price.

Table 2 also shows:

i)   the type of brand (manufacturer's brand, distributor's own label etc.) and the origin (home-produced, imported etc.,) since it is useful to know if the widest price differences (between the sales points in the sample) are to be found on imported or home-produced goods;

ii)   the pricing methods (normal price structure or special offer), since we must know this in order to assess the price differences.

1.3.6.   Table 3

Table 3 gives a breakdown on the comparative statics approach, it can be used to compare price variations over a given period. The products (items) are ranked according to the difference in price variations (ϵ As), i.e. according to the difference between the percentage increase (or reduction)from one shop to another. The sales point which has shown the highest price increase is also shown, as are the prices on dates t and t + i. The same details are given for the sales point which shows the smallest price increase (or reduction) over the period in question. Thus the figures do not refer to the maximum or minimum prices but to the prices of those articles which have increased the most (or the least) in a specific shop in relation to the increases recorded for that same article over the period in question in the other shops in the sample. Columns 8 and 9 (pricing methods) are of particular interest since it is essential to know whether the item was on special offer on a given date (t or t + i) in order to appreciate fully a given price increase (or reduction) for a given product (item).

Other information on each product covered by the survey and on its manufacturer may be useful for research into the causes and factors influencing the price increases or reductions.

1.3.7.   Table 4

In Table 4 the products (items) are ranked according to the <u>maximum rate of price increase</u> recorded in a particular shop.

It follows that if a product frequently appears at the top of the table because its price has increased heavily in several shops it would be reasonable to conclude that the price increases depend primarily on the manufacturer (and/or wholesaler or dealer), rather than on the retailer. Table 4 will, therefore, be extremely useful for the study proposed in Chapter I (section 1.2.)

1.3.8.   Table 5

Most of the notes on Table 2 apply equally well to Table 5. It will be interesting to compare the average mark-up with the median mark-up. It must be remembered that the information obtained on mark-ups generally corresponds broadly to the <u>official</u> mark-up rates, i.e. they are often understated. In fact, major retailers often obtain more favourable terms from their manufacturers, especially in connection with bulk buying and delivery dates. Given that special terms of business are often treated as business secrets it is impossible to know what mark-ups are actually applied. In certain cases and for certain retailers they can be considerably higher than the official mark-ups entered in Table 5. We will attempt to deal with this problem in Chapter II (Section 1.2.7.).

Despite these limitations, Table 5 gives an interesting picture since the figures are shown from the angle of comparative statics, meaning that the mark-ups recorded during an earlier survey are shown in brackets. Since the approved discount scales generally refer to the manufacturer's official terms and prices, any change in <u>official</u> mark-ups may be reflected in <u>actual</u> mark-ups, with the resulting benefit for certain major retailers.

1.3.9.   <u>Table 6</u>

In Table 6 the products (items) are ranked in decreasing order according to the percentage represented by the highest mark-up; the items at the top of the table produce the highest profit for the retailers involved (the salient features of the products are also shown).

- the names of these retailers;
- the selling prices (total and unit) recorded during a previous survey as well as the most recent in order to show whether or not the increased mark-up is linked to a recent increase in prices.

1.3.10.   <u>Table 7</u>

Table 7 gives a detailed list of all the products (items) classified by "product group" (Criterion No. 2), e.g. "CON", "ENF", "SOU", "EPI", in order to show:

(i)   The price difference between sales points for each product group, as well as the two sales points charging the maximum and the minimum price respectively for each specific item;

(ii)   The value of certain standard indices such as:
           - standard deviation, or SD (sigma),
           - the variation coefficient in % (V),
           - the relative difference in % (ε Rp).

It will be noted than within each product group ("CON", "ENF", etc.) each specific item is ranked according to the relative difference (εRp), so that the reader can immediately see which product group displayes the largest differences.

For each product group the overall price (average, maximum, minimum) is established on the basis of the arithmetical averages calculated for all the articles in each product group, as stated in Note 2 to Table 7.

By comparing the most recent results with those obtained from an earlier survey (figures in brackets) the reader will be able to answer the following questions:

- Do the differences in prices charges by two sales points always apply to the same items, or do they vary from one survey to another?

- Are certain sales points always the most expensive (or the least expensive), or do the price-leaders vary from one survey to another?

1.3.11   Table 8

Table 8 owes its originality to the fact that:

- identical or similar products marketed under different brand names or in different packages are listed and compared with one another on the basis of their unit price on the date $t + i$ $(t + i_{pu})$;
- the indices measuring the price spread and price trends (namely; V, $\mathcal{E}$ Rp,$\mathcal{E}$ As) are based not on the selling price of each specific item but on the unit price of each product. There will, therefore, be only one index (V, $\mathcal{E}$Rp,$\mathcal{E}$ As) for the whole range of items falling under the same product/brand heading.

The table will also help to interpret Tables 4, 10/A and 11/A. It will also be especially useful for the analysis in Chapter II. It will also be useful to compare the average price with the median price.

1.3.12   Table 9

At this stage, the research programme includes only one table designed to make comparisons between one Community country and another.

Its primary purpose it to enable the researcher to select products (items) which can usefully be compared from one country to another. Table 8 - one table for each of the relevant countries - provides the basic material.

It should, however, be noted that:

- only columns 1,2,3,4,6,15 and 17 in Table 8 are used in Table 9, which means that any reference to material obtained from a previous survey (t) is omitted;

- all the prices are converted into Belgian francs and also expressed in European units of account(rather than in the local currency);

- the price variations between t and $t + i$ are not taken into account.

For each product and each country there may be two sets of prices in Belgian francs and EUA, corresponding respectively to the two alternative methods of converting to the local currency:

a)   the rate based on purchasing power parities and/or exchange markets
        for the Belgian franc (Bfr);

b)   the rate based on the exchange market, for European units of account
        (EUA).

1.3.13   Tables 10/A and 10/B and 11/A and 11/B

These tables have been explained in paragraphs 1.1.27 (Scrutiny of trends and
Concept of Combined Table.......) and 1.1.28 ("Identical Data".....as a sign of concerted
practices).

1.3.14   The two central issues in the study of prices

All the tables listed above provide, in one way or another, the raw material
which needs to be sifted, refined and clarified before the two central issues in the study of
prices can be properly dealt with. These two issues are:

i)   country-to-country differences in buying prices/producer prices.
        (the static approach);

ii)   country-to-country comparison of price trends (the dynamic approach).

I.   (Static Approach)

There are very serious complications involved in ascertaining and studying the
buying prices actually paid by major retailers - i.e. the prices which should technically
correspond (in integrated trade) to the producer prices actually charged and actually
received by the producers themselves.

These prices must, however, be known and studied if we are to analyse:

a)   the strategies and practices engaged in by the producers and by major
        retailers;

b)   the level and components of the major retailers' mark-ups. In other
        words, a straightforward survey of retail selling prices that is not
        closely linked to a survey of actual buying prices would not lead the
        way to this type of "operational analysis",which seeks to establish
        the existence of legal and economic bases for applying Articles 85
        and 86 of the Treaty, and which alone can justify the setting-up of
        such a large-scale programme. The use of the "thermometer" - the
        retail prices paid by the final consumer - is admittedly an essential
        first stage in the search for a diagnosis and, later, for a solution
        to the situation, but it is not enough.

Before going any further, we should just mention a few special conditions and advantages. They cannot be readily quantified, but, nevertheless a country-by-country comparison of these buying prices and producer prices should help to detect, and above all to prove the existence (or otherwise), the importance and the impact of:

- discriminatory prices, where it is found that the price of a specific product varies considerably between one Community country and another (possibility of applying Article 86 where prices differ because of action taken by a dominant firm;)

- unfair prices, where, in one or more countries, the existence of an obviously excessive price is ascertained after all the components making up the cost price have been meticulously investigated (possibility of applying Article 86 where the excessive price can be charged because a firm occupies a dominant position);

- concerted prices, fixed at an artificially high level by means of agreements or concerted practices between undertakings (possibility of applying Article 85 where the dynamic analysis demonstrates the existence of this type of action in concert.)

We also propose to include another table in this Chapter (Table 9), which will highlight the differences in retail prices from one Community country to another on a specific date.

The table uses two conversion rates so that prices can be compared on an international scale from two different angles:

- the rate based on purchasing power parities, used for converting local currency into Belgian francs (or any other currency);

- the rate based on exchange market quotations for converting local currency into European units of account (or any national currency).

If both conversion methods give unequivocal and converging results we will have an objective and quantitative basis for attacking competitive anomolies, where the Commission might consider own-initiative to be called for under Articles 85 and 86.

II.   (Dynamic Approach)

Table 9 has two distinct limitations:

a) it deals only with retail prices, i.e. it looks no further than the "thermometer";

b)   It is <u>static</u>, in that it does not tackle the problem of comparative trends.

Table 9 is, however, a stepping-stone towards more interesting developments since it helps to:

- <u>select</u> a list of "critical products" whose progress along the economic pipeline from production to final consumer must be traced so that the role played by each cost component can be established;

- <u>complete the dynamic analysis</u> which will make it easier to monitor and distinguish the strategies and practices adopted by undertakings.

This dynamic approach should enable us to produce supplementary evidence of:

- the existence of <u>price co-ordination</u> (possibility of applying Article 85;)

- the existence of unfair prices, whose illegality will be established by means of a detailed study of the relationship between, on the one hand, <u>price variations</u> (at the retail, wholesale and manufacturing stages) between countries, towns and shops and, on the other, <u>variations in the components</u> that make up prices, mark-ups and costs (possibility of applying Article 86).

Chapter II will set out the guidelines of the research by which, it is hoped, the extreme complexity of price studies can be directly resolved with a view to achieving the "<u>operational objectives</u>" to which we referred in the Introduction (The Research Programme - Its Aims and Stages").

Detailed results by sales point and product.

No.of survey:
Date   :
(figures in parenthesis are for previous survey No.........)

TABLE 1

COUNTRY :.........
TOWN   :.........
CURRENCY :.........

SALES POINT.......... PRODUCT GROUP.......... TYPE OF SALES POINT.......... LOCATION.......... GROUP..........

Product	Product Group	Importance	Origin	Pricing Method	Size	Brand	Type of Brand	Manufacturer	Nationality of Manufacturer	Aggregate Selling Price	Aggregate Buying Price	Aggregate Mark-Up	Coefficient	Unit Selling Price	Unit Buying Price	Unit Mark-Up
										( )	( )	( )		( )	( )	( )
										( )	( )	( )		( )	( )	( )
										( )	( )	( )		( )	( )	( )
										( )	( )	( )		( )	( )	( )
										( )	( )	( )		( )	( )	( )

SURVEY OF PRICES AND MARK-UPS

TABLE 2

Products ranked according to price differences (εRp) between sales points (%).

No. of survey: ....   COUNTRY : ....
Date   : ....   TOWN   : ....
(figures in parenthesis are for previous survey No........)   CURRENCY : ....

Ranking	Rp (%)	Detailed description of the item (type,brand,size)	t+i, pj*: aggregate selling price,max, min, average 2	n* = number of observations.	Sales points involved.	Major cat.	Detailed cat.	Name of owner	Product Group	Type of brand	Origin	t	t + i	Name	Nationality	Other max. prices 3	Sales point involved.
						Type of Business						Pricing		Manufacturer or Distributor (OL)		(Where Applicable)	
1	2	3	4	5	6	7	8	9	10	11	12	13	14	15	16	17	18
1		...	( )										-			2nd	
			( )													3rd	
2		...	( )													4th	

1. εRp = $\dfrac{\text{Maximum price} - \text{minimum price}}{\text{Minimum price}} \times 100$

2. Highest selling price or first maximum.

3. In order of magnitude :2nd, 3rd, 4th highest.

The average price is not, of course, the mean between the maximum and the minimum, but the average of all the prices recorded at all the sales points in the sample for a given article.

SURVEY OF PRICES AND MARK-UPS

Products ranked according to the differences in the price variations (Σ As) (Column 12) between two given surveys.

No. of Survey:.............
Date   :.............
(Figures in parentheses are for a previous survey No.........)

TABLE 3
to be established for each country.

INDUSTRY :.............
COUNTRY :.............
CURRENCY :.............

Ranking	Detailed description and number of the item.	Product Number	Product Group	Type of Brand	Origin	Pricing			Manufacturer		ΣAs. Absolute deviation in % (in decreasing order)	Prices and Variations (between t and t + i)								
									No.	Nat.		Price		No. corr. sales point	Var. Max.	Price		No. corr. sales point	Var. Min.
						t	t + i	n*			12 = 16-20	t	t + i		t+i Sj in %	t	t + i		t+i Sj in %
												p_j	p_j		(var. max)	p_j	p_j		(var. min)
1	2	3	4	5	6	7	8	9	10	11	16-20	13	14	15	16	17	18	1)	20

13, 14, 17, 18 : p_j = Total Selling Price for the item considered in the given Sales Point.

TABLE 4

CLASSIFICATION OF PRICE CHANGES IN DECREASING ORDER,
SAMPLING ALL ITEMS AND SALES POINTS.

| $t + i$ Sj
Price change
(in %) | vPj
Total price | | vPu
Unit price | | Product, size,
brand | Sales point |
	t	$t + i$	t	$t + i$		No. and name of owner.

N.B: The above table will show a total number of n^*y^* price changes; for each article/
sales point combination the entry in the table should indicate the price change
($\pm$) in % between time t and time $t + i$ (where i = 1, 2, 3, ...). Those items
which have experienced the largest price increases (in each sales point) will appear
at the upper end of Table 4, while those items which have experienced no price change
or indeed have experienced a price reduction, will appear at the lower end of
Table 4.

TABLE 5

SURVEY OF PRICES AND MARK-UPS

Products ranked according to relative difference between mark-ups $(3\ qj)$

No. of survey.............
Date   ....
(Figures in parentheses are for a previous survey No......)

COUNTRY : ....
TOWN   : ....
CURRENCY: ....

Ranking	qj: Difference(%)	Detailed descr- iption of item prod,size,brand	qj:maximum ( ) minimum ( ) average ( )	n* number of observations	Sales points involved	Type of business		Name of owner	Product Group	Type of Brand	Origin	Pricing Method		Manufacturer/ Distrib. (OL)		Other max. prices. 3	Sales point involved
						Major cat.	Detailed cat.					t	$t + i$	Name	Nat.		
1	2	3	4	5	6	7	8	9	10	11	12	13	14	15	16	17	18
1		...	( ) ( ) ( )													2nd	
			( ) ( ) ( )													3rd	
2		...	( ) ( ) ( )													4th	

1. Difference in % = qj = maximum mark-up - minimum mark up.
2. Highest selling price for first maximum.
3. In order of magnitude; 2nd, 3rd, 4th highest.

The average price is not, of course, the mean between the maximum and the minimum, but the average of all the prices recorded at all the sales points in the sample for a given article.

66

TABLE 6

CLASSIFICATION OF MARK-UPS IN DECREASING ORDER,
SAMPLING ALL ITEMS AND ALL SALES POINTS.

$t + i$ qj Mark-ups (in %)	Total price vPj		Unit price vPu		Product, size, brand	Sales point No. and name of owner.
	t	t + i	t	t + i		

N.B.   The above table will have a total number of n*y* mark-ups, derived by multiplying the number of different items by the number of sales points which actually market those items. Those items that show the highest mark-ups in a given sales point at time t + i (where i = 1, 2, 3,.....) will appear at the upper end of the tables, while those items showing a very low mark-up, or indeed a negative mark-up, in a given sales point will appear at the lower end of Table 6.

SURVEY OF PRICES AND MARK-UPS

Measures of price differences by product group

No.of survey : ....
Date : ....
(figures in parenthesis are for previous survey No...............)

Product Group	Identity Code				n* (1)	Average and total price	Maximum Price			Minimum Price			Standard Deviation (S.D.) or (Sigma)	Standard Error (S.E.)	Variation coefficient in % (V)	Relative difference in % (≤ Rp) 3.
	Detailed description & no. of the item	Size/weight product	No.	Brand			Price	Sales Point		Price	Sales Point					
								No.	Wide Group		No.	Wide Group				
CON.																
total						(2)	(2)			(2)						
ENF.						(2)	(2)			(2)						
total																

(1) r.* = Number of observations
(2) The Arithmetic mean of different items constituting the Group, this mean being calculated on the Maximum Prices (or the minimum) registered for each item in the different Sales Point. In other terms, the basic hypothesis is that one man buys each item separately in the "Sales Point" where it costs more (or less).
(3) Within each Product Group the items are ranked according to the relative difference (≤ Rp)

68

SURVEY OF PRICES AND MARK-UPS

Regrouping of products/brands ("own-labels" included) according to the unit price and evolution of the unit price (1)

No. of survey:.........
Date   :t + i

TABLE 8
to be established for each country.

INDUSTRY:............
COUNTRY :............
CURRENCY:............

Description of items regrouped (2)	Identity Code Product No.	Identity Code Brand No.	n* (3)	Unit Price Average Price for each group t	Unit Price Average Price for each group t + i	Unit Price Average Price for each group Diff. in %	Unit Price Maximum Price for each group t	Unit Price Maximum Price for each group t + i	Unit Price Maximum Price for each group Diff. in %	Unit Price Minimum Price for each group t	Unit Price Minimum Price for each group t + i	Unit Price Minimum Price for each group Diff. in %	V (4) t	V (4) t+i	Rp 3 (in %) t	Rp 3 (in %) t+i	Price Variations between t and t+i (in %) MAX.	Price Variations between t and t+i (in %) MIN.	Price Variations between t and t+i (in %) As 3 in %
1	2	3	4	5	6	7	8	9	10	11	12	13	14	15	16	17	18	19	20

(1) All data are indicated for each item of the "Product/Brand" considered.
(2) Items referring to each "Product/Brand" are ranked in decreasing order of the Unit Price, within each "Product/Brand" class, taking into account the "Average Price for each Group" (Column 6), at time t + i.
(3) n* = Number of observations for each item at time t + i (in parentheses, at the right side in the same column, number of observations at time t).
(4) V = coefficient of variation.

All prices are expressed in national currency.

69

TABLE 9

SURVEY OF PRICES AND MARK-UPS

List of products comparable at international level on the basis of unit price.

No.of survey............
Date ....
(Figures in parentheses are for previous survey No.....)

COUNTRY : ....
TOWN : ....
CURRENCY : ....
Exchange rate : ....Bfr. (1)
 EUA (1)

Country	Description of items surveyed in each country(prod. size, brand)	Identity Code		n*	Pricing methods	Total price (in local currency)			Unit price in Bfr,and/or EUA and/or other			V (3)	ε Rp (4)
		Product	Brand			Average (2)	Max.	Min.	Average price(2.)	Max. price	Min. price		
D									(5) (6)				
F									(5) (6)				
I									(5) (6)				
NL									(5) (6)				
B									(5) (6)				
UK									(5) (6)				
IRL									(5) (6)				
DK									(5) (6)				

1. The following exchange rates were used to calculate prices in Bfrs and EUA respectively: DM.......and.......; FF........ and ......; Lit .... and .... etc.,
2. As elsewhere in these tables, the average price is calculated on the basis of all prices recorded at all sales points in the sample, rather than on maximum and minimum prices.
3. V = variation coefficient
4. ε Rp = relative difference (in %) = $\dfrac{\text{maximum price} - \text{minimum price}}{\text{minimum price}} \times 100$
5. Price based on purchasing power position.
6. EUA price based on free market rates.

SURVEYS OF PRICES AND MARK-UPS ON FOODSTUFFS AND BEVERAGES

CURRENCY CONVERSION TABLES

In European Units of Account (EUA)
In Belgian Francs (Bfrs)*

Equivalent in national currency of 1 EUA (1)

Country	National Currency	1976 January	1976 July	1977 January	1977 July
D	DM	3.03223	2.82434	2.68045	2.62517
F	FF	5.21284	5.31728	5.57233	5.57637
I	LIT	817.999	918.364	985.151	1014.236
NL	FL.	3.11146	2.99359	2.80409	2.80437
B	FB	45.7650	43.5582	41.1509	40.8048
UK	£	0.574278	0.614228	0.654430	0.666835
IRL	£IRL	0.574278	0.614228	0.654430	0.666835
DK	DKR	7.17504	6.76205	6.60115	6.85440

In Bfrs., (1), (2)

Country	National Currency	Conversion Rate	1976 January	1976 July	1977 January	1977 July
D	1 DM	(1)	15.092	15.422	15.352	15.543
		(2)	16.982	17.256	17.564	17.722
F	1 FF	(1)	8.7792	8.1918	7.3848	7.3174
		(2)	8.3991	8.3210	8.3003	8.1029
I	1 LIT	(1)	0.055947	0.047430	0.041771	0.040232
		(2)	0.069570	0.065340	0.061241	0.058985
NL	1 FL.	(1)	14.708	14.550	14.675	14.550
		(2)	15.884	15.818	15.896	15.794
B	1 FB	(1)	1	1	1	1
		(2)	1	1	1	1
UK	1 £	(1)	79.69	70.915	62.880	61.191
		(2)	101.62	99.650	93.916	90.345
IRL	1£IRL	(1)	79.69	70.915	62.880	61.191
		(2)	103.95	99.835	95.879	94.310
DKR	1 DKR	(1)	6.3783	6.4415	6.2339	5.9531
		(2)	5.8509	5.7034	5.6018	5.4372

1. Conversion rates based on free market exchange rates. See Eurostat (monthly general statistics bulletin) 1-1978, pp.167-168, Brussels, Luxembourg.¾

2. Conversion rates based on purchasing power parities calculated by the SOEC (General Statistics, Statistical Methods and Liaison Activities Directorate).

* The figures may also be expressed in other national currencies, calculated on the basis of the EUA conversion rates (free market exchange) indicated in the left-hand section.

COMBINED TABLES FOR ZONES PROPOSED BY REMO LINDA

TABLE 10/A
to be completed for one
or more countries and/or
regions.

A. CLASSIFICATION OF PRODUCTS

Rank	Product				Maker		Number of cases occurring in each zone												Total			
	Detailed description of item.	Product Group	Brand	Origin	No.	Nat.	I. (t+ i Sj) Variation of prices (Table 3a)				II. (t + i qj) Measurement of Mark-ups (Table 5a)				III. (*C_4) Concentration of product at national level (Table 1)				I	II	III	
							red	orange	yellow	green	red	orange	yellow	green	red	orange	yellow	green	red	orange	yellow	green

Products are classified according to the number of cases coming within the red zone of price variations (t + i Sj) and subsidiarily in the orange zone.

The list does not include products for which no case of "price variations" comes within the red or orange zone.

COMBINED TABLES FOR ZONES PROPOSED BY REMO LINDA

TABLE 10/B
to be completed for one
or more countries and/or
regions.

B. CLASSIFICATION OF SALES POINTS

Sales point				Number of cases coming within each zone.									
				I. (t + i Sj) Price variations (Table 3a)			II. (t + i qj) Measurement of mark-ups (Table 5a)			Total I and II		
Rank	No. and name	Type of Business		Name of owner.	red	orange yellow	green	red	orange yellow	green	red	orange yellow	green
		Broad Group	Detailed Cat.										

Sales points are classified according to the number of cases coming within the red zone of price variations (t + i Sj) and subsidiarily in the orange zone.

The list does not include sales points for which no case of price variations comes within the red or the orange zone.

73

COMBINED TABLES OF IDENTICAL DATA PROPOSED BY REMO LINDA

TABLE 11/A
to be completed for one or more countries and/or regions.

A. CLASSIFICATION OF PRODUCTS

| Product | | | | | Manufacturer | | Identical Data | | | | | | | | | | |
| | | | | | | | Price Variations | | | For reference $t+i$ S_j | | | Mark-Ups | | | For reference $t+i$ q_j | | |
Rank	Detailed description of item	Product Group	Brand	Origin	No.	Nat.	Identical $t+i$ $S_j > 1$ (%)	Number of cases	Names of sales points involved	Max.	Min.	Ave.	Identical $t+i$ $S_j > 1$ (%)	Number of cases	Names of sales points involved	Max.	Min.	Ave.

The list includes only products for which an identical variation of retail selling price has been recorded at at-least two sales points in the relevant period.

Identical refers to all rates exceeding by less than 4% the identical reference value ($t + i$ $S_j > 1$ or $t + i$ $q_j > 1$).

Products are classified by decreasing order of identical rate of variation $t + i$ $S_j > 1$. For reference, however, the rates $t + i$ S_j MAX (maximum variation), $t + i$ S_j MIN (minimum variation) and $t + i$ S_j AV (average variation) are also given.

74

COMBINED TABLES OF IDENTICAL DATA PROPOSED BY REMO LINDA

TABLE 11/B
to be completed for one or more countries and/or regions.

B. CLASSIFICATION OF SALES POINTS

Rank	Sales Point				Identical Data													
	No. and name	Type of Business		Name of Owner	Price Variations				For reference $t+i$ S_j			Mark-ups				For reference $t+i$ q_j		
		Broad Group	Detailed Category		Product	Identical $t+i$ $S_j > 1$ (%)	Number of cases	Names of other sales points involved	Max.	Min.	Ave.	Product	Identical $t+i$ $S_j > 1$ (%)	Number of cases	Names of other sales points involved	Max.	Min.	Ave.

The list includes only products for which an identical variation has been recorded. All rates exceeding the identical reference value ($t+i$ $S_j > 1$ or $t+i$ $q_j > 1$) by less than 4% are considered to be identical.

Sales points are classified in decreasing order of the number of products for which each sales point has applied a rate of variation (increase or decrease) identical with the rate applied by at least one other sales point, as regards price variations, and subsidiary as regards measurement of the mark-up.

All products for which sales points apply either an identical price variation policy or an identical mark-up policy are included in this table.

75

CHAPTER TWO

THE SECOND STAGE

POWER INTERPLAY BETWEEN RETAILERS AND PRODUCERS

2.1. THE SETS OF "ATOMS OF INFORMATION"

2.1.1. Description of the programme

The second stage of the research programme represents the bulk of the work to be done during the next few years.

It aims to outline and stress a variety of aspects of the :

"Power Interplay between Retailers and Producers".

Generally speaking, the "producer" is either an importer/exporter of agricultural or basic commodities or a manufacturer/processor, but it is well to remember that the power interplay may also involve primary or secondary wholesalers and agents. Our methodology - as regards the present Chapter Two - plans a clear distinction between the manufacturers/processors and the importers/wholesalers. [1]

Our approach will therefore extend to the intriguing question of the analysis of the structure and evolution of the complete economic channels through which the basic goods pass - with or without being submitted to manufacturing or processing - from the producing countries to the final western consumers. The fifth and sixth tables are, in particular, prepared for the purpose of such an analysis. See sections 2.5., 2.7. and 2.8.

All the raw data collected at the pilot stage, and especially at the first stage, will continue to be used to give a picture of the evolution of competition as concerns relationships :

- between retailers and consumers ;

- between retailers and producers.

In this respect, the reader is referred to the following concise schemes and tables referring to Chapter Two :

- First Reference Table, concerning structure (retail prices, mark-ups and buying prices) ;

- Second Reference Table, concerning evolution (retail prices, mark-ups and buying prices) ;

- Third Reference Table, concerning "Power Interplay", "Shop Efficiency" and "Loss Leaders" ;

- Fourth Reference Table, concerning excessive prices, breakdown of the final price and national and local concentration.

---

[1] A distinction will be made between "integrated" distributive firms, buying direct from the producer, and "independent" distributors, buying from wholesalers. Thus there will be two types of buying price, generally higher in the latter case than in the former.

Commentaries on the questions and tables will be found in the following sections of Chapter 2:

- the sets of atoms of information (2.1.)

- the brands and sizes available (2.2.)

- the selective historical series (2.3.)

- analysis of shop efficiency (2.4.)

- evolution of actual price structures for selected products (2.5.)

- negative mark-ups - loss-leading (2.6.)

- retail buying prices and power interplay (2.7.)

- completion of the monographic approach by product: excessive prices and their causes. And particularly the breakdown of prices (2.8.)

- completion of the firm-by-firm monographic approach: national and local concentration
(2.9.)

- crucial points of the research (2.10.)

International comparisons will play a leading role here. If these comparisons are to have real economic significance and operational value, they must satisfy certain basic conditions:

- comparisons must not be confined to retail selling prices in the various countries but must also extend to the various producer prices and possibly also dealer or wholesaler prices, thus highlighting the comparative effect of taxation in the various countries;

- the comparisons must be based not only on an average price for each country but also on the highest price (possibly even the highest two, three or four prices), the lowest price, and of course the average price (and possibly also the median price) observed in each local sample surveyed in each country;

- comparisons must not be confined solely to prices but must also consider retail mark-ups and, where the independent trade is involved, wholesale or trade mark-ups, thus again highlighting the effect of taxation in each country, so as to give comparisons of pre-tax mark-ups.

But it must be emphasised with particular force that the need is for price comparisons relating not only to identical products but also to comparable products. There are two aims here:

- to ascertain the range of choice available to consumers in each country and each town or city studied;

- to obtain pointers to the possible existence of market-sharing agreements or to the existence of particular barriers to trade between states, depriving consumers in this or that country or town of access to this or that brand or type of product of a given manufacturer.

This chapter of the research programme proposes a set of 140 questions designed to bring out every facet of the phenomena we are studying.

FIRST REFERENCE TABLE CONCERNING STRUCTURE (Retail Prices, Mark-ups and Buying Prices)

Corresponding questions

N°	RETAIL PRICE	N°	RETAIL MARK-UP	N°	BUYING PRICE
XIV (14)	Product: degree of dispersion of unit prices for the product.	XXXIX (39)	Product: degree of dispersion of mark-ups for the product.	LXV (65)	Product: degree of dispersion of buying prices for the product.
XV (15)	"Own Label" products: Unit prices of "O.L." products in relation to branded products.	XL (40)	"Own Label" products: Retailers' mark-ups in relation to branded products.	LXVI (66)	"Own Label" products: Buying prices paid by retailers for "O.L." products in relation to branded products.
XVI (16)	Imported products: Unit prices of imported products in comparison with home-produced goods.	XLI (41)	Imported products: Retail mark-ups in comparison with home-produced goods.	LXVII (67)	Imported products: Buying prices paid by retailers for imported products in comparison with home-produced goods.
XVII (17)	Shop identity: Highest (or lowest) unit price, all items considered.	XLII (42)	Shop identity: Absolute highest (or lowest) mark-up, all items considered.	LXVIII (68)	Shop identity: Highest (or lowest) unit buying price paid by retailers, all items considered.
XVIII (18)	Shop identity: Most expensive shop in relation to the shop's minimum unit price available.	XLIII (43)	Shop identity: Shop recording the highest mark-up.	LXIX (69)	Shop identity: Shop recording the highest unit buying price paid in relation to the minimum unit buying price of the shop.

Questions I to XII are examined in Section 2.2. — "The brands and sizes available".

FIRST REFERENCE TABLE CONCERNING STRUCTURE (Retail Prices, Mark-ups and Buying Prices)

Corresponding questions

N°	RETAIL PRICE	N°	RETAIL MARK-UP	N°	BUYING PRICE
XIX (19)	Shop identity: Highest (or lowest) unit price and choice available to consumers	XLIV (44)	Shop identity: Highest (or lowest) mark-up and choice available to consumers.	LXX (70)	Shop identity: Highest (or lowest) buying price and choice available to consumers.
XX (20)	Shops policy: Uniform or differentiated unit prices on different brands of the same manufacturer's product.	XLV (45)	Shops policy: Uniform or differentiated mark-ups on different brands of the same manufacturer's product.	LXXI (71)	Producers' policy: Retailers' unit buying prices paid for different brands of the same manufacturer's product.
XXI (21)	Shops' policy: Degree of dispersion of prices between different shops, for identical items.	XLVI (46)	Shops' policy: Degree of dispersion of mark-ups between different shops, for identical items.	LXXII (72)	Producers-retailers interplay: Degree of dispersion of buying prices between different shops for identical items.
XXII (22)	Shop identity: Dearest (or cheapest) shops selling identical items.	XLVII (47)	Shop identity: Shops applying highest (or lowest) mark-ups for identical items.	LXXIII (73)	Producers-retailers interplay: Shops paying the highest (or lowest) buying prices for identical items.
XXIII (23)	Shops' policy: Brands for which we have the highest degree of dispersion of prices. Countries (or regions) having the highest (or lowest) prices for identical items.	XLVIII (48)	Shops' policy: Brands for which we have the highest degree of dispersion of mark-ups. Countries (or regions) having the highest (or lowest) mark-up for identical items.	LXXIV (74)	Producers' policy: Brands for which we have the highest degree of dispersion of buying prices paid by retailers. Countries (or regions) having the highest (or lowest) buying price for identical items.

FIRST REFERENCE TABLE CONCERNING STRUCTURE (Retail Prices, Mark-ups and Buying Prices)

Corresponding questions

N°	RETAIL PRICE	N°	RETAIL MARK-UP	N°	BUYING PRICE
XXIV XXV (24/25)	Multi-shop operators' policy: Uniform or differentiated prices for identical items between different shops of the chain – different questions and hypotheses.	XLIX L (49/50)	Multi-shop operators' policy: Uniform or differentiated mark-ups between different shops – different questions and hypotheses – existence of endogenous competition.		
		LI LIII (51/53)	Multi-shop operators' policy: Hypotheses as to the causes of uniform retail prices charged by different shops of the same chain.		

SECOND REFERENCE TABLE CONCERNING EVOLUTION (Retail Prices, Mark-ups and Buying Prices)

Corresponding questions

N°	RETAIL PRICE	N°	RETAIL MARK-UP	N°	BUYING PRICE
XXVI (26)	Products: Variation of degree of dispersion of unit selling prices.	LIV (54)	Products: Variation of degree of dispersion of mark-ups.	LXXV (75)	Products: Variation of degree of dispersion of unit buying prices.
XXVII (27)	Product identity: Variation of the dearest or cheapest Brand/Size.	LV (55)	Product identity: Variation of the Brand/Size having the highest (or lowest) mark-up.	LXXVI (76)	Product identity: Variation of the Brand/Size having the highest (or lowest) buying price.
XXVIII (28)	"Own Label" products: Price increases for "O.L." products in relation to manufacturers' branded products.	LVI (56)	"Own Label" products: Increase or decrease in mark-ups in relation to manufacturers' branded products.	LXXVII (77)	"Own Label" products: Increase in buying prices for "O.L." products in relation to manufacturers' branded products.
XXIX (29)	Imported products: Price increases for imported products in comparison with home-produced goods.	LVII (57)	Imported products: Increases or decreases in mark-ups in comparison with home produced goods.	LXXVIII (78)	Imported products: Increases in unit buying prices for imported products in comparison with home-produced goods.

SECOND REFERENCE TABLE CONCERNING EVOLUTION (Retail Prices, Mark-ups and Buying Prices)

Corresponding questions

N°	RETAIL PRICE	N°	RETAIL MARK-UP	N°	BUYING PRICE
XXX (30)	Shop identity: Variation of the dearest or cheapest shop.	LVIII (58)	Shop identity: Variation of the shop applying the highest (or lowest) mark-up.	LXXIX (79)	Shop identity: Variation of the shop paying the highest (or lowest) unit buying prices.
XXXI XXXII (31/32)	Shop policy: Relationship between price increases and several factors qualifying the shop policy (range of products, imported goods, etc.)	LIX LX (59/60)	Shop policy: Relationship between increases and decreases in mark-ups and the factors indicated in question 31.	LXXX LXXXI (80/81)	Shop policy: Relationship between increases in buying prices and the factors indicated in question 31.
XXXIII (33)	Shop policy: Changes in manufacturers' brands.				
XXXIV (34)	Shop policy: Elimination of "own label" products or manufacturers' branded products and price variations on substitute products.	LXI (61)	Shop policy: Elimination of "own label" products or manufacturers' branded products and variations in mark-ups for substitute products.	LXXXII (82)	Shop policy: Elimination of "own label" products or manufacturers' branded products and variations in buying prices of substitute products.

SECOND REFERENCE TABLE CONCERNING EVOLUTION (Retail Prices, Mark-ups and Buying Prices)

Corresponding questions

N°	RETAIL PRICE	N°	RETAIL MARK-UP	N°	BUYING PRICE
XXXV (35)	Shop policy: Changes in size and/or packaging and increase in unit prices.	LXII (62)	Shop policy: Changes in size and/or packaging and variations in mark-ups.	LXXXIII (83)	Manufacturers' policy: Changes in size and/or packaging and increase in buying prices paid by retailers.
XXXVI (36)	Producers' and retailers' policies: Explanation given by producers and retailers on changes of brand/size/packaging.				
XXXVII (37)	Multi-shop operator Group: Uniform or differentiated price increases for identical items sold by different shops of the chain.	LXIII (63)	Multi-shop operator Group: Uniform or differentiated variations of the mark-up applied by the different shops of the chain.		
XXXVIII (38)	Regional and international comparisons of price variations in relation to several factors (questions 26 to 37 and 11 to 13).	LXIV (64)	Regional and international comparisons of variations in mark-ups in relation to several factors (questions 26 to 37 and 11 to 13).	LXXXIV (84)	Regional and international comparisons of variations in buying prices paid by retailers in relation to several factors (questions 26 to 37 and 11 to 13).

THIRD REFERENCE TABLE CONCERNING: - POWER INTERPLAY
SHOP EFFICIENCY
"LOSS LEADERS"

List of relevant questions

	POWER INTERPLAY (Section 2.7.): QQ 85-94
LXXXV (85)	Comparative evolution of prices (buying, producer's, unit retail prices) considering the maximum, minimum and average - identification of firms benefiting or suffering from the evolution.
LXXXVI (86)	Ranking of countries (and/or regions) according to the increases in different types of price.
LXXXVII (87)	Ranking of countries (and/or regions) according to the increases in differences between the different types of price - Explanatory causes.
LXXXVIII (88)	Identification of firms and countries (and/or regions) benefiting or suffering from the evolution - Quantitative breakdown of individual profits and losses.
LXXXIX (89)	Comparison between products - Ranking according to the increases in different types of price.
XC (90)	Comparison between products - Ranking according to the criteria indicated in question 87.
XCI (91)	Comparison between products - Ranking, by country, according to absolute sizes of different types of mark-up - retail, trader, importer, exporter - considering the maximum, minimum and average.
XCII (92)	Quantity discounts and rebates.
XCIII (93)	Discounts and rebates linked to exclusive rights.
XCIV (94)	Discounts and rebates under different forms - Difficulties of concrete evaluation.

THIRD REFERENCE TABLE CONCERNING: — POWER INTERPLAY
                                 SHOP EFFICIENCY
                                 "LOSS LEADERS"

List of relevant questions

	SHOP EFFICIENCY (Section 2.4.): QQ 95—103
XCV (95)	Identification of "the best (or the worst) shops", as concerns separately selling prices, mark—ups and buying prices.
XCVI (96)	General definition of efficiency — Identification of shops.
XCVII (97)	Degree of brand monopolisation and shop efficiency.
XCVIII (98)	Relationship between time in stock and retail buying price.
XCIX (99)	Relationship between time in stock and retail mark—up.
C (100)	Countries (and/or regions) having the most (or least) efficient shops.
CI (101)	Evolution of "shops" averages (unit selling and buying prices) — Breakdown by countries (and/or regions).
CII (102)	Identification of shops whose efficiency increases or deteriorates.
CIII (103)	Changes in ranking of shops according to the overall efficiency score.

List of relevant questions

	"LOSS LEADERS" (Section 2.6.): QQ 104-115
CIV (104)	Identification of shops opting for a loss leading policy, at a given moment.
CV (105)	Evolution of mark-ups and changes in loss leaders.
CVI (106)	Long term analysis and identification of retailers more attached to the loss leading policy.
CVII (107)	Explanatory causes – Hypothesis of predatory pricing.
CVIII (108)	Identification of products and brands chosen as loss leaders.
CIX (109)	Effects of loss leading on time in stock.
CX (110)	Effects of loss leading on retailers' buying prices.
CXI (111)	Effects of loss leading on retail selling prices.
CXII (112)	Loss leaders and own label products.
CXIII (113)	Loss leaders and imported products.
CXIV (114)	International comparisons, as regards products chosen as loss leaders as well as the different effects seen under QQ. 109-113.
CXV (115)	Attitudes of manufacturers towards loss leaders – Different questions.

FOURTH REFERENCE TABLE: EXCESSIVE PRICES
                         BREAKDOWN OF THE FINAL PRICE
                         NATIONAL AND LOCAL COMPETITION

List of relevant questions

	EXCESSIVE PRICES (Section 2.8.): QQ 116–118
CXVI (116)	Excessive prices – list of products and firms concerned – use of maxima (prices, mark-ups, differences, increases) – share of sole distributors.
CXVII (117)	Ranking of suspect products and firms by degree of probability of excessive pricing – role of exclusive agreements.
CXVIII (118)	Ranking of suspect products and firms according to the speed at which prices downstream react to changes in producers prices.

	BREAKDOWN OF THE FINAL PRICE (Section 2.8.): QQ 119–123
CXIX (119)	Table of comparative statics – comparative evolution of prices, mark-ups and components of margins and costs (reference to question 85 – shares accounted for by taxes).
CXX (120)	Explanations of trends observed in answering question 119.
CXXI (121)	Link between profits made by certain firms and the existence of dominant positions and/or restrictive agreements and practices.
CXXII (122)	Detailed breakdown of the mark-up (reference to question 91) – share accounted for by taxation.
CXXIII (123)	Detailed breakdown of producers prices into their various components.

FOURTH REFERENCE TABLE: EXCESSIVE PRICES
BREAKDOWN OF THE FINAL PRICE
NATIONAL AND LOCAL COMPETITION

List of relevant questions

	NATIONAL AND LOCAL CONCENTRATION (Section 2.9.): QQ 124-136
CXXIV (124)	Possible correlation between dominance of producers on a product market and level of retail selling prices.
CXXV (125)	Price increases and intensity of dominance.
CXXVI (126)	Dominance of producers and trends of prices at the various levels.
CXXVII (127)	Survey of dominant positions on national product markets held by the 100 largest agri-food firms in the western world.
CXXVIII (128)	Possible correlation between the dominance of a producer and the comparative profitability of the dominant firm.
CXXIX (129)	Possible correlation between price levels on a given product market and the profitability of the producer firm. Role and effects of exclusive agreements.
CXXX (130)	Price increases and profitability.
CXXXI (131)	Trends of prices and variations (uniform, identical) and profitability of the firms concerned.
CXXXII (132)	Evolution of the shares of the ten principal retail buyers in the aggregate sales of the ten principal manufacturers of food and beverages. The most profitable competitors.
CXXXIII (133)	Evolution of the shares of the ten principal manufacturing suppliers in the aggregate sales of the ten principal retail distribution groups. Alternative suppliers.
CXXXIV (134)	Possible relation between the development of producers prices and the absolute and relative shares bought by wholesalers and retail distributors.
CXXXV (135)	Special terms and advantages granted by producers in relation to the quantities bought by certain wholesalers and retail distributors.
CXXXVI (136)	List and market shares of the ten principal retail distribution groups on the national market and in a number of selected large conurbations – indicators of local concentration.

FOURTH REFERENCE TABLE: EXCESSIVE PRICES
                         BREAKDOWN OF THE FINAL PRICE
                         NATIONAL AND LOCAL COMPETITION

List of relevant questions

	NATIONAL AND LOCAL CONCENTRATION (Section 2.9.): QQ 137-140
CXXXVII (137)	Development over the last ten years of the market shares of the ten principal groups nationally and in selected conurbations – indicators of local concentration.
CXXXVIII (138)	Comparison between the evolution of concentration in distribution nationally and locally.
CXXXIX (139)	Individual sheet for each selected shop, comparing its pricing policy with the policy of other shops in the local sample (table XII).
CXL (140)	Comparative analysis and final conclusions on the basis of the overall results of the surveys: – relation between the market power of retail distributors locally and the relative levels of prices and mark-ups; – increase in concentration in local distribution and increase in prices and mark-ups; – existence of excessive or unfair prices by reason of the dominance enjoyed by producers; – detection of a number of practical cases (dominant positions, anti-competitive agreements, exclusive agreements); – value – necessity even – of broadening the surveys.

2.1.2. The problem of selecting essential data (products, retailers, producers)

The selection aims to extract a more restricted and more meaningful sample from the bulk of data available on:

a) products,

b) retailers (operator groups),

c) producers

and submit it to thorough analysis.

This manifold analysis will be situated in a dynamic framework, in order to bring out the relationships if any between the levels, disparity (or dispersion) and evolution of retail prices and:

- one one side: the level, disparity and evolution of buying prices and retail mark-ups,

- on the other side: the pricing policies and profitability of the retailers and producers concerned.

2.1.3. Comparisons based on unit prices

Accordingly, the comparisons will be based on the unit prices of different items, since the objectives set out above imply the need to compare a great number of brands and sizes - also including a great number of "own labels" - sold in a great number of shops and countries.

A specific analysis - in this dynamic framework - will concern each relevant product taken from the given sample on the basis of a set of six tables: "Selective Historical Series", based on the unit prices and data.

2.1.4. A set of six tables concerning only the selected products

Six tables concerning only the chosen relevant products (a) will therefore be the starting point for concrete and wider analyses - also taking into account all available financial, economic and legal information - on the bargaining power and actual behaviour of the selected:

- retailers (b)
- producers (c).

Further historical series tables are planned in order to bring out the evolution of turnovers and market shares and of all meaningful data for the main retailers as well as the main producers (Tables VII, VIII, IX, X, XI and XII).

SELECTIVE HISTORICAL SERIES

— concerning some relevant products taken from the sample —

TABLE I
UNIT SELLING PRICES: vPu
by shops and brands/sizes

PRODUCT:

COUNTRY: CURRENCY:

ENQUIRY		BRAND (AND SUPPLIER)	SIZE	ACTUAL PRODUCER OR MANUFACTURER
	RANK (R) AND CODE NUMBER (C) OF THE SHOP			
No. Date	R / I / II / III / IV / V / VI / .... / XXX			

| TOTAL No. OF BRANDS /SIZES IN EACH SHOP | (GB) (F) |
| SHOP AVERAGE EFFICIENCY SCORE RANK | T̄j (GB)(F) / vPu (GB)(F) / (GB)(F) |

REMARKS

EXPLANATORY NOTES REFERRING TO THE FIRST TABLE

- Shops of the sample are ranked according to the degree of "Brand/Size Monopolization" at time t, i.e. at the date of the first enquiry. Thus the first shop from the left is the one offering the smallest number of brands and/or sizes to the consumer, and the last shop (on the right) — whose ranking corresponds to the total number of shops in the sample — will be the shop offering consumers the broadest choice of brands and/or sizes. At the bottom of the table it is possible to see the range of choice available for the given product in each shop in each country.

- Horizontal broken lines separate data referring to two countries taken into account.

- Data given only by way of example are indicated in parentheses.

- The code number for each shop makes it possible to know the actual name of the shop (and of the operator group or chain) according to the lists referring to each country (in our example, two different lists for Great Britain (GB) and France (F) will be examined).

- The own label corresponds to the given shop selling the relevant product. Thus, as regards Great Britain, we will have different own labels for instant coffee for each retailer, such as Sainsbury, Key Markets, Safeway, Cater Bros., Waitrose, Tesco and so on. As regards France, in our example, we have the "Coop" own label.

- When a given brand and/or size is not available in one country but only in the other one, "n.a." (not available) will be indicated on the corresponding horizontal line for this country.

- In our example, it has been assumed that the sample is of 30 shops both in Great Britain and in France.

- As concerns the dates of surveys indicated in the table, 1977/1 indicates the survey carried out in the first half of the year (January/February), 1977/2 the survey carried out in the second half (July/August).

- Imported products are designated by an asterisk.

- The symbol "+" indicates the highest priced product/shop (or the highest mark-up) and the symbol "-" the lowest one.

- The last column (on the right) gives the name of the actual producer or manufacturer, which is not the same as the supplier when the latter is a wholesaler or dealer (exporter, importer).

- The bottom of the table gives, for each shop:
  - stock turnover period (time in stock) — Tj,
  - average unit selling price $(_vP_u)$; the second and third tables give the mark-up (q) and unit buying price $(_aP_u)$,
  - the score of each shop, from which an efficiency ranking can be derived (see at 2.2.6. and 2.4.3.).

SELECTIVE HISTORICAL SERIES

— concerning some relevant products taken from the sample —

TABLE II
RETAILERS' MARK-UPS: q
by shops and brands/sizes

PRODUCT:

COUNTRY:

CURRENCY:

ENQUIRY		RANK (R) AND CODE NUMBER (C) OF THE SHOP								BRAND (AND SUPPLIER)	SIZE	ACTUAL PRODUCER OR MANUFACTURER
No. Date	R / C / C	I	II	III	IV	V	VI	.....	XXX			
	(GB)											
	(F)											

OWN LABELS

TOTAL No. OF BRANDS /SIZES IN EACH SHOP	(GB) / /								
	(F) //								

REMARKS

SHOP AVERAGE EFFICIENCY

SCORE / RANK

SELECTIVE HISTORICAL SERIES

- concerning some relevant products taken from the sample -

TABLE III
UNIT BUYING PRICES: a.Pu
by shops and brands/sizes

PRODUCT:

COUNTRY: CURRENCY:

ENQUIRY			RANK (R) AND CODE NUMBER (C) OF THE SHOP								ACTUAL PRODUCER OR MANUFACTURER
No. Date		R	I	II	III	IV	V	VI	.....	XXX	SIZE
	(GB)	C									
	(F)	C									BRAND (AND SUPPLIER)
	(GB)	/									
	(F)	/									
	(GB)	/									
	(F)	/									
	(GB)	/									
	(F)	/									OWN LABELS
		/									
		/									
		/									REMARKS
TOTAL No. OF BRANDS /SIZES IN EACH SHOP	(GB)	/									
	(F)	/									
EFFICIENCY SCORE	T j (GB)	/									
	(F)	/									
	aRu (GB)	/									
	(F)	/									
SHOP AVERAGE RANK	(GB)	/									
	(F)	/									

97

SELECTIVE HISTORICAL SERIES

- concerning some relevant products taken from the sample -

TABLE IV

SYNTHESIS : RETAILERS UNIT
SELLING PRICES

PRODUCT: ....

Country: ....   Currency: ....

$\varepsilon R\ _v p_u$ = ...%; V_u = ...%

| Enquiry | | | MAXIMUM (1) | | MINIMUM (1) | | AVERAGE (2) |
No	Date						
		- UNIT SELLING PRICE	..		..		..
		corresponding to:					
		1) Shop : name (and Code No)	..		..		..
		2) Brand/Size : name					( )
		3) Actual Producer or Manufacturer : name	( )		( )		
		4) Other brands : I)... II)... III)...					
		5) No of brands x sizes in the shop	.. x .. = ..		.. x .. = ..		.. x .. = ..

- RETAIL PRICE INDEX AND SHOP (Code No)	INDEX	SHOP	INDEX	SHOP	INDEX	SHOP
base : 1977/1 = 100	..	( )	..	( )	..	( )
1977/2 = 100	..	( )	..	( )	..	( )
1977/3 = 100	..	( )	..	( )	..	( )

(1) They are the highest (or lowest) unit selling prices ($_v p_u$) in absolute terms, considering all items for a given product (question 17), corresponding therefore to the dearest (or cheapest) shop in the sample.

(2) The average price has been calculated on all items (brands, sizes, ..). The shop outlined in the table is the one in the sample which is closest to the average price.

- "O.L." designates the own label products sold by a given retailer.

- Imported products are indicated by an asterisk.

SELECTIVE HISTORICAL SERIES

TABLE V

— concerning some relevant products taken from the sample —

SYNTHESIS : RETAILERS MARK-UPS

PRODUCT: ....

Country: ... Currency: ...

Enquiry		$\varepsilon R_q = \quad\%; \quad V_q = \quad\%$	MAXIMUM (1)	MINIMUM (1)	AVERAGE (2)
No	Date				
		— MARK-UP (RETAILER)	..	..	..
		corresponding to:			
		1) Shop : name (and Code No)	.. ( )	.. ( )	.. ( )
		2) Brand/Size : name			
		3) Actual Producer or Manufacturer : name			
		4) Other brands : I)... II)... III)...			
		5) No of brands x sizes in the shop	.. x .. = ..	.. x .. = ..	.. x .. = ..
		6) Tj—(Ranking in Tj)—(Ranking in overall shop efficiency)	..-(..)-(..)	..-(..)-(..)	..-(..)-(..)
		7) Unit Buying Price — (Date of purchase)	( )( )	( )	( )( )
		8) Producer's or Manufacturer's Unit Price	( )	( )	( )
		9) Unit Retail Price	( )	( )	( )

(1) They are the highest (or lowest) mark-up (q) all items considered (question 42), corresponding therefore to the shop in the sample applying them.

(2) The average mark-up has been calculated on all items (brands, sizes, ...). The shop mentioned in the table is the one in the sample which is close to the average mark-up.

— "O.L." designates the own label products sold by a given retailer.

— Imported products are indicated by an asterisk.

SELECTIVE HISTORICAL SERIES

– concerning some relevant products taken from the sample –

TABLE VI

SYNTHESIS : RETAILERS UNIT BUYING PRICES

PRODUCT: ....

Country: ...   Currency: ...

$$\epsilon R_{a}p_{u} = \quad \%; \quad V = \quad \%$$

Enquiry No	Date		MAXIMUM (1)			MINIMUM (1)			AVERAGE (2)		
			BUY-ING	PRO-DUCER	RETAIL	BUY-ING	PRO-DUCER	RETAIL	BUY-ING	PRO-DUCER	RETAIL
		– UNIT BUYING PRICE – (Date of purchase) corresponding to:	( )			( )			( )		
		1) Shop : name (and code No)	... ( )			... ( )			... ( )		
		2) Brand/Size : name	... ( )			... ( )			... ( )		
		3) Actual Producer or Manufacturer : name									
		4) Other Brands : I) ... II) ... III) ...									
		5) No of brands x sizes in the shop	.. x .. = ...			.. x .. = ...			.. x .. = ...		
		6) Tj – (Ranking in Tj) – (Ranking in over-all shop efficiency)	..–(...)–(...)			..–(...)–(...)			..–(...)–(...)		
		7) Retailers Mark–up	( )			( )			( )		
		8) Producer's or Manufacturer's Unit Price	( )			( )			( )		
		9) Unit Retail Price	( )			( )			( )		
		– BUYING PRICE INDEX (compared with retail price index) base : 1977/1 = 100 1977/2 = 100 1977/3 = 100									

(1) They are the highest (or lowest) unit buying prices ($_{a}p_{u}$) in absolute terms, all items considered (question 68), corresponding therefore to the shop in the sample which buys at the highest (or lowest) price.

(2) The average buying price has been calculated on all items (brands, sizes, ...). The shop mentioned in the table is the one in the sample which is close to the average price.

– "O.L." designates the own label products sold by a given retailer.

– Imported products are indicated by an asterisk.

100

2.1.5. Comparisons between retailers' buying prices and retail selling prices

The structure and behaviour of each firm – retailers as well as producers, manufacturers and/or traders included in the "restricted" sample – will be analysed, focusing also on any possible long-run effect on the level, disparity and trend of:

- buying prices (paid by retailers)
- retail prices (paid by consumers)

2.1.6. General features of the programme

A long-term analysis on this basis will give a living picture of the actual working of competition in a field of the greatest interest both to the consumer and to the authorities.

In conclusion the second stage is essentially

- selective since it implies the choice of a more limited number of products, retailers (groups) and suppliers;

- dynamic since it considers all the chosen data in their long-run connection;

- comprehensive since it considers all kinds of data and information, both quantitative and qualitative, which might be helpful for attaining its objectives.

2.1.7. The two fields of the research: Market – consumer and producer stage

There is no doubt that in recent years power relations have been changing between the manufacturers of goods (suppliers) and the major retailers (purchasers), and this has brought into existence new trends and features in the working of the competition mechanism.

Because of the complex interdependence of the phenomena under study, the analysis will have to work from several starting points and angles, in order to:

- follow each stage of the channel through which a given product or brand moves from producer to final consumer,

- see how retail prices are compared, correlated and evolving.

Let us distinguish two main starting points:

I) Retail stage exclusively: relationship between retailers and consumers;

II) Intermediate stage: relationship between producers and retailers.

As regards the "retail stage exclusively", it is helpful to distinguish two sub-groups of data:

Ia) those acting directly on consumers and easily and automatically emerging from the prices and mark-ups surveys carried out by the Commission – retail prices;

Ib) those acting on the retail prices, but not known by the final consumer since they imply a specific survey and analysis – retail mark-ups.

As regards the "intermediate stages", two sub-groups of data will be distinguished:

IIa) quantitative data, to be summarized in the "historical series tables", such as: evolution of retailers' buying prices compared with the evolution of retail selling prices, turnover and market shares (from the suppliers' viewpoint and from the customers' viewpoint) and so on;

IIb) qualitative data, expressed by legal and financial arrangements, tying clauses in the contracts, discount terms and so on.

2.1.8. References to the tables of Chapter One

Sub-group Ia) refers to data — i.e. brands and prices — and indices having certain characteristics in common:

- they are collected in the framework of the research programme on prices and mark-ups, on the basis of the principle: "go to the shop, see and compare",

- they can therefore be said to be the "atoms of information" that ought to be available to each consumer or housewife,

- however, one complete econometric elaboration of those "atoms of information" provides the material for a large, comprehensive picture of certain significant features of the major retailers' business strategies.

The set of eleven tables described in Chapter One of this report gives several instances of how much of what information and what conclusions can be obtained from a volume of elementary data ("atoms of information") which, as single items, should be there for each housewife to see.

2.1.9. "Atoms of information" — structural and evolutionary viewpoint

The "atoms of information" constitute the ground for elaborations, viewed from two basic angles:

- from the structural (or static) angle, at a given moment,

- from the evolutionary angle, over a given reference period.

Let us consider, firstly, the structural angle.

2.1.10. Basic data: brands and relative prices

The "atoms" taken into account in the structural (or static) framework and hypothesis are the following:

I) the brands (and sizes/weights) of each product on sale at each shop, outlining more particularly the origin (country of production, name and nationality of the manufacturer or of the distributor) and, generally speaking, all the essential characteristics (shelf life, importance to the consumer, etc.) of each item considered;

II) the relative prices of each brand (and size/weight) which differ, sometimes considerably, according to the shop investigated and the time of the survey.

From the evolutionary angle, the analysis will consider the changes in position taking place between the same thousands (or millions) of "atoms" considered in the structural (or static) approach, over one or more reference periods.

All these analyses imply, as we have seen, the prior selection of "relevant products" if the research is not to sink in the sea of millions of "atoms of information".

Initially the following products have been considered by the Commission and the researchers working with it:

1) instant coffee and, where appropriate, ground coffee or beans;

2) sugar;

3) pure chocolate, in powder and solid form, and/or cocoa;

4) homogenized baby foods: (a) desserts (fruit), (b) mixed vegetables with meat, fish, chicken;

5) margarine and/or other edible oils (groundnut oil, corn oil, etc.);

6) tinned peas (natural);

7) tinned and packet soups (vegetable – minestrone, vermicelli – chicken, tomato, pea, mushroom);

8) beer (bottled and in cans);

9) mineral water;

10) cola beverages.

Account has also been taken of the high degree of concentration on the various national markets for most of these products (see Table VIII at 2.9.2.).

Each national research institute is asked to add to this list two further products of specific interest for national market structure.

2.2. THE BRANDS AND SIZES AVAILABLE

2.2.1. Choice of the consumer, "own label" products, imported goods

In each shop there is generally a number of brands (sizes and weights) for each product at a given moment ("structural" or static approach).

In the research programme the structure of the range of products offered to the consumers will be analysed for each shop according to:

  I) the number of brands actually available for each product;

 II) the share of own labels, in relation to manufacturer's branded products,

III) the share of imported products.

2.2.2. References to tables 1, 2, 4, 8, 10 and 11 of Chapter One

The number of brands actually available for each product implies a series of analyses from three basic angles:

a) product; b) spatial or geographic; c) evolutionary.

Let us refer back to Tables 1, 2, 4, 8, 10 and 11 of the first stage (Chapter One) which give a full picture of all products and items taken into account in all the sample shops.

Table 8, for instance, shows all basic data collected, referring to different brands (and sizes/weights) available for each product, all items being ranked in decreasing order of unit price at the time of the most recent survey (i.e. t+i). However, as a starting point for further analysis it is necessary to ascertain at each shop in the sample whether any brand or item (of each given product) has been neglected, and whether there has been any error in recording price differences, especially for the extreme (i.e. dearest and cheapest) items.

It is obvious that Table 8, taken with Tables 1, 2 and 4, is of crucial importance to the attainment of the objectives of our research, for these tables reveal that:

- the number of items is very high (almost a thousand) in each survey country;

- it is neither possible nor fruitful to take the analysis further for all the items in the sample of products;

- there is meaningful quantitative information in tables 1, 2, 4, 8, 10 and 11 enabling us to determine what are the most "relevant" products which actually deserve more refined investigation.

2.2.3. Criteria for selecting the products to be analysed at the second stage

The products to be submitted to more sophisticated analysis must be selected according to criteria permitting:

a) comparison of the products (and relative data: prices, mark-ups, and so on) over a given period of time and among the different countries and regions;

b) analysis of the negotiating power as between retailers and manufacturers. Accordingly, preference will be given to products which are:

  - available in all the countries and shops taken into account for the analysis;

  - manufactured by companies operating world-wide;

  - relatively homogenous as regards quality, in order that comparisons based upon the "unit prices" are not misleading: it is not very fruitful to compare the unit price for tinned caviar with the unit price for tinned sardines;

- sold under several brands and sizes, including possibly a large number of own labels.

2.2.4. References to the first stage

As we have seen, it is in fact the analysis of the results from the first stage of the research (see particularly the above mentioned tables 1, 2, 4, 8, 10 and 11 in Chapter One) which will allow us to pass on to the second stage of the research based primarily on the "Selective Historical Series".

Because of the continuity of the development of the analysis, we may sometimes appear somewhat repetitious in presenting, elaborating and commenting on data, but this, however tedious, is unavoidable if we wish to investigate all facets of complex phenomena really thoroughly.

2.2.5. Choice of brands and sizes - QQ. 1-13

The first Table of the "Selective Historical Series" stresses the geographical or spatial dispersion of prices for the same product according to brand and size, but especially according to the sales point.

In fact, the first Table outlines many relevant aspects of the pricing system and distribution structure.

First of all answers are given to the following detailed and specific questions, concerning the range of choice open to final consumers:

I) (1) How many brands and sizes of one product are available in one given shop of the sample?

II) (2) Is there, or is there not, a reasonable choice of brands and sizes for the consumer?

III) (3) Is the range of choice broadly the same for all shops in the local sample, or are there strong differences among the shops in the sample?

IV) (4) The same question, but referring to an inter-regional comparison, that is: is there broadly the same range of choice - concerning given brands and sizes - in all the regions surveyed (for example: 1) Greater London, 2) Greater Manchester, 3) Greater Glasgow) or does this range of choice vary considerably from one region to another in the same country?

V) (5) The same question, but referring to an international comparison. Does the range of choice differ - concerning given brands and sizes - among the different countries considered?

VI) (6) Are the same brands and sizes, produced by the same manufacturers, available in all countries, regions or shops, or do the names and sizes of those brands (as well as the names of their manufacturers) vary according to country, region or shop?

VII) (7) What is the share of own labels and/or imported products analysed in different countries (or regions)?

VIII) (8) Are the more popular sizes sold under own labels or under manufacturers' brands?

IX) (9) Are actual manufacturers of own label products the same as of manufacturers' branded products or are they different?

X) (10) Are imported products more widespread among the own label products or among the manufacturers' branded products?

XI) Is there a tendency – in the sample of shops – towards stability of brands,
(11) manufacturers and sizes sold in each given shop or is there a tendency towards
continual change?

XII) Is there a tendency towards an increase in the share of own label items in the
(12) sample of shops, or is there a tendency towards an increase in manufacturers'
branded products? The same question for imported products in relation to
home-produced goods?

XIII) In a more general way, is there a general or common tendency towards a widening
(13) of the range of brands and sizes available to the final consumer (and therefore
towards an increase of competition among brands sold in each shop) or is there,
on the contrary, a tendency towards a reduction in the number of brands and
sizes available in each shop?

We must point out the "double meaning" of the word "share" ("what is the share",
questions 7 and 12):

– number of items (brands and sizes),

– percentage of the retailers' total sales of the given items (own labels and imported
goods).

2.2.6. Unit Retail Selling Prices: contents of the first table

The first table of the "Selective Historical Series" is designed to illustrate:

– spatial and geographical comparisons,

– evolutionary comparisons.

In the same scheme it is planned to indicate together, for comparison purposes, two
countries (or two regions of the same country) and also the code number of each shop,
the name and owner of the shop being identified from the separate lists of Sales Points
for each country.

These shops are ranked according to the same criterion – in decreasing order of the
degree of brand monopolization, the first shop (on the left) being the one where the
consumer has the narrowest range of choice of brands and sizes and the last shop (on
the far right) being the one where the range of choice is the widest.

All the brands, sizes and manufacturers, even if they are available only in one of the
countries (or regions) compared, are specified on the right of the table, as well as the
whole range of own label products available in each of the countries (or regions).

The names of the shops (and of their owners or groups) are specified in the lists attached
to the first table.

Moreover, conclusions about the distribution structure in several member countries can be
drawn from comparison of more "couples" of tables (each one for two countries or regions).

The bottom of the first table indicates, for each shop

– the stock turnover rate or time in stock (Tj);
– the average unit selling price;
– the "SCORE" for each shop, used to calculate the efficiency rankings (as we will
see at 2.4.: "Analysis of shop efficiency").

2.2.7. <u>The set of the first tables: by product, by country, by survey date</u>

For the study of structural evolution, the first table has to be established for each survey (and generally these enquiries will be six-monthly). Thus, one series of these tables, covering a sufficient number of six-monthly surveys, will outline the evolution of each distribution structure as well as the existence of common and/or divergent features in the comparative evolution as between member states or between different regions studied.

Therefore, several first tables regarding different countries (and regions) as well as different surveys (carried out at different times over a sufficiently long period) will be the subject of cross comparisons and of further summary tables.

In order to underline salient and more meaningful data from the first table, it is planned to establish a "Summary Table" (fourth table) concerning more particularly the evolution of the "Unit Retail Selling Price". Similar "Summary Tables" will have as their subject the evolution of "Retailers Mark-Up" (fifth table) and the evolution of "Unit Retail Buying Price" (sixth table).

2.3. THE "SELECTIVE HISTORICAL SERIES"

2.3.1. Basic presentation of the First, Second and Third Tables

The layout of the first table is the same as that of the second and third tables, though the data to be entered in them is different even if they are closely related, since all three tables take into account:

- the same product and the same brands, sizes, manufacturers and own labels;

- the same surveys (No. and date);

- the same countries (or regions), generally two for each table;

- the same sample of sales points (or shops), each one with the same name and code number in each of the three tables.

But, what is more important is that the shops (or "sales points") are ranked in exactly the same order in the three tables, the first shop (or the second, third, etc.) being exactly the same (same ranking, same name) in all three.

In this way, since:

- the first table outlines the "Unit Selling Price" (to final consumers),

- the second table: the "Retailer's Mark-up",

- the third table: the "Unit Retail Buying Price",

it is possible to investigate thoroughly the structures considered, in order to point out the salient aspects of the quantitative relationship between the buying price and the selling price.

From cross comparisons based on the set of these three tables it is possible to draw valuable conclusions that will help to improve our knowledge of the behaviour of major retailers. Let us examine separately the quantities outlined in each table:

- unit selling prices (first table);

- retail mark-ups (second table);

- unit buying prices (third table).

All these tables also consider, at the bottom, the shops' average "stock turnover rate" (Tj) for the given product (or time in stock), suggesting fruitful comparisons and remarks, in relation to averages concerning unit selling and buying prices and mark-ups.

2.3.2. The unit retail selling prices - QQ. 14-20

The first table aims to answer the following questions, concerning unit prices in particular:

XIV) What is the degree of dispersion of unit prices between the different brands and
(14) sizes - including own label products - for the same product?

XV) Generally speaking, how are the own label products priced in relation to
(15) manufacturers' branded products:

    a) are they cheaper?

    b) are they more expensive?

    c) are they sometimes cheaper and sometimes more expensive?

    Does the difference in price correspond to a real difference in quality?

XVI) The same question, as regards imported products in comparison with home-produced
(16) goods.

XVII) In which shop of the sample will we find the highest (or lowest) unit price? For
(17) which brand and size? Do those prices refer to own label products and/or to
imported products?

XVIII) Referring to the lowest unit price charged in each shop (regardless of brand and/or
(18) size), which is the most expensive shop in the sample?

XIX) Is the shop with the highest (or lowest) unit price the one where the choice of
(19) brands and sizes is widest (or narrowest)? Or is there no significant relationship
between the number of brands and sizes and the price level?

XX) When the shops of the sample sell one product made by the same manufacturer but
(20) under different trade marks – including own label ones – which brand, and in which
shop, costs more (or less) and why?

2.3.3. The selling prices of "identical items" – QQ. 21-25

One aspect of great interest is the comparison and analysis of unit prices of "identical
items" (same brand and size), that can be found in more than one shop.

Thus we will put questions such as:

XXI) What is the degree of dispersion of prices between the different shops selling
(21) a given "identical item" (same brand and size)?

XXII) Which are the dearest (or cheapest) shops for each "identical item", exactly defined
(22) as above (same brand and size)?
Are these shops the same as the dearest shops as regards the unit price of the
product when no distinction is made as to either brand or size (as we have done
in question 18)?

XXIII) Which are the brands and the actual producers or manufacturers for which the
(23) highest degree of dispersion of prices is observed as between:

a) the shops constituting the local sample?

b) the different countries or regions surveyed?

c) which countries (or regions) have the highest or lowest prices for the same
"identical items" (ie. same brand, same size, same actual manufacturer)?

XXIV) It is possible to consider the following alternatives:
(24)
a) does the retailer group have some of its shops specializing in the more
expensive brands (prestige brands) while other shops sell only more common,
cheaper brands?

b) do all the shops of the group sell more or less the same brands and sizes,
without any specialization as to quality?

For the latter hypothesis, the following question will arise.

XXV) What is the pricing policy of the operator group? It may be that:
(25) a) in all shops of the group the prices of "identical items" are the same;

b) in some shops, prices are higher for some "identical items" and lower for others;

c) some shops are always more expensive and others are always cheaper.

The problem is very complex. It may be helpful to refer to the fundamental
questions regrouped under 49, 50 and 51.

2.3.4. The evolution of selling prices – different aspects – QQ. 26–38

By comparing two or more fourth tables (extracted from the respective first tables), relating to different points in the reference period ($\underline{t}$, $\underline{t+1}$, $\underline{t+2}$, etc.), it is possible to draw conclusions on the evolution of the structure considered. Questions will be put about[1]:

XXVI) Does the degree of dispersion of unit prices, between the different brands
(26) and sizes – including own label products – increase or decrease between $\underline{t}$, $\underline{t+1}$, $\underline{t+2}$, $\underline{t+3}$, etc.? (See also question 14).

XXVII) Is it always the same brand/size that is the most expensive or the cheapest?
(27)

XXVIII) Does the (average) unit price increase more for own label items or for
(28) manufacturers' branded products? Or can no clear trend be observed? (See also question 15).

XXIX) Does the (average) unit price increase more for imported products or for
(29) home-produced goods?

XXX) Is it always the same shops that sell the more expensive items or the less
(30) expensive ones (in terms of unit price)? (See also questions 17 and 18).

XXXI) Are the shops with the highest (or lowest) increases in the (average) unit
(31) prices those where:

    a) the choice of brands and sizes (including own labels) is wider or narrower? Or is there no significant relationship? (See also question 19).

    b) the choice of brands and sizes (including "own labels") has become wider or narrower during the reference period? Or is there no significant relationship?

    c) the share of own labels has increased (or decreased) in relation to manufacturers' brand products?

    d) the share of imported products has increased (or decreased) in relation to home-produced goods?

    e) an important change of the brands, manufacturers, sizes and packages took place during the reference period? (See also question 11).

XXXII) Is there a significant relationship between the increase in unit prices and an
(32) important change in the brands and sizes sold by a given shop?

XXXIII) Is the change affecting a given manufacturer's brand sold in a given shop due to:
(33)
    a) removal of the brand from the manufacturer's catalogue and production line;

    b) a change of supplier by the retailer, though in favour of another manufacturer's brand;

    c) replacement of the manufacturer's brand by an own label, the product still being made by the <u>old manufacturer</u>;

    d) replacement of the manufacturer's brand by an own label, the new product being:
        d1) made by a <u>new manufacturer</u>,
        d2) imported, whereas before it was home-produced,
        d3) home-produced, whereas before it was imported.

---

1. In point 4 we will refer to the <u>normal hypothesis</u> of an "<u>increase in prices</u>", but the same questions and remarks are usually valid when, as an exception, there is a <u>decrease in prices</u> and not an increase.

XXXIV) Which own labels or manufacturers' brands have been dropped by the retailers?
(34) Do they concern home-produced or imported goods? Which are the substitute products if any, and how much more (or less) do they cost than the items dropped? Is there a tendency towards a sharp increase (or decrease) in unit prices for substitute products in comparison with the own labels or manufacturers' brands that have been dropped?

XXXV) Has the change in the size and/or packaging of a given product — whatsoever the
(35) brand concerned: manufacturer's brand or own label — caused an increase in the unit price that is:

a) greater than the average increase in the unit price of the product?

b) smaller than the average increase in the unit price of the product?

XXXVI) Which reasons have been advanced by manufacturers and/or retailers for
(36) explaining the changes eventually recorded in the above mentioned questions?

XXXVII) When one operator group owns several shops, is the increase in the unit prices
(37) for identical items of the given product absolutely the same for all shops of the group, or do these increases in unit prices differ according to the item and shop?

XXXVIII) Are the answers to all questions of this point — from 26 to 37, as well as to
(38) questions from 11 to 13:

a) much the same for all countries and/or regions surveyed, or at least for most of them?

b) divergent from one country and/or region to another?

2.3.5. The retail mark-up — Contents of the Second Table — QQ.39-45

The second table has as its subject the retail mark-up by shops and brands/sizes.

Before examining this table it is worth considering the first two reference tables (one on structure, the other on evolution) summarizing, in a comparative way, the contents of the questions related to each of the three tables as regards unit retail prices, retail mark-ups and buying prices.

Answers will be given to the following questions:

XXXIX) What is the degree of dispersion of mark-up between the different brands and
(39) sizes — including own label products — for the same product?

XL) What is the size of the mark-up applied to own label products, in comparison
(40) with manufacturers' branded products:

a) are they lower?

b) are they higher?

c) are they sometimes lower and sometimes higher?

XLI) The same question, as regards the mark-ups on imported products in comparison
(41) with home-produced goods.

XLII) In which shop of the sample will we find the absolute highest (or lowest) mark-up?
(42) For which brand and size? What is the size of those mark-ups? Are they applied to own label products, and/or imported products?

XLIII) Referring to the lowest unit price which is available in each shop (whatever
(43) the corresponding brand and/or size):

    a) which is the shop applying the highest (or lowest) mark-up?

    b) does this shop coincide or not with the most expensive (or cheapest)
       shop considered in questions 17 and 18?

    c) does this shop coincide with one of the shops indicated in question 42?

XLIV) Are the shops recording the highest (or lowest) mark-ups (questions 42 and 43)
(44) the ones where the choice of brands and sizes is wider (or narrower)? Or is
there no significant relationship between the number of brands and sizes and
the level of mark-ups?

XLV) When the shops of the sample sell one product made by the same manufacturer,
(45) but under different trade marks - including own labels - which brand, and in
which shop, has the highest (or lowest) mark-up?

2.3.6. The mark-ups applied to identical items - QQ. 46-48

Let us now consider each item separately, defined jointly by brand and size, in order
to come to some conclusion as to the comparison between identical items where they are
sold in more than one shop.

XLVI) What is the degree of dispersion of mark-ups between the different shops
(46) selling a given identical item, (same brand and size)?

XLVII) Which are the shops recording the highest (or lowest) mark-ups for each
(47) identical item, defined exactly as above (ie. same brand and size)?
Do the names of those shops coincide or not with the shops mentioned at
questions 43, 17, 18 and 22? In which cases and to what extent?

XLVIII) Which are the brands and the actual producers or manufacturers for which
(48) we observe the highest degree of dispersion of "mark-up":

    a) between the shops constituting the local sample analysed?

    b) between the different countries or regions surveyed?

    c) which countries (or regions) record the highest (or lowest) mark-ups for
       the same identical items (ie. same brand, same size, same manufacturer)?

2.3.7. The retailer groups operating several shops - Q. 49

A major problem may arise with the following question:

XLIX) Referring to the hypothesis at question 25 - the major retailer groups operating
(49) several "sales points" - what is the pricing policy of the group? Since it is
reasonable to assume that one given group buys all identical items sold in its
shops at the same price, it seems evident that the present question coincides
substantially with question 25. In fact, if the buying price is the same and if
an identical mark-up is applied by all shops, there will also be an identical
"retail price". So hypotheses 25 (a), (b) and (c) refer equally to final unit
retail prices as well as to retail mark-ups. But transport facilities and the
cost of capital and land vary according to both location and size of different
shops - even if they are controlled by the same operator group - and so accurate
analyses are needed about:

    a) the buying price paid by the retailer to obtain delivery of the goods at a
       given warehouse or storage point,

    b) the full, actual cost borne by the retailer in order to have goods ready
       for sale in each of the different shops of the group.

In principle, the mark-up must be calculated on the buying price (a) and not on the full, actual cost of the good (b).

Thus the answer to question 49 entails making an accurate analysis of the different mark-ups applied by different shops in the same group, to determine to what extent the differences in final unit retail prices are linked to differences in the full, actual costs, varying according to shop.

2.3.8. The competitive price for each shop and endogenous competition - Q. 50

A common answer to questions 49 and 25 should highlight the working of competition in the different areas surveyed.

From the purely economic viewpoint, it seems evident that:

- each shop (owned by the same retailer (operator group), as it is on our hypothesis) has to contend with a different competitive situation depending on its location and on the number, importance and pricing policies of competing shops, that is those existing in the relevant area;

- accordingly, each shop will have to adapt its prices to the prices of its actual competitors in this relevant area and the prices ought to vary between shops controlled by the same operator group as a normal effect of competition;

- it is obvious that in this case, the mark-up - for each shop - should be fixed in such a way as to obtain the "competitive price" characterizing each shop. One of the most efficient retailers in the UK has four different price levels and four different pricing policies, depending on the location of individual shops.

The preceding remarks aim to demonstrate that competitive as well as efficient behaviour by the retailers automatically implies endogenous competition[1] between shops controlled by the same operator group.

We therefore put the question:

L) Assuming several shops to be owned by the same operator:
(50)
  a) is there endogenous competition between those shops in one or more relevant areas analysed, so that a high degree of dispersion of prices between them is observed?

  b) what is the comparative degree of dispersion for prices and mark-ups between the different shops?

  c) for which operator groups and in which regions and countries is endogenous competition stronger, in relation to the answer given to question 48 (b)?

  d) are prices lower in areas where several shops are controlled by several retailers competing against one another? How many competing shops are there? How many competing retailers?

2.3.9. Shops of the same groups apply uniform prices - Q. 51

Let us now consider the hypothesis of uniform prices by putting the following question:

---

1. See R. LINDA, Methodology of Concentration Analysis applied to the Study of Industries and Markets, September 1976, point 58, pages 79-80.

LI) If prices are the same for all shops controlled by the same retailer, one of the
(51) following hypotheses will occur:

   a) either the retail price of a given item (ie. product determined by the brand,
      size and package) is fixed by the manufacturer himself for all shops selling
      this product in one or more regions or countries;

   b) or there is an agreement between the operator groups owning the shops existing
      in a given relevant area to refrain from price competition for this product;

   c) or the operator group is fixing a uniform mark-up based exclusively on a common
      buying price, calculated artificially for all shops of the group on the basis
      of the suppliers' invoices.

If the hypotheses 51 (a) and (b) do occur we can conclude that:

- there is no competition on the product, owing to the restrictive behaviour of the
  manufacturer (hypothesis a);

- there is no competition on the product, owing to the restrictive behaviour of the
  retailers (hypothesis b).

This latter hypothesis would justify a thorough and comprehensive investigation into
the behaviour of given retailers in order to see if similar agreements also concern
other products, seriously affecting competition in the relevant area.

2.3.10. Explanatory hypothesis of uniform prices - QQ. 52-53

Let us finally examine hypothesis 51 (c), that is, prices are derived from the
application of a general mark-up on a uniform buying price, both being common to
all shops of the operator group. In this case we have the dilemma:

LII) Either the competitive pressures on the retail side in the relevant area are
(52) relatively weak (no competing shop nearby, or only a higher priced shop) and
     so it is possible to disregard competition, and particularly prices in other
     shops, in the relevant area, without the profitability of the shops under
     study being affected;

LIII) Or those competitive pressures are fairly strong (several low priced shops
(53) nearby) in which case a rigid, uniform pricing policy is bound to be inefficient
     since it neglects the actual specific environment of each shop.

But the "profitability" and "efficiency" issue is taken into consideration by joint
analysis of the set of data (average stock turnover rate for each shop as well as the
shop's average unit retail price, retail mark-up and unit buying price) at the bottom
of the first, second and third tables.

At any rate it is worth noting that such an analysis has to distinguish between the efficiency of the single shop and the efficiency of the aggregate operator group, the latter being
obtained by aggregation of the "efficiency score" of all the individual shops in the
restricted sample (of shops as well as of products), always assuming this sample to be
representative.

2.3.11. The evolution of "mark-ups" - QQ. 54-64

If the analysis is to be complete answers must also be given to questions concerning the
evolution of mark-ups ("q") (questions 54-64), which are similar to questions concerning
the evolution of unit retail prices (questions 26-38). There is no need to reformulate
those questions.

Later, in section 2.7. we will analyse in detail the problems concerning the unit buying
price ("aPu"), distinguishing between structure (questions 65-74) and evolution
(questions 75-84), with additional questions concerning more particularly the "power
interplay" (questions 85-94). In this respect, it is helpful to recall the reference
tables mentioned in point 5:

- first reference table concerning <u>structure</u> (retail prices, mark-ups and buying prices),

- second reference table concerning <u>evolution</u> (retail prices, mark-ups and buying prices),

- third reference table concerning "<u>power interplay</u>" (85-94); <u>shop efficiency</u> (95-103) and the <u>loss leading</u> policy (104-115).

- fourth reference table concerning excessive prices, breakdown of the final price and national and local competition (116-140).

These tables summarize all questions from 14 to 140. It is useful to recall that questions 1 to 13 concern the more general problem of the choice actually available to the consumers.

2.3.12. <u>The problem of defining and calculating the retailers' buying prices - QQ. 65-94</u>

The analysis of the relationship between selling (or retail) prices, mark-ups and buying prices is an essential step in the study of the power interplay between retailers and producers[1]. Even if, in the initial stage of the research, it may be very difficult to answer most of the 140 questions, the target of the research as defined above has to be kept in mind. In this way, the 140 questions can be regarded as guidelines for a multiple-stage long-term research project.

It might be helpful to formulate a number of additional remarks on the treatment of buying prices.

The collection of buying prices is particularly fruitful for analysis of:

I) the comparative viewpoints of retailers and producers,

II) the mark-up policy of the major retailers.

As concerns the first point, it will be necessary to check the buying prices declared by retailers with the manufacturers' prices. If these prices are divergent, an appropriate survey will be needed in order to seek possible explanations:

a) manufacturers are not selling directly to major retailers but to commercial distributors or wholesalers; in this case it is helpful to analyse the margins of those traders;

b) buying prices declared by retailers are not exact or manufacturers' prices are not exact, owing to errors or to other causes to be discovered;

c) retailers consider a peculiar definition of "buying price", which does not correspond with the "manufacturers' price"[2].

----

1. It is for this reason that it seems helpful:
   - to regroup all the questions concerning the retailers' buying price (QQ. 65-84) with the closely connected questions concerning the basic aspects and tendencies of power interplay (QQ. 85-94),
   - to examine these questions later at 2.7.: "Retail Buying Prices and Power Interplay".

2. The effect of taxes on the relevant product will have to be considered.

In principle, the "buying price" represents the cost of the good plus other costs for delivery to the warehouse or to the retailer's shop (c.i.f.). It is therefore possible that transportation and insurance costs account for the difference between the manufacturers' price (f.o.b.) and the retailers' net buying price. The way different sorts of discounts and facilities granted to big retailers are registered and disclosed by the retailers and by the manufacturers is a problem that will be considered later at 2.7.24. and 25.

2.3.13. The "formal" and the "actual" mark-up

The date of purchase of the goods may also be relevant in these times of inflation. Knowledge of the buying price is vital if we are to check the size of retail mark-ups declared by the retailers themselves, by comparing retail selling prices with their actual buying prices.

The problem is very important:

- Are all retailers considering the same conception of the mark-up, or is each using a different definition?

- Is it possible to distinguish between a formal and an actual mark-up?

The simplest approach would be to take from the third table the buying price, to add the mark-up from the second table and thence to obtain the selling price, which ought to be the same as in the first table.

It is an essential task for each research institute to check, in this way, the consistency of data linked by these three tables. But it is easy to forecast that the selling price calculated from the second and third tables will rarely correspond to the price in the first table. In this case, appropriate analyses will then have to be undertaken in order to provide explanations, such as:

a) the mark-up has been calculated on a buying price which is different from the buying price currently applied at the time of the retail price survey;

b) the retail price has changed since the mark-up was calculated.

In these hypotheses it is easy to see that we have a formal mark-up (that is, a given "q" applied to the buying price) and an actual mark-up (that is, the actual percentage indicating the difference between the actual selling price and the actual buying price).

2.3.14. Relationship between buying price, time in stock and "actual" mark-up

In practice the retailer will find it quite easy to know the formal mark-up, since he himself fixes the percentage to be applied. But in inflationary times it may be difficult to know the actual mark-up, since the prerequisite would be knowledge of the actual date of purchase and of the actual buying prices for any item sold by the shop. When a product is bought at several times at different prices, it is necessary to take into account the time in stock in order to calculate an average buying price and an average mark-up.

The institutes must therefore take care to try to collect relatively comparable and homogenous data as regards buying prices and mark-ups, outlining all existing discrepancies and differences between the second and third tables on the one hand and the first table on the other. It is also obvious that specific analysis of the time in stock, linked to the problem of the "shop efficiency", is justified by the objectives of the research programme.

116

2.4. ANALYSIS OF "SHOP EFFICIENCY"

2.4.1. Time in stock

At the bottom of each of the three tables just examined, there is one highly relevant point:

- the stock turnover rate, or time in stock (T_j), which is outlined for each shop of the sample.

It is noteworthy that this T_j (j indicating the code number of the shop) is only an average calculated on different brands and sizes of the given product sold by the shop. It is suggested that the stock turnover rate should be expressed by the number of days during which the product is kept in the shop or in its warehouses, that is the number of days between the delivery date from the supplier and the selling date to the final consumer (for example, for canned vegetables – 140 days; for eggs – 8 days). For this reason it is better to speak of time in stock. It is evident that, ceteris paribus, the more efficient shops are those where the time in stock is shortest.

In this way it is possible to analyse the relationships between time in stock and:

- the unit selling price;

- the mark-up;

- the unit buying price.

2.4.2. The concept of shop efficiency

In this framework, it is possible to elaborate a general approach to shop efficiency from two angles:

- the benefit to the shop;

- the benefit to the consumer (social angle).

From the first angle:

- a shorter time in stock (T_j); and a

- lower buying price,

mean that the shop is more efficient than others with a longer time in stock and/or a higher buying price.

From the second angle:

- a lower unit selling price; and a

- lower mark-up,

indicate that the benefit arising from the shop's efficiency is passed on to the consumer.

117

2.4.3. The efficiency score and the ranking of the shops

It is possible to rank the shops by efficiency in order of scores.

To begin with, all shops will be ranked - each one having a given rank number - by increasing order of the time in stock, unit selling price, mark-up, unit buying price.

The more efficient shop will therefore rank as number 1 on each of those parameters.

In the first table, the "best shop" will have a score equal to 2, that is: ranking 1 for the time in stock and ranking 1 for the unit selling price, that is the cheapest price of all the shops in the sample. The least efficient shop might possibly have a score equal to 60, that is: given a sample of 30 shops, it would rank 30th by time in stock and 30th by unit selling price (it would therefore be the most expensive shop in the sample.

In the second table, the score ranking will be founded on the time in stock and on the size of the mark-up (the "best shop" being the one applying the lowest mark-up), while in the third table, the score ranking will be founded on the time in stock, as usual, and on the unit buying price (the "best shop" being the one paying the lowest buying price).

2.4.4. Aspects of shop efficiency - QQ. 95-100

Answers to the following questions might be helpful[1]:

XCV) Do the efficiency rankings of the three tables coincide, that is: the best
(95) (or the worst) shops are always the same in each of these tables?

XCVI) If it is possible, given the necessary data, to calculate an overall score -
(96) by adding the shops' rankings in the three tables - which would be the most (or least) efficient shops, according to the definitions given above?

XCVII) Since all shops are ranked according to the number of brands and sizes available
(97) to the consumer (degree of brand monopolization) it is easy to see if the most "product monopolistic" shops, at the left side of the table, are also the most (or least) efficient shops in the sample.

XCVIII) Does it happen that shops recording the lowest buying prices have to bear a
(98) longer time in stock since they usually buy more than they need in order to reap substantial discounts?

XCIX) When comparing the second tables referring to different products, is there evidence
(99) of a relationship between the time in stock and the size of the mark-up? Does this relationship exist in none, in some, in most or in all shops of the sample? In one, in several or in all countries surveyed?

C) Which are the countries (and/or regions) which have the most (or least)
(100) efficient shops?

---

1. It will be observed that we have not yet examined QQ. 65-94 concerning jointly the unit retail buying prices and power interplay, but given the strategic importance and considerable complexity of both, it is helpful to postpone this analysis until Section 2.7., after having cleared the ground by examining shop efficiency (QQ. 95-103) and the loss leading policy (Section 2.6.; QQ. 104-115).

2.4.5. The evolution of shop efficiency – QQ. 101–103

Under the evolutionary viewpoint it will be helpful to answer the following questions:

CI)   As regards the evolution of "shops' averages" – time in stock as well as unit
(101) selling and buying prices – do they tend to increase, and if so to what extent
       and in which countries (and/or regions) in particular?

CII)   Which shops are tending to become "better" (that is, cutting their time in stock,
(102) mark-ups and possibly even the buying and selling prices) and which shops are on
       a deteriorating trend?

CIII) Do the overall efficiency scores resulting from the three tables, and the three
(103) individual efficiency scores change considerably in time or not? Which shops are
       the best (or worst) in the long run?

2.5. THE EVOLUTION OF CONCRETE PRICE STRUCTURES FOR SELECTED PRODUCTS

2.5.1. References to the basic contents of the first, second and third tables

The first, second and third tables give a breakdown of the structure and its evolution, by analysing each shop, product, brand and supplier (producer, manufacturer) in the "restricted" sample.

It is helpful to recall the fundamental goals of the research programme:

To analyse both the structure and the evolution of:

- the power interplay between retailers and producers and their patterns of behaviour,

- the working of competition in the distribution channels through which given products and brands move from producer to final consumer,

- the effects of the competition mechanism on final retail prices and on the consumers' freedom and behaviour.

2.5.2. The analysis of concrete price structures as a top priority

The analysis of answers given, even to only some of the 140 questions, enables us to draw meaningful conclusions. These questions concern more particularly the concrete structure and evolution of the prices of selected products.

The analysis of the concrete structure and evolution of prices is, in our view, a top priority for any further analysis of relations between retailers and producers in general terms.

It may be objected that this supposedly detailed analysis extends only to a very restricted sample of selected products[1] so that there can be no question of drawing general conclusions on the patterns of behaviour of retailers and producers.

However, it will be noted that the three "observation posts" — unit retail selling prices, retail mark-ups, unit retail buying prices — play a threefold function:

a) first, they enable the reliability of data collected to be checked as to homogeneity and consistency;

b) second, they provide an illustration of the working of competition between retailers;

c) third, they provide a means of measuring the evolution of the balance of power and dominance as between retailers and producers.

Why and how? Let us see.

2.5.3. Rigorous definitions are a sine qua non of several comparisons

As regards (a), this statement seems to us to be self-evident, considering the need for a comparative analysis of the behaviour of shops and retailers with different price policies and structures and the highly specific situations of individual regions and countries. The great number of questions aim to check that data are classified according to comparable definitions and approaches, and thus to avoid all ambiguity.

---

1. See 2.1.10.

2.5.4. The THREE KEYS

As regards (b) and (c), we need three keys for analysing the answers to the various questions, or at least to some of them:

- key one: the analysis of evolution,

- key two: international (and if possible interregional) comparisons of this evolution,

- key three: comparison between products.

The Summary Tables (the fourth, fifth and sixth) are a good example of the way in which we may approach some general conclusions, having recourse to key one and to key two. Later analysis will highlight the role of key three.

2.5.5. KEY ONE: The analysis of evolution - The summary concerning the retail selling prices (fourth table)

The fourth table, concerning the unit selling price, will give several pointers to the working of competition between retailers, by setting out the answers to the basic questions:

- 26: variation of degree of dispersion of unit selling prices,

- 27: change in the dearest or cheapest brand/size,

- 30: change in the dearest or cheapest shop.

When those answers show that:

- the degree of dispersion of prices remains high or increases in the time; and

- the dearest and cheapest brand/size changes continuously,

- the dearest and cheapest shop changes continuously;

there is evidence of keen competition:

- between brands/sizes

- between shops.

If moreover, it is found that:

- differences between maximum and minimum price increases are widening and even, on the minimum side, there is a price decrease;

- the names of shops with the highest or lowest increases in the prices are changing;

this corroborates the evidence in favour of effective competition.

We are assuming that:

- competition tends to develop dynamically, and is visible through the continuous changing of relevant data and factors[1],

---

1. See: R. LINDA, Concurrence oligopolistique et planification concurrentielle internationale, in "Economie Appliquée", Archives de l'ISEA, 1972, No. 2-3, pages 340-341, 367-369.

- differing prices or differing price increases are a <u>sign</u> of competition, albeit of a probably "<u>imperfect</u>" form, but at least fairly workable, whereas uniform prices and uniform increases tend to point to <u>restrictions</u> of competition. And on the whole we prefer <u>imperfections of competition</u>, since it still works, rather than <u>restrictions</u> of it[1].

Here it is worth emphasising the utility of the index of dispersion, which offers a summary quantitative picture of the effects on prices jointly exerted by imperfections and by restrictions of competition.

The index $\varepsilon R_v p_u$ (Relative Difference) expresses the percentage difference between the <u>highest</u> unit price recorded in any shop (most expensive shop) and the <u>lowest</u> unit price recorded elsewhere (cheapest shop)[2]. If $\varepsilon R_v p_u$ exceeds <u>40%</u> it may be concluded that the conditions of competition are very different for the two <u>extreme priced shops</u> of the sample. But it is noteworthy that the <u>existence</u> of different conditions of competition surrounding at least two shops in the sample – owing essentially either to their location or specialization or both – constitutes <u>per se</u> a <u>sign of competition</u>. This sign of competition will be even more meaningful and reliable if we have a <u>coefficient of variation</u> $(_p V_u)$ exceeding <u>20%</u>. Such a high coefficient of variation will demonstrate and confirm that the difference in conditions of competition concern not just two shops in the sample but the <u>whole sample</u>, since each shop has a <u>different</u>, <u>specific unit price</u> of its own.

2.5.6. <u>The number of brands and sizes as a sign of competition</u>

Another relevant factor is the number of brands and sizes available in the shop (question 13):

- with the highest selling price,

- with the lowest selling price.

If this number is increasing both in the most expensive shop and in the cheapest one and, under the evolutionary viewpoint, even the names of those shops are changing from <u>t</u> to <u>t+1</u>, <u>t+2</u>, <u>t+3</u>, we have a further sign of competition:

- between brands,

- between shops.

It seems reasonable therefore to argue that shops are widening the range of brands available to consumers in order to become more attractive to them.

Analysis of the evolution of retail prices by means of a set of fourth tables can also offer pointers to the evolution of power relations between retailers and producers, though these pointers may be felt to be somewhat ambiguous. The need for reference to the fifth and sixth tables is evident. See our commentaries on the sixth table.

---

1. R. LINDA, <u>Methodology</u>, <u>op. cit.</u>, 1976, point 65.

2. The formula is $\varepsilon R_v p_u = \dfrac{\text{Maximum Price} - \text{Minimum Price}}{\text{Minimum Price}} \times 100$

    See: Commission of the European Communities, <u>Sixth Report on Competition Policy</u>, Luxembourg, April 1977, points 312-315.

2.5.7. Some signs of restrictions of competition

Conversely, it is possible to identify certain signs of restriction of competition:

- It is always the same shop and the same brand which are the dearest or cheapest. This means that there is some source of resistance to competition between brands (quality, prestige, etc.) and between shops (location, specialization, etc.);

- The percentage price increases are uniform for all brands and for all shops. This means that an agreement definitely exists between suppliers (producers, manufacturers) and/or retailers;

- The number of brands and sizes available in each shop is continuously decreasing, each shop tending to specialize in only one or two brands. If this sign is accompanied by other negative signs, competition would seem to be sharply restricted.

2.5.8. The synthesis concerning the retail mark-ups (Fifth table)

While the fourth table represents but a first step in the analysis, and is easy enough to fill up since it is sufficient to obtain information simply by visiting the shops of the sample, the fifth table as a rule requires the direct cooperation of shops themselves or of public authorities.

Let us recall the basic questions:

54: variation of degree of dispersion of retail mark-ups,

55: change in the brand/size having the highest (or lowest) mark-up,

59: change in the shop applying the highest (or lowest) mark-up.

In principle, the degree of dispersion of mark-ups between different shops — at a given moment — may be a sign of competition, since:

- each shop has a different cost structure, as a result of the scale of quantities purchased, location, size, stock turnover rate (T_j);

- each shop has to encounter different kinds of competing shops, in relation to its location, the available means of communication, etc.

Hence the application of a uniform mark-up by all shops in the sample is the sign of collusive behaviour or of public measures to fix the maximum mark-up. But, the public authorities generally fix a maximum mark-up to be observed by all shops only when competition is not exerting sufficient pressure on retailers to cut their mark-ups.

2.5.9. Sharp decrease of the retail mark-ups as a sign of competition

Under the evolutionary viewpoint, it is possible to have the following hypotheses in the process from time t to $t+1$, $t+2$, etc.:

Hypothesis	Remark
- The degree of dispersion of mark-up among shops is increasing	- Probable sign of competition
- The average mark-up is sharply decreasing, as are both the maximum and the minimum mark-up	- Definite sign of keen competition: Three hypotheses: (a), (b), (c)
- The brand/size having the highest (or the lowest) mark-up is changing	- Sign of competition
- The shop having the highest (or lowest mark-up is changing	- Sign of competition

It is evident that a _sharp_ decrease of the mark-up is a _definite_ sign of competition. But the question is: between whom?

In this respect it is possible to formulate three hypotheses:

a) existence of competitive pressures from other shops;

b) increase in bargaining power of the retailers' suppliers (producers, manufacturers);

c) combination of factors (a) and (b).

From this it follows that:

- we are confronted with real "multiple competition", many factors and facets being strictly interdependent,

- we need to take into account _separately_ the price structure and evolution of _each_ product, for each shop in the sample, in order to extract individual causes of a complex of results.

This is a point that must be heavily emphasised. As we are to analyse "multiple competition", it is not possible to consider cumulative relationships and cumulative data, covering and concealing contradictory and amalgamated factors, tendencies and effects.

To analyse phenomena linked to "multiple competition" we will have to keep in mind _at the same time_:

- not only _key one_ recording the sharp decrease in the evolution of mark-ups (or the opposite hypothesis of a sharp increase), but also:
  - _key two_: international comparisons, and
  - _key three_: comparisons between products;

- not only the mark-up evolution, but also:
  - the evolution of unit retail prices, and
  - the evolution of unit buying prices.

2.5.10. Sharp increase in retail mark-ups

Let us now consider the hypothesis of a sharp increase in the mark-up applied by one or more shops in the sample, from time t to $t+1$, $t+2$, and so on, resulting from a chronological set of fifth tables.

This _sharp increase_ may concern:

a) the maximum mark-up

b) the minimum mark-up

c) the average mark-up.

The fifth table enables us to focus further investigation on shops (and especially operator groups) recording:

- higher mark-ups at any given moment,

- higher increase in the mark-up during the period considered.

124

2.5.11. Structural viewpoint (at a given moment)

It seems prima facie that a high (or the highest) mark-up is a sign of market power, but the questions are: On which side? And against whom?

- To the detriment of final consumers, since there is no effective competition from other shops;

- To the detriment of suppliers, since the retailer – who has considerable negotiating (or purchasing) power – can buy at a very low price without having to pass his saving on the buying price on to the consumer.

These phenomena are closely linked, as we have seen in paragraph 9. But one must not neglect the following hypothesis:

- a given retailer is obliged to apply a higher mark-up because his cost structure is heavier than at other shops due to inefficiency (excessive personnel costs, excessive time in stock);

- consequently, as the high mark-up is reflected on the retail selling price, the turnover of the shop is reduced under the pressure of competition from other shops, resulting in lower prices.

An appropriate detailed analysis seems therefore necessary concerning the shops (and operator groups) recording the highest mark-up, and the chronological set of fifth tables will in this case act as a warning light. See in particular Table XII (Q. 139, point 2.9.11.).

2.5.12. Evolutionary viewpoint – Explanatory hypotheses about an increase in mark-ups

Mark-ups may also increase as a result of several tied, combined and even contradictory factors:

 I) inflationary tendencies (first and foremost);

 II) discontinuation of special offer and/or loss leader policies pursued in previous periods; see section 2.6., "The negative mark-up: loss leading";

III) slacker competitive pressures from other shops, owing either to the elimination of some shops (or operator groups) or to the adoption of a collusive (or non-agressive) price policy followed by all shops in the region, no further commentary being necessary;

IV) increase of negotiating (or purchasing) power enjoyed by retailers vis-à-vis the suppliers: see section 2.7.: "Retailers' buying prices and power interplay";

 V) heavier cost structure at the shop (and/or of the operator group) owing to an increase in personnel costs and/or overheads and so on, no further commentary being necessary.

We must now draw attention in particular to point I: "Effects of sharp increases in the retailers buying prices".

2.5.13. Purchases by big retailers as an inflationary factor

In an inflationary period, a sharp increase in the mark-up may be the result of a series of facts, which can be illustrated as follows: A big retailer forecasts a probable sharp increase in the (retailers' buying) price of a given product and therefore buys an enormous quantity just before the price increase takes place.

We must now look at what may happen:

a) It may be that the weight of this **purchase** anticipates and amplifies the impact of the forecasted price increase of the product, this big purchase therefore playing an inflationary role. And so, for example, the current retail buying price will rise by 20% instead of 10%.

b) The big retailer must afterwards choose between three price levels and hence three price policies.

2.5.14. First pattern of price policy

He fixes a relatively low retail selling price (for example: + 2%) in order to meet competition from other shops and possibly increase his market share.

In this hypothesis we will have, as regards the above mentioned retailer:

- a relatively low "actual" mark-up;

- a shorter time in stock;

- a unit retail selling price increasing by less than the corresponding increase in the buying price (paid by the other retailers after the forecasted increase has taken place) and probably also lower than the increase in the selling price of other competing shops.

2.5.15. Second pattern of price policy

He fixes a retail selling price proportionate to the increase in the retail buying price (in our example: 20%). He will do this if he does not want to provoke a price reaction from other competing shops, because if he increases the retail selling price by less than the increase in the buying price, competitors might align their prices, so that there was no change in the retailers' market shares.

This price policy is based on the principle of "peaceful coexistence" ("quieta non movere") that represents the normal and most widespread pattern of behaviour in modern oligopolistic structures.

In this hypothesis we will have, as regards the above mentioned retailer:

- a relatively important increase in the "actual" mark-up, since this retailer has benefited from a lower buying price (his purchase taking place on a date just before the forecasted increase in buying prices);

- a longer time in stock for the product concerned, since this retailer is not willing to try to attack the market shares and positions of his competitors and so, having bought an enormous quantity of the product, he has to stock the goods longer before the whole quantity is sold. Moreover, even if all other things remain unchanged, a price increase naturally entails an increase in the time in stock in proportion to the demand elasticity of the product, since final consumers will tend to reduce their consumption of products whose prices are going up.

2.5.16. Third pattern of price policy

He raises his retail selling price by an increase (for example: 50%) far greater than the increase in the retailers' buying price (in our example: 20%).

He can do this if he is not hampered by the competitive pricing policies of other shops (and operator groups), since:

- either this big retailer dominates the market, (hypothesis: existence of dominance),

- or, even without the existence of this dominance, the relationship between different retailers is so friendly and well cultivated that all of them will follow our given retailer passively and promptly in making this very sharp increase in the retail selling price (hypothesis: existence of price leadership).

In this hypothesis we will have, as regards the above mentioned retailer:

- a very sharp increase in the actual mark-up,

- a probable sharp increase also in the time in stock, in proportion to the demand elasticity of the product.

In the present hypothesis, we can conclude that the existence of collusive conduct in the field of retail distribution renders competition virtually non-existent.

Moreover, the benefit of the operation would be much greater for our retailer in the event of relatively rigid or unelastic consumer demand (sugar, coffee, tea cocoa), since total sales would not be affected by the retail price increase.

2.5.17. The possible influence on inflation

In our analysis we refer to the actual mark-up[1], since that alone will enable us to illustrate:

- the actual behaviour of retailers, who have the power to make use of inflationary tendencies in order to reap considerable profits,

- the impact of this retailers' pattern of behaviour on the propagation of the inflationary process.

In this respect it seems evident:

a) that big retailers can play a decisive role in curbing (first pattern: point 2.5.14.) or alternatively stimulating (third pattern: point 2.5.16.) the inflationary process;

b) that big retailers have the power to stimulate the inflationary process only where:
  - the market structure is very highly concentrated, with strong power of dominance;
  - there is no real competition between these retailers;

---

1. The problem of the discrepancy between the "formal" and the "actual" mark-up has already been evoked in Section 2.3.: "The selective historical series", points 13 and 14. Let us recall that in order to take into account the "formal" mark-up, it is sufficient:
   - to consider the unit retail buying price, not at the moment of the purchase of the product concerned, but at the moment of the survey,
   - to compare it with the unit retail selling price at the same moment.

   In contrast, to calculate the "actual" mark-up, it is necessary to take into account the actual unit buying price, at the moment in which the purchase was made and then to calculate the percentage mark-up resulting from the difference between the unit retail selling price, at the moment of the survey, and the actual unit buying price. This very essential point will be examined in more detail in section 2.7. "Retailers' Buying Prices and Power Interplay".

c) that the public authorities must therefore keep a very close eye on the situation so
   that retailers cannot use (and abuse) their dominance against the general interest.

In this respect, we must point out that the chronological set of fifth tables (Retail
mark-ups) highlights several important aspects of the above phenomena. And if we also
analyse the chronological set of sixth tables (Unit retail buying prices), it will be
possible to draw up decisive conclusions as regards the products and the retailers
surveyed.

2.5.18. KEY ONE and KEY TWO — Role played by fourth, fifth and sixth tables in the
         development of the analysis

The fourth, fifth and sixth tables are designed to set out all fundamental data for
analysing phenomena described at points 2.5.10 to 17, provided that we have recourse to
the two keys:

- key one: the analysis of evolution;

- key two: the international comparison of this evolution.

With these tables we can:

   I) ascertain the shops (and the operator groups) following a given pattern of behaviour,
      owing especially to the distinction and contrasts between Maximum and Minimum:

      - unit retail selling prices;

      - retail mark-ups;

      - unit retail buying prices;

  II) detect the existence of excessively sharp increases in unit retail selling prices
      and/or in mark-ups and/or in unit buying prices, by measuring their actual size
      via comparisons between Maximum and Minimum;

 III) compare the evolution in different countries (and/or regions), and more particularly
      measure the differences in the increases — or decreases — in retail selling prices,
      mark-ups and retail buying prices there;

  IV) compare the levels and the variations of the time in stock in the different countries
      (and regions), this being a meaningful indicator of shop efficiency.

If the trend of the more important data (prices and mark-ups) diverges in the different
countries (and regions), this will help to establish and quantify the impact on final
prices, and more particularly on the inflationary process, exerted by the different
structures of trade and competition in these different countries (and regions).

It will also be possible to establish and quantify the effects both of dominance and
of collusive practices relating to specific products in specific countries (and regions).

2.5.19. Crucial products — Establishment of additional monthly tables

The use made of key one and key two may be further refined if circumstances so require.
For example, if a given product is found to be subject to sharp and/or frequent variations —
possibly increases — in current international prices (such as coffee, cocoa) a further
development of the analysis, based on the above tables, will be necessary.

We have seen that all surveys and all tables are intended to be established every six
months; but this frequency is inadequate for the collection of meaningful data for analysis
of the working of market mechanisms for certain products. Therefore, if the research
institutes notice that there are or have just been important changes in the price structure
of a given product, they should forthwith:

- identify between one and four of the <u>most important retailers</u> operating in the country (or region) surveyed;

- establish additional fourth, fifth and sixth tables in a new, revised version not only every six months but every two months or even every month.

2.5.20. <u>Contents of the new revised version of the additional tables (fourth A, fifth A, sixth A)</u>

The <u>new revised version</u> of the additional tables (fourth A, fifth A, sixth A) will be established monthly — or every two months — for the one or two given products whose price structures are undergoing important changes. They will indicate:

- in the place of the three columns:

MAXIMUM	MINIMUM	AVERAGE

- one or more columns, one for each **retailer** chosen for more thorough analysis as regards the given product(s); taking the example of distribution in the United Kingdom, we have:

TESCO	SAINSBURY	ALLIED SUPPLIERS (CAVENHAM GROUP)	FINE FARE (Associated British Food: ABF Group)

It will **then** be possible to monitor the behaviour of these retailers and the impact on the structure of prices very closely.

It is obvious that the additional tables — established every one or two months — will omit all non-essential or non-consistent data (for example: the indexes of dispersion: $ER_{a}p_{u}$ and $V_{a\,u}$).

2.5.21. <u>The speed at which retail prices react to changes in producers' prices</u>

We must again stress the <u>fundamental purpose</u> of the new revised versions of the additional tables, fourth A, fifth A and <u>most especially</u> sixth A. If the latter <u>is established</u> monthly it will highlight more particularly the <u>speed at which specific retail prices</u> — in the different countries, regions and shops surveyed — <u>react to the changes in the producers' prices</u>. Knowledge of this <u>speed of reaction</u> is of basic importance for competition policy.

Let us take two examples:

a) If the producers' price of coffee (or seed oils, or margarine) increases on 1 December 1976 by 20%:

- on which date will this <u>increase</u> occur in the different countries, regions and shops surveyed?
- by how much (5%, 10%, 20%, 50%, 100%) will the different shops in the sample actually increase the **retail** price of the different makes and types of coffee?

b) If the producers' price of coffee (and/or seed oils, or margarine) <u>decreases</u> on 1 July 1977 by 10%:

- on which date will this <u>decrease</u> occur in the different countries, regions and shops surveyed?
- by how much will the different shops reduce the retail price of the different makes and types of coffee?
- are there countries, regions and shops where there is <u>no reduction at all</u> in the retail price? Why and how?

The value of establishing the sixth A table <u>monthly</u> is self-evident.

2.6. NEGATIVE MARK-UP: "LOSS LEADING"

2.6.1. Negative mark-ups - QQ. 104 and 105

The fifth table will reveal the existence of any loss leaders, that is items sold at a retail price below the buying price. The warning signal is given by a negative mark-up. A warning signal concerning the loss leading policy may result from several tables of the first stage research (Chapter One) under the column Pricing, where one can distinguish whether we have:

- a special offer, that is a temporary reduced price offered to consumers for advertising purposes;

- standard pricing;

- an undefined pricing pattern.

Obviously not all special offers constitute loss leading; on the contrary, it may be that some products are always offered below their unit buying price, without there being a special offer.

The following hypotheses and questions must be answered[1]:

CIV) At a given moment:
(104)
    - only one or a few shops select a given product as a loss leader. In this case the minimum mark-up will be negative;

    - several (or all) shops select the same product as a loss leader. In this case, not only the minimum mark-up, but also the average and maximum mark-ups will be negative or close to zero.

CV) The evolution of mark-ups from time t to t+1, t+2, and so on shows:
(105)
    - the product is no longer used as a loss leader;

    - it is always the same shops that select the given product as a loss leader;

    - the product is selected as a loss leader first by one shop and then by another.

2.6.2. Identification of retailers - Purposes of the loss leading policy - QQ. 106 and 107

If, in the analysis of evolution, one product seems to be preferred by one or more shops as a loss leader, it is essential to develop further investigation in order to ascertain:

CVI) Which retailers more frequently have recourse to this practice.
(106)

CVII) For what reasons do they do so: to eliminate one specific competitor (a small
(107) business or a big one) or simply to promote the expansion of the shop and increase turnover.

In the hypothesis of predatory pricing further analysis and action might be helpful since a negative mark-up - for the purpose of eliminating competitors - is a sign of degeneration of competitive behaviour, which is not socially beneficial.

---

1. It will be observed that we have not yet examined QQ. 65-94 concerning jointly the unit retail buying prices and power interplay, but given the strategic importance and considerable complexity of both, it is helpful to postpone this analysis until Section 2.7., after having cleared the ground by examining shop efficiency (QQ. 95-103) and the loss leading policy (Section 2.6.; QQ. 104-115).

2.6.3. Set of effects linked to the loss leading practice – QQ. 108–111

Four points in particular must also be outlined as concerns the loss leading practice.

CVIII) Is it always the same brand belonging to the same manufacturer which is selected
(108) as a loss leader, or does it change from one moment to another?

CIX) What are the after-effects of loss leading for the retailers, as concerns more
(109) particularly:

- a decrease in time in stock (Tj) for the brand and shop involved in the loss leading;

- an increase in time in stock (Tj) for brands and shops not having recourse to this practice.

CX) What are the after-effects of loss leading for the manufacturer, as concerns more
(110) particularly an anomalous increase or decrease in retail buying prices:

- for brands used as loss leaders;

- for other brands.

CXI) What are the after-effects of loss leading for the final consumer, as concerns more
(111) particularly an anomalous increase or decrease in unit retail selling prices, that
is does an anomalous increase or decrease in unit selling prices concern shops and
brands having previously indulged in loss leading or other shops and brands?

2.6.4. Own label products and imported goods – QQ. 112 and 113

Two particular questions must also be outlined:

CXII) Is loss leading practised more particularly with own label products (O.L.) or with
(112) manufacturers' branded products? Is this tendency confirmed by surveys carried out
over a relatively long period?

CXIII) Is loss leading practised more particularly with imported goods or with home-produced
(113) goods? Is this tendency confirmed by surveys carried out over a relatively long
period?

2.6.5. KEY TWO: International comparisons – QQ. 114 and 115

The analysis of loss leading has to be taken a stage further by means of international
comparisons (key two).

CXIV) In general, are the same products and brands selected as loss leaders in different
(114) countries? Are the effects for retailers, manufacturers and final consumers
(questions 109, 110, 111, 112, 113) broadly the same in different countries and
regions?

CXV) Do the manufacturers all take the same attitude to loss leading? Hostility or
(115) cooperation with retailers practising it? Is there any change in their attitude?
Does it vary according to the product, retailer and country (or region)?

2.6.6. Analysis of the pricing policy of a selected retailer (shop "A" as regards a given product

The problem of the possible discrepancy between the "formal" and the "actual" mark-up was
considered in connection with the evolution of concrete price structures for chosen
products.

EXAMPLE OF TABLE FOR ANALYSING THE PRICING POLICY OF A GIVEN RETAILER FOR A GIVEN PRODUCT

BUYING PRICES			SELLING PRICES				TIME IN STOCK (days)	
Date of quotation	Date of purchase for shop "A"	Current buying price	Date of survey	Current selling price	Selling price of shop "A"	Mark-up of shop "A"	Average of all shops	for given shop "A"
1/ 9/1976	1/ 9/1976	100	15/ 9/1976	110	120	+ 20%	30	180
1/10/1976	-	100	15/10/1976	150	120	+ 20%	30	180
1/11/1976	-	120	15/11/1976	160	120	+ 20%	30	180
1/12/1976	-	140	15/12/1976	200	120	+ 20%	30	180
1/ 1/1977	-	150	15/ 1/1977	250	120	+ 20%	30	180
1/ 2/1977	-	160	15/ 2/1977	300	130	+ 30%	30	180
1/ 3/1977	1/ 3/1977	200	15/ 3/1977	300	150	- 25%	30	60
1/ 4/1977	-	220	15/ 4/1977	300	150	- 25%	30	60
1/ 5/1977	1/ 5/1977	240	15/ 5/1977	300	216	- 10%	30	60
1/ 6/1977	-	200	15/ 6/1977	300	216	- 10%	30	60
1/ 7/1977	-	180	15/ 7/1977	280	216	- 10%	30	60

In our inflationary times, the concept of loss leaders might be extended and revised. Let us suppose the following hypothesis: compare the current average of the buying and selling prices of all shops in the sample with the individual selling price of one given shop "A", at different moments.

It will be possible to isolate and analyse the pricing policy of shop "A" and possibly to identify a particular type of loss leading policy.

2.6.7. Positive mark-up and loss leading in inflationary times

The example in the table shows all the difficulties of the analysis. The example is meaningful in itself. Shop "A" (operator group) bought (on 1 September 1976) a very large quantity of one given product (corresponding more or less to increased retail sales over a six month period) and so he does not care at all about the very sharp increases in current prices, but he tries to operate a predatory policy directed against rival shops. In this way, even if the mark-up is positive in December 1976 and January 1977 (+ 20%) as well as in February 1977 (+ 30%) this product is in fact being used as a loss leader, since shop "A" sells it at a price very much lower than not only the current retail selling price, but also the current retail buying price.

This pricing policy might be considered to be somewhat similar to the first pattern of pricing policy, considered in section 2.5., point 14, ("The evolution of concrete price structures for selected products"), if one important difference did not have to be underlined. In the present case, we have undoubtedly a very extreme pattern of behaviour, the selling price of the shop "A" being well below the current retail buying prices (even if the selling price is higher than the "actual" buying price), the loss leading policy might be a weapon used to eliminate competitors.

Therefore, even a positive mark-up may conceal, in inflationary times, a highly agressive loss leading policy.

2.6.8. Extension of the analysis of the individual retailer's pricing policies

It would be helpful to establish the above table not only for the products and for the shops or retailers (operator groups) operating loss leading policies but also for other products and shops, in order to ascertain, for each relevant product and shop, the actual evolution of each big "retailer's" individual behaviour and policy in the competitive framework surrounding him. But, in order to do so, many theoretical and practical problems have to be solved. In section 2.7., we will analyse more thoroughly the problem of the actual buying price, in order to highlight the actual working of market and competition mechanisms between retailers (buyers) and producers or manufacturers (suppliers).

2.6.9. Special offer

One aspect of the retailer's attempts to promote sales by underpricing some products is the Special Offer.

In principle special offers are available for a certain length of time only (two or three weeks) and sometimes the unit selling prices of the items chosen may be below the unit buying price.

But even when the mark-up is positive, the special offer constitutes an anomalous reduction in gross income from the product, the counterpart being found in an increase in gross income from other products sold by the shop. Therefore it is helpful, in analysing the evolution of mark-ups relative to a given product, to outline the basic features of the special offer policies followed by one or more retailers.

The raw material for doing this is to be found in the different tables planned in the first stage of the research (Chapter One).

2.7. RETAIL BUYING PRICES AND POWER INTERPLAY

2.7.1. Summary of retail buying prices (Sixth Table)

The sixth table (retail buying prices) deserves particular attention since it summarizes all the essential data so far assembled.

An analysis of the evolution of retail buying prices taken as far as possible, constitutes an essential element for assessing the power interplay between retailers and producers (or manufacturers). Accordingly, it will be necessary to examine the sixth table in connection with the third table, the latter showing the breakdown of retail buying prices by shops and brands and sizes, in order to illustrate all signs and indices as to the rules that govern competition between retailers and producers.

2.7.2. The degree of dispersion of retail buying prices - Q. 65

Before examining the sixth and third tables together, it is fruitful to glance at the first two of the three reference tables (one concerning structure, the other concerning evolution) summarizing, in a comparative way, the contents of the questions relating to each of the three "observation posts":

- unit retail selling prices,

- retail mark-ups,

- unit retail buying prices.

Answers will be given to the following questions:

LXV) What is the degree of dispersion of the retail buying price between the different
(65) brands and sizes - including own label products - for the same product?

We have two possible extreme hypotheses: a) The degree of dispersion is very high;
b) The degree of dispersion is very low.

Moreover, it must be ensured that prices are comparable, being those either of the integrated trade or of independent retailers. Some analysis of terms of delivery may be necessary.

2.7.3. Hypothesis a): The degree of dispersion is very high

Hypothesis a): The power interplay between retailers and producers does not work as between two closely united armies struggling vigorously against each other. On the contrary, each army is divided within by competitive behaviour and tendencies since there are:

- on the one side, several retailers competing against each other to buy at the lowest price,

- on the other side, several producers (or manufacturers) also competing against each other to sell to the competing retailers at the highest price.

The effect of this situation is that since each retailer (or buyer) is surrounded by specific conditions of competition - owing, above all, to his size and the total quantity he is able to purchase - each will also be able to negotiate a different buying price. Hence the degree of dispersion will be very high, since:

- the retailer with the greatest bargaining power will get the lowest buying price,

- the retailer with the weakest bargaining power will have to bear the highest buying price.

Such a situation of keen competition on both sides of the market will be expressed quantitatively:

- by a relative difference $(\epsilon R_{a^p u})$ of more than 10%,

- by a coefficient of variation $(_a V_u)$ of more than 5%.

If these indices become too high, the relative difference exceeding 20% or 30% and coefficient of variation exceeding 10% or 15–20%, it might be argued that:

- the <u>conditions of competition</u> are too unequal, seriously hindering both retailers (those having the weakest bargaining power) and manufacturers (those being obliged to supply some retailers at too low a price);

- this inequality in the conditions of competition might ultimately result in the elimination of some competitors (both retailers and manufacturers), thus provoking a <u>sharp increase in the degree of concentration</u>, in both retail distribution and manufacturing;

- such a sharp increase in the degree of concentration might seriously hinder competition (and market) mechanisms;

- therefore, excessive competition might in itself result in a very dangerous process of monopolization;

- this monopolization process attributes too much power to retailers, allowing them to speculate on purchases and to abuse their power in the retail trade.

However, before proceeding with the analyses described above, it is helpful to ascertain to what extent the "<u>quality</u>" of the different brands of the same product is <u>homogenous and comparable</u>.

In some very special cases, the high degree of dispersion of buying prices may reflect no more than an <u>important difference</u> in the quality of the brands considered[1].

2.7.4. <u>Hypothesis b): The degree of dispersion is very low</u>

Hypothesis b): If the degree of dispersion of buying prices is relatively low, three explanations are possible. There exists:

(1) a high degree of market transparency and strong competition;

(2) collusive agreements, or at least concerted practices;

(3) concealed discounts and special buying terms.

As regards point (1), no comment is necessary since this is the situation of perfect competition with which all readers will be familiar.

As regards point (2), it may occur that:

- either retailers have entered into collusive agreements in order to obtain <u>lower prices</u> to the detriment of suppliers (manufacturers or producers);

- or suppliers (manufacturers or producers) have entered into collusive agreements in order to obtain <u>higher prices</u> to the detriment of buyers (or retailers);

- or both hypotheses are confirmed, the structure being, in this case, close to the "bilateral monopoly" model.

---

1. International price discrimination by a manufacturer against retailers in different countries might be a case for action under the EEC Treaty rules on competition.

As regards point (3), it is evident that it will not be possible to ascertain the actual buying price achieved by some big retailers, who are known to enjoy considerable bargaining power. It is beyond doubt therefore that they could benefit from special buying terms. This point will be examined later on in this section (points 24-25).

2.7.5. The degree of dispersion and the working of competition

The prima facie conclusion is that:

- when the degree of dispersion is low, we have ambiguous and contradictory signs, indicating both monopolistic (or collusive) and competitive behaviour;

- when the degree of dispersion is high, we have a positive sign of the existence of competition.

Even in the latter hypothesis, we must search for other signs and indices in order to highlight the power interplay between retailers and producers, because:

- if competition is really keen and the conditions of competition (surrounding the different operators) are very unequal,

- it is evident that some retailers (those having the greater bargaining power) can benefit from this inequality whilst others suffer badly.

It follows that retail selling prices will ultimately be set in one of the two following ways, there being no apparent alternative:

- either the retailers who buy at the lowest prices will follow a policy of peaceful coexistence in relation to selling prices, thus reaping much more substantial profits than other, less favoured retailers;

- or they will seek to eliminate their competitors by passing on to the retail selling price the saving on the buying price.

In the latter hypothesis the degree of dispersion of mark-ups would be very similar to the degree of dispersion of unit buying prices, since each retailer will tend:

- to apply the same mark-up;

- to charge therefore a different unit selling price, depending on the unit buying price.

2.7.6. Relationship between retail selling price and buying price

If we place our analysis in the logical framework of classical "perfect competition" the conclusion is inevitably pessimistic, since any substantial saving on the unit buying price - for a given retailer - will be of no benefit to the consumer.

Why is this so?

Because, either this saving (on the buying price) constitutes extra profit for the given big retailer or it constitutes a weapon by means of which he can eliminate his competitors, monopolize the market and hence abuse the monopolistic power thus given to him at the expense of the consumers. The explanation is plain and clear: the classical conception of "perfect competition" is based on the principle that it is not possible to have an equilibrium situation with several different prices for the same product; according to the classical theory, we can have only one price (equilibrium price) in any given market[1].

---

1. See: R. LINDA, Concurrence oligopolistique et planification concurrentielle internationale, in "Economie Appliquée", Libraire Droz, Genève, 1972, nn. 2-3, pages 327-328, 334-342; and Méthodology ...., op. cit., point 65.

But the classical theory is erroneous and not borne out by reality. The price surveys carried out in the different member countries of the Community have demonstrated that, in the same town or region, it is possible to observe several different retail selling prices for an identical product or item, and the degree of dispersion of retail selling prices is in fact indeed very high.

This point is of vital importance.

2.7.7. The bases of "multiple competition" and the existence of multiple equilibrium prices

If we accept the erroneous principle (inherited from the classical theory) that there can be only one equilibrium price in any one market, we will reach an important conclusion for economic policy:

- since any difference in the unit buying price cannot ultimately benefit the final consumer,

- that public authorities must fix this single equilibrium price at the lowest possible level in order to benefit the consumer and to curb inflation.

But the principle of a classical perfect economy is erroneous as we have seen, since it is possible to observe several very different retail selling prices for the same product at the same moment in the same market. Therefore:

- it is neither possible nor fruitful to fix a single official price (to be charged by all shops) because:

- this single price will correspond either to the highest price (most expensive shop) or to the lowest price (cheapest shop) or to the middle of the range;

- consequently, either the single, official price will provide a rent (or extra profit) for the more efficient shops, this extra profit being both socially undesirable and inflationary, or this single, official price will drive the "marginal" shops (ie. the least efficient) off the market.

On the contrary, we must realize that the real-life situation is based on the phenomenon of multiple competition, which implies the existence of a situation of equilibrium, even if:

- unit retail selling prices differ from one shop to another, even in the same town or region;

- the mark-ups applied by different retailers are also different;

- unit retail buying prices also differ.

The state of equilibrium is a result, therefore, of dynamic forces working from a combination of different, divergent and opposing data and situations surrounding firms, this inequality (or diversity) being the catalyst to the competition process. The crucial problem is not eliminating this inequality (or diversity), because this would simply mean eliminating competition as well, but rather of finding out the ceiling of inequality (or of diversity), above which the competition mechanism would be hindered by the emergence of dominance.

In a sense, our analyses aim to determine and to describe the "living space" between the ceiling and the floor of inequality (or diversity), within which competition can develop its endogenous process.

2.7.8. Pricing of own label items - The problem of the quality of the products - Q. 66

Further questions must be put as regards own labels and imported products.

LXVI) Generally speaking, how do the prices at which retailers buy own label products
(66) compare with the prices of manufacturers' branded products:

    a) are they **cheaper**?

    b) are they more expensive?

    c) are they sometimes cheaper and sometimes more expensive?

    Does the difference in price correspond to a real difference in quality?

The answers to this question may give some indication of the actual market power of the retailers, if they are compared with answers given to questions 15, concerning the unit retail selling prices, and 40, concerning retail mark-ups.

Thus we can distinguish four (or even six) hypotheses:

	RETAIL SELLING PRICE	BUYING PRICE	MARK-UP
	+	−	+
Own	−	+	−
label	−	−	±
products	+	+	±

Before examining the above hypotheses, it is essential to analyse the real quality of the items considered, in order to see if the own label products are:

(a) of better quality;

(b) of poorer quality;

(c) of the same quality.

For instance, the quality of block chocolate may vary considerably according to the percentage content of cocoa butter, sugar, etc.

This point is also very meaningful for our analysis of the behaviour of retailers as regards own label products. Are they sold either on the basis solely of "price competition", these products being therefore either of poorer quality or of much the same quality (as the branded products), or on the basis of a "non-price competition" pattern, the retailer's policy aiming to create a particular quality image for his own labels.

In this case it will be necessary to analyse also the retailers' advertising policy as regards their **own labels**.

2.7.9. Different hypotheses concerning the pricing of own label items.

The first hypothesis indicates that a certain degree of market power is enjoyed by the retailers, since they pay less for the own label products (than for the manufacturers' branded products), while they are able to sell them at a higher price.

The second hypothesis opens up two **opposite** and indeed contradictory explanations:

− either the retailer is launching an advertising campaign in order to replace the manufacturers' branded products by his own label products and, if this campaign is successful, we have a sign of the retailer's strong bargaining power;

- or the retailer cannot obtain from the manufacturers the quantities of manufacturers' branded products which he needs and so he is obliged to use other, more expensive sources of supply; in this case, we conclude that the retailer is negotiating with the manufacturers from a position of weakness.

Which of these two explanations occurs in the specific case?

The third hypothesis deserves particular attention since - especially in the case of a high mark-up for own label products - it indicates the existence of considerable bargaining power in the hands of the retailers vis-à-vis the manufacturers who actually make the retailers' own label products. These manufacturers are hardly competing with manufacturers' branded products, and the retailer takes the opportunity to reduce the proportion of manufacturers' branded products sold by him.

The fourth hypothesis calls for no particular comment.

All the above hypotheses must be checked against the answers given to other related questions:

- What is the share of own labels? (Q. 7);

- Are the more popular sizes sold as own label items? (Q. 8);

- Is there a tendency towards an increase in the share of own label items in the sample of shops? (Q. 12).

2.7.10. Comparison of retail buying prices as between imported goods and home-produced goods - Q. 67

Similar methods of analysis will be used for the answer to question:

LXVII) Generally speaking, how do the prices paid by retailers for imported products
(67) compare with those for home-produced goods;

    a) are they cheaper?

    b) are they more expensive?

    c) are they sometimes cheaper and sometimes more expensive?

    Does the difference in the buying price correspond to a real difference in quality?

2.7.11. Identification of retailers with the strongest (or the weakest) bargaining power - QQ. 68 and 69 and 72 and 73

Further questions to be examined are:

LXVIII) Which shop in the sample pays the highest (or lowest) unit buying price? For
(68) which brand and size? Do these prices refer to own label products and/or to imported products?

LXIX) Referring to the minimum unit buying price that one shop is paying (whatever may
(69) be the brand and/or size), which is the shop that is obliged to bear the highest unit buying price?

The answer to question 68 will identify both the retailers with the weakest (or strongest) negotiating power and the manufacturers or producers with the strongest (or weakest) negotiating power.

The answer to question 69 will confirm the identity of the retailer with the weakest bargaining power.

All this information is of basic utility in a long-term analysis, as we shall see later. But the answers to questions 68 and 69 must be linked up to the answers to questions:

LXXII) What is the degree of dispersion of buying prices between different shops for
(72) identical items?

LXXIII) Which shop pays the highest (or lowest) buying prices for identical items?
(73)

Hence, **if it is assumed that:**

- the degree of dispersion is very high as regards both the buying price (product unit price) under question 65 and the buying price (identical item) under question 72; and that

- it is always the same shop (or retailer) that pays the highest (or the lowest) buying price as regards questions 68 and 69 as well as question 73,

it is possible to ascertain the identity of the retailers that actually have the strongest and weakest bargaining power respectively.

2.7.12. Large scale purchases and choice for consumers — Q. 70

Answers to questions 70 and 71 may help to **reveal** the retailers' purchasing policy.

LXX) Is the shop paying the highest (or lowest) unit buying price the one where the
(70) choice of brands and sizes is widest (or narrowest)? Or is there no significant relationship between the number of brands and sizes and the level of buying prices?

The answer to this question will indicate the extent to which some retailers prefer to **buy** very considerable quantities of only one brand of a given product, in order to get substantial discounts (in return for exclusivity and/or for quantity)[1]. The generalization of this policy results in a shop offering only one brand for each existing product, no choice therefore being available to the consumer.

Is this a sign that strong bargaining power is enjoyed by the retailer? Or is it, on the contrary, a sign of weak bargaining power?

In this respect, it will be necessary:

- to compare the evolution of sales, mark-ups and gross income of retailers working under the single brand policy;

- to ascertain whether there is a free decision by the retailer to base his policy upon only one brand or whether, on the contrary, there are important producers or manufacturers who simply refuse to supply him;

- to ascertain whether this policy, based on one single brand, is the effect of inter-locking shareholdings or directorates between the retailer in question and the producer or manufacturer from whom alone he buys.

2.7.13. Several brands made by the same manufacturer — Q. 71

It is of the greatest interest to know the pricing policy of a given manufacturer in relation to different products manufactured by his firm but presented under different brand names. We will therefore put the following question:

---

1. The analysis of time in stock as set out in Section 2.4. (Analysis of shop efficiency) **provides** the means of describing and explaining the various features of the major retailers' policies.

LXXI) When shops in the sample sell one product made by the <u>same</u> manufacturer but under
(71) different trade marks – including own labels – which <u>brand</u>, and in which shop, costs
      more (or less) and why?

Previous analysis will highlight whether the difference in trade mark and price correspond
to a difference in quality.

Further analysis will establish:

- whether the difference in brand name and price conceals a difference in negotiating
  power enjoyed by different retailers buying the different brands from the same producer
  or manufacturer;

- whether the brands having the highest buying price are artificially pushed up by
  intensive advertising campaigns by the producers (or manufacturers) and/or by the
  retailers concerned;

- whether the brands having the <u>highest buying price</u> have a proportionate <u>highest selling
  price</u> to final consumers and, on the contrary, whether the brands having the <u>lowest
  buying price</u> are used for the purpose of special offer campaigns by retailers, with or
  without the consent of the producers (or manufacturers).

2.7.14. <u>KEY THREE</u>: <u>The comparisons between products in relation to international
         comparisons – Q. 74</u>

The following set of questions implies, among other things, the use of <u>key three</u> already
proposed at point 2.5.4. (comparisons between products):

LXXIV) Which are the brands and the actual producers or manufacturers for which we
(74)   observe the highest degree of dispersion of buying prices:

       (a) between the shops constituting the local sample surveyed?

       (b) between the different countries or regions surveyed?

       (c) which countries (or regions) record the highest (or lowest) buying prices
           for the same identical items (ie. same brand, size and manufacturer)?

In our belief, the answers given to the set of questions at 74, connected with the
answers given to the set of questions at 48 (retail mark-ups), will enable us to outline
the <u>real substance of negotiating power</u> on both sides of the market: the supply side
(producers or manufacturers) and the demand side (retailers).

Above all, it will be possible to ascertain the <u>brands</u> and <u>producers</u> for which the
phenomenon of <u>power interplay appears to be the most marked and especially the most
variegated</u>, owing to the high degree of dispersion of buying prices.

Furthermore, through the international comparisons, it will be possible to ascertain:

- in which countries (or regions) the negotiating power balances out in favour either
  of producers or manufacturers (higher buying prices) or of retailers (lower buying
  prices, possibly but not necessarily accompanied by higher retail mark-ups);

- in which countries (or regions) and to what extent the <u>lower</u> buying prices are passed
  on to the final consumers in the form of a <u>lower</u> retail selling price.

In this respect it will be necessary to compare:

- all the answers – referring to a given product or brand – to the set of questions at 23
  (retail price) with the answers given to the sets of questions at 48 (mark-ups) and 74
  (buying prices);

- all those answers with the answers to questions 65, 66, 67, 68 and 69 to see if <u>the
  strongest (or the weakest) bargaining power</u> enjoyed by individual retailers always concerns
  <u>the same brand and size</u> (an <u>identical item</u>) or sometimes one brand and one product and
  other times other brands and other products.

2.7.15. The summarizing role of the Sixth Table: "arrival" and "departure"

Analysis of the evolution of buying prices and of all the questions connected wit it enables us:

- to use together the three keys defined at Section 2.5. (key one: the analysis of evolution; key two: the international – and the inter-regional – comparison of this evolution; key three: the comparison between products);

- to approach the core of the power interplay between retailers and producers.

But it is obvious that if we are to make progress in the evolutionary or dynamic approach, we are faced with the problem that the data to be taken into account will expand in volume with the number of surveys to be compared and analysed. Hence the further development of our analysis requires the advance summary of the main results if we are to have a really intelligible and **meaningful** picture.

This can be done by means of the sixth table, which plays a dual summarizing role ("arrival" and "departure"), as do the fourth and fifth tables, that is:

(a) the "arrival" role, made possible by its concise structure, is based on three "warning lights":

- the maximum;

- the minimum;

- the average.

The table summarizes salient features described analytically (by shops and brands/sizes) in the first three tables and obtained from data such as: unit buying prices, retail mark-ups, unit retail prices, shops, actual producers and time in stock;

(b) the "departure" **role**, introducing new data for further comparative analysis.

As concerns the latter role, it is noteworthy that the sixth table gives essential additional information (left out of the first to third tables because of lack of space) such as:

- date of purchase;

- unit producer or manufacturer price;

- trend of indexes of buying prices, producer prices and retail prices.

All these data are selected according to the above breakdown according to the three "warning lights" (maximum, minimum and average).

Lastly, we must emphasize that, as regards both the summary roles (of the sixth table) and the data set out in the first to sixth tables, these tables always indicate whether a given datum refers:

- to an own label product (designated by "O.L."), manufacturers' branded products therefore being determined by exclusion;

- to an imported product, which is indicated by an asterisk, home-produced goods therefore being determined by exclusion.

It is clear then, that the sixth table enables essential conclusive data to be extracted from an enormous bulk of atoms of information.

2.7.16. The evolutionary viewpoint: various aspects – QQ. 75-78

To the question "How are we to analyse the sixth table?" the answer is: "by using the three keys already proposed."

As regards the evolutionary viewpoint (key one), we will have to answer the following questions, by comparing two or more sixth tables (extracted from the first, second and third tables), relative to different moments of the reference period (t, $t+1$, $t+2$, etc.):

LXXV) Does the degree of dispersion of unit buying prices among the different brands
(75) and sizes – including own label products – increase or decrease from t to $t+1$, $t+2$, etc.?

LXXVI) Is it always the same brand/size that has the highest or lowest unit buying
(76) price?

LXXVII) Does the (average) unit buying price increase more for own label items or for
(77) manufacturers' branded products? Or is no clear trend apparent?

LXXVIII) Does the (average) unit buying price increase more for imported products or for
(78) home-produced goods?

2.7.17. Interpretation of an increase in the degree of dispersion of the unit buying price

As a rule, an increase in the degree of dispersion of the unit buying price as between retailers in the sample will mean that:

– terms of supply are becoming more unequal among the retailers purchasing the product;

– therefore, some retailers are probably acquiring stronger bargaining power at the expense:

a) apparently, of the producers (or manufacturers) or dealers selling the product,

b) possibly of the other retailers who have to face a sharp increase in their unit prices as manufacturers (or producers) pass on to them the loss they themselves have suffered as a result of better terms granted to the stronger retailers,

c) consequently, of the final consumers, if the average retail selling price increases very considerably as a result of the increase in the unit buying price suffered by the other retailers.

It is necessary to check what may be a very important economic conclusion, namely that an increase in the degree of dispersion of the retail buying price may be a contributory factor in the inflationary process.

Comparison of the evolution of mark-ups between the retailers receiving much better terms of supply and those who suffer in consequence show:

– that the increase in negotiating power is a real phenomenon for some retailers;

– whether this increase in the negotiating power will benefit or damage the final consumer.

These conclusions will be confirmed and possibly enlarged by the answer given to question 46.

On the other hand, a decrease in the degree of dispersion of unit buying price means that terms of supply are becoming more equal among the retailers, but this conclusion opens the way to contradictory explanations about the evolution of the retailers' bargaining power, depending on the answers to other connected questions in our system.

Answers to questions 77 and 78 may be helpful, but they also have to be interpreted in the general framework of our system of questions.

2.7.18. The set of questions concerning the retail buying price (QQ. 79-84) and power interplay

The set of connected answers to the four questions considered above therefore brings out only some aspects of the basic trend of the negotiating power as between retailers and producers or manufacturers.

The set of answers have therefore to be linked to **other**, more detailed questions, in order to establish the exact identity of given retailers in terms of stronger (or weaker) bargaining power vis-à-vis producers or manufacturers.

More particularly, further analysis will take into account the answers to all the questions below:

I) Questions about the evolution of the buying price - QQ. 75-84.

II) Questions about the evolution of the retail mark-ups - QQ. 54-62.

III) Questions - Q. 85 - about the comparative evolution of
   - unit buying prices
   - unit producers prices
   - unit retail selling prices.

IV) Questions about the international (or inter-regional) comparative evolution of the data at III, using key two - QQ. 86-88.

V) Questions about the product-to-product comparative evolution of the data at III, using key three - QQ. 89-91.

VI) Questions about the determination of actual buying prices, discounts and rebates - QQ. 92-94.

As regards the wording of the questions concerning the evolution of the unit buying price (QQ. 79-84), it will be very similar to those concerning the evolution of retail selling prices: see Section 2.3.: "The selective historical series", point 4, (QQ. 30-38).

2.7.19. An approach to the power interplay - Q. 85

It is now possible to refine the analysis of power interplay by focusing on the structure and evolution of retail buying prices in comparison with other prices and data available.

As we have already underlined, the three keys constitute a fundamental tool for attaining our research purposes.

As concerns especially point III (key one: analysis of evolution) we will put the following question:

LXXXV) What is the comparative evolution of unit retail buying prices, unit producers
  (85) prices and unit retail selling prices? Is it possible to work out price indexes
       (see bottom of sixth table) taking into account separately the average increases
       and the maximum and minimum increases? What explanations can be given as to the
       cause of a divergent evolution? Increase in transport costs, in taxes, and so on?

2.7.20. <u>International comparisons concerning the evolution of retail buying prices and other prices — QQ. 86-88</u>

As concerns more particularly point IV (key two), we will put the following set of questions:

LXXXVI) How are the <u>different countries</u> (or regions) ranked according to the following
(86) criteria:

    (a) increase in the <u>unit buying prices</u> (maximum, minimum and average prices indicated in the <u>sixth table</u>)?

    (b) as (a), referring to the <u>unit producers prices</u> if it is not the same as unit retail buying price?

    (c) as (a), referring to the <u>retail selling price</u>?

Two further questions will have to be discussed:

LXXXVII) How are the <u>different countries</u> (or regions) ranked according to the following
(87) criteria:

    (a) average increase (or decrease) in the <u>difference</u> between the unit retail selling price and the unit retail buying price?[1]

    (b) average increase (or decrease) in the <u>difference</u> between the unit retail buying price and the producers (or manufacturers) price?[1]

    (c) (d) (e) (f): as (a) and (b), but referring to the <u>maximum</u> and <u>minimum</u> <u>increases</u> in price differences, specifying the names of the relevant retailers in each country?[1]

    (g) evolution of the rates of taxes affecting the various stages of distribution?

LXXXVIII) In <u>which countries</u> (or regions) do we find the retailers, producers (or
(88) manufacturers) or traders:

    (a) who benefit from the evolution in question 87?

    (b) who suffer from it?

    See also questions 118 and 121 (Section 2.8.).

2.7.21. <u>Ranking of products according to different criteria — The regional differences and the role of traders (importers, exporters) — QQ. 89-91</u>

As regards the fifth and last point (key three: comparisons between products), we shall put three basic questions:

LXXXIX) How are the different <u>products</u> ranked according to each of the following criteria:
(89)
    (a) increase in <u>unit retail buying prices</u>, indicating <u>separately</u> the average, maximum and minimum prices (as in the sixth table)?

    (b) as (a), referring to unit <u>producers</u> prices?

    (c) as (a), referring to unit <u>retail</u> selling prices?

What is the breakdown of the shares accounted for by transport and insurance costs and taxes in:

    — unit retail buying prices (average, maximum, minimum)

    — unit producers prices (average, maximum, minimum)

    — unit retail selling prices (average, maximum, minimum).
    See also questions 119 <u>et seq</u>.

---

1. See also 2.5.21. — <u>The speed at which retail prices react to changes in producers' prices</u>.

XC) How are the different products ranked according to each of the different criteria
(90) indicated in question 87?

XCI) How are the different products ranked by country in decreasing order for each of
(91) the following data, as obtained from the most recent survey:

    (a) absolute size of average retail mark-up, that is: the difference between the
        retail selling price and the unit retail buying price, specifying the amount
        accounted for by taxes;

    (b) absolute size of the maximum retail mark-up, specifying the name of the
        relevant retailer for each country, and also the amount accounted for by taxes;

    (c) absolute size of the minimum retail mark-up, specifying the name of the relevant
        retailer for each country, and also the amount accounted for by taxes;

    (d) absolute size of the average wholesale (or import/export) mark-up, that is:
        the difference between the unit retail buying price and the unit producers (or
        manufacturers) price, before deduction of any transport and insurance costs borne
        by the trader (amount to be specified);

    (e) absolute size of the maximum wholesale (or trade) mark-up, before deduction of
        any transport and insurance costs borne by the trader (amount to be specified).
        The name of the relevant wholesaler (or trader) for each country will also be
        indicated;

    (f) absolute size of the minimum wholesale (or trade) mark-up, before deduction of
        any transport and insurance costs borne by the trader (amount to be specified).
        The name of the relevant wholesaler (or trader) for each country will also be
        indicated.

    See also question 123.

Here it is worth remembering that the sixth table illustrates the differences:

- between the retail buying price and the actual producers' (or manufacturers') price,
  as regards both structure and evolution, in the different countries;

- between the retail selling price and the actual producers' (or manufacturers') price,
  as regards both structure and evolution, in the different countries.[1]

From the answers to questions 87-91 we can discover:

- whether there is discrimination in producers' (or manufacturers') prices according to the
  country (and/or region) where a given product is bought;

- in which countries (and/or regions) the distributive system is most and least
  expensive to the final consumer, assuming a uniform producers' (or manufacturers') price.[1]

What we now need is a quantitative breakdown of all these factors, that is:

- an attempt at estimated figures for each cost and/or profit element (transport and
  insurance costs, storage costs, various forms of taxes, exceptional profits and so on);

- identification of the producers, traders or retailers concerned (whether they are
  benefiting or being damaged), special attention being also paid to the differences in
  taxation depending on product and country.

---

1. See also 2.5.21. - The speed at which retail prices react to changes in producers
   prices

146

2.7.22. The problem of calculating the actual retail buying price

It is apparent from the above questions that there is a need for a very thorough analysis of:

I) the distributive system, in relation to the production (and/or manufacturing) system, considered in terms of:

   - international trade;

   - each selected product submitted to the very thorough analysis;

II) the concept (definition and measure) of:

   - the unit retail buying price; and

   - the unit producers price; or

   - the unit manufacturers price.

The crucial problem, as we have seen, is calculating the actual retail buying price of a given item, this calculation presupposing knowledge of the actual date of purchase.[1]

On this basis it will be possible to calculate:

- the actual mark-up.

How are we to determine the actual date of purchase, in order to know the actual retail buying price?

And then: how are we to determine the different forms and sizes of discounts, rebates and so on?

2.7.23. Practical ways and means of determining actual retail buying prices

Briefly speaking, we can indicate four suitable ways:

(a) direct questions to retailers; (b) indirect or mediate questions to retailers; (c) direct questions to all suppliers concerned (producers and/or traders); (d) estimations based on analysis of chronological and international sets of tables and data.

(a) The retailer has to be asked, on the occasion of each six-monthly survey, about:

   - the date of purchase and the retail buying price - at the actual date of purchase - of a given item (product), which exists in the shop at the time of the survey;

   - the retail buying price for the corresponding item (product), currently payable at the time of the survey.

The first point is necessary for calculation of the actual mark-up, to be recorded in the present survey, while the second point will be utilised for analysing and determining actual retail buying prices and mark-ups in future surveys (see letter (d)).

(b) Another question to be put to the retailer on the occasion of each survey concerns the average time in stock, which will enable the research institute:

   - to ascertain the actual date of purchase of the items (products) concerned;

   - to check these calculations (and estimations) with other information directly supplied by the retailers concerned, as regards the actual date of purchase, retail buying price and retail mark-up (see letter (a)).

---

1. This knowledge is essential for calculating more particularly the speed at which the retail selling price reacts to changes in the retail buying price. See also 2.5.21.

(c) By contacting the retailers' main suppliers, such as producers, manufacturers, wholesalers, importers and/or exporters, it will be possible to double-check the information given by the retailers as regards actual dates of purchase and actual retail buying prices (resulting from letters (a) and (b)).

(d) It is possible to estimate and to double-check the actual dates of purchase and the actual buying prices by analysing data collected in previous surveys (see the second question in letter (a), as well as questions (b) and (c)). As concerns more particularly the actual buying prices, where they are fixed internationally, it is possible also to derive useful information from surveys carried out in other countries.

The conclusion is obvious:

- determining and estimating the actual dates (or times) of the purchase, the actual retail buying prices and the actual mark-up is a very difficult task, but not an impossible one. And in **any** case importance of such knowledge justifies all the efforts made in fulfilling the task;

- key one (the analysis of evolution) requiring systematic and continuous development of the research over time - in a long-term context and programme - as well as key two (the international comparison) requiring international cooperation between the European Commission and the national research institutes, **both** play a decisive role in highlighting the pattern of behaviour of the major retailers as well as the working of market and price structures.

2.7.24. Discount and rebate scheme - QQ. 92-94

There exist different forms of discount and rebate schemes. The research institutes will answer the following questions:

XCII) In the determination of the unit buying price, has it been possible to find out
(92) whether some retailers (specifying their name) receive the following rebates or discounts, and if so what is the probable percentage of purchases affected:

    (a) a rebate linked to the aggregate quantity bought by the retailers at a given time or in a given period. How is this period determined and how does the rebate scheme operate?

    (b) a rebate linked to the rate of increase of quantities purchased by the retailers in relation to a previous year (or other fixed period)?

XCIII) As 92, as **regard**s rebate linked to exclusivity (in respect of purchases or of
(93) sales or of both).

XCIV) Are some retailers **benefiting** from special terms that it is difficult to express
(94) as sums of money because they concern:

    (a) the terms and conditions of transport, delivery and storage of the goods purchased (eg. for supplementary services demanded by buyers);

    (b) other special terms agreed between the retailer (buyer) and the seller (**p**roducer, manufacturer or wholesaler)?

2.7.25. Standard contracts between suppliers and buyers

We must emphasise that it is the actual buying price, ie. the full price minus all discounts and rebates allowed to the retailer, that must be taken into account. The calculation and estimation of those discounts - granted under different forms and in different ways - constitutes a very delicate operation. In this respect, it may be helpful to consider the standard contracts that some big retailers (buyers) and manufacturers or wholesalers (suppliers) currently apply in their business relationship. It is noteworthy however that exceptions are often allowed from the standard contracts and terms in dealings with very big retailers (**b**uyers). The report of the research institute will specify in detail how the different forms of discount have been worked out, calculated and/or estimated, so as to give a very precise view of the reliability of the buying price taken into account, and to what extent it is really the actual buying price.

The actual buying prices have to be compared, both from the evolutionary and the international viewpoints, and for this reason they must be defined very strictly.

2.7.26. The circle is complete – Reference to the analyses of shop efficiency (QQ. 94–103) and loss leading (QQ. 104–115)

The research on price structures now reaches the final stage, as though the circle were completed, since it is now possible to integrate:

– the results of analysis of retail buying prices and power interplay (QQ. 65–93)

– with further and deeper analysis:
  – of shop efficiency (QQ. 95–103);
  – of loss leading (QQ. 104–115).

Indeed it is now possible to give the names of retailers in each of the different countries and regions who are buying the selected products from producers and/or manufacturers and/or traders,

– at the lowest price, those retailers therefore having the greatest bargaining power,

– at the highest price, those retailers therefore having the weakest bargaining power.

If those retailers' names are broadly the same for all products, we must now see what kind of relationship exists between strength of retailer bargaining power (against the suppliers) and:

(a) shop efficiency (Section 2.4.);

(b) loss leading (Section 2.6.);

(c) the level and the trend of concentration in actual regional (or local) retail distribution and in national retail distribution in each given country in general.

2.7.27. Shop efficiency at the final stage of analysis – Reference to QQ. 95–103

The next stage in the analysis will show how far the strongest retailers (in terms of bargaining power) make use of their power:

I) either:
  – by reducing their retail selling prices and mark-ups, therefore **benefiting the** final consumer;
  – by reducing the time in stock of the different products, owing to an increase in their sales helped by lower prices;

II) or:
  – by doing so in some of their shops operated but not in others.

In the latter case an attempt will be made to ascertain the actual long-term goals of the policy pursued by the retail operator group:

– is it trying to concentrate the benefits acquired by virtue of this stronger bargaining power and to practice predatory retail pricing in order to drive certain troublesome competitors off one (or more) regional (or local) markets?

On the other hand, further analysis – using certain essential data already seen (as regards retail selling prices, mark-ups and time in stock) – will show the degree of probability of the weakest retailers (in terms of bargaining power) being driven off the market sooner or later.

International comparisons of the evolution (key three) will help to forecast the expected trends in each country and/or region analysed.

2.7.28. Loss leading at the final stage of analysis – Reference to QQ. 104-115

The research institutes, after estimating the actual date of purchase and the actual retail buying price, will be able to move on to a detailed analysis of the loss leading policy.

It is in almost all respects a highly ambiguous "two souls" policy (Zwei Seelen wohnen ach! in meiner Brust – Goethe), since it is difficult to define and anyway it may reflect:

I) either the existence of strength and efficiency,

II) or the existence of weakness and inefficiency.

I) In the first case loss leading may be an active – even aggressive – policy of a strong retailer for curbing his competitors and even eliminating them. His considerable bargaining power (vis-à-vis the suppliers) enables him to follow a very effective and dangerous policy without enduring substantial losses (points 2.6.6. to 8.). And so, without bearing either risks or losses, this retailer can eliminate competitors in some regions or towns and thus restrict the "competitive arena".

But, on the other hand, does this policy benefit the final consumer by helping to combat inflation? After all, this retailer, in our inflationary times, is in practice working against those who speculate on anticipated price rises!

A loss leading policy, in other words, acts as a barrier to artificial price increases:

– both at the producers' level, as regards the trend of international trade;

– and at the regional (or local) level, as regards consumer prices.

A meaningful indication of whether the good or bad "soul" is animating the loss leading policy will be whether the policy is fairly widespread among all the shops of the retailer operator group or applied solely in selected shops in crucial regions or towns (point 2.7.27.II).

II) In the second case, the loss leading policy expresses the existence of weakness and of inefficiency because the weak retailer, who is obliged to buy at an excessively high price from his suppliers, is also obliged to sell some products below his buying price.

In this case, there are two possible explanations:

a) The "weak" retailer is weak because he is small.

Since he is small, he can buy only small quantities and thus has a weak bargaining power (vis-à-vis suppliers).

Since he is small, he is also inefficient because he is not able to reap economies of scale in distribution, his personnel is utilized below capacity, therefore his selling prices are too high and he has also to endure a longer time in stock.

In this case, a loss leading policy is the last resort and the retailer may well be heading for bankruptcy.

b) The "weak" retailer is a big operator group.

Since he is too big, his management is not able to run the business efficiently or else his management is simply of poor quality, so that there is no relationship between corporate size and profitability. The real difficulty in analysing the efficiency of a big group is shown by the fact that, since this group is operating many undertakings in different lines of business and in different regions, it can use profits that may arise from the abuse of dominance (or monopoly) power in some markets to offset losses incurred in other markets.

In a big group also the quality of management may be highly variable (ranging from the excellent to the very poor manager) and the best managers may wish to preserve the distinction between themselves and the "poorer" managers by keeping the latter in jobs as long as the overall financial position of the conglomerate group is out of the red.

Anyway, the analysis of the "buying price" in this section should seek to establish whether the big retailer is actually using his strong bargaining power to obtain the best terms from his suppliers, as is most probable.

In any case, the practice of loss leading has to be analysed very thoroughly in order to ascertain whether:

- it aims to conceal the inefficiency of some shops and branches of the retailer operator group, offset by excess profits in other shops or branches and/or for other products; or

- it is possible because of large volume of overall sales in the shops practising it, these shops being in a position to finance their own loss leading.

The comparison of time in stock in relation to different products and shops might be helpful here.

2.8. COMPLETION OF THE MONOGRAPHIC APPROACH BY PRODUCT: EXCESSIVE PRICES AND THEIR CAUSES - AND PARTICULARLY THE BREAKDOWN OF PRICES

2.8.1. A monographic approach by product

The foregoing considerations have highlighted the complexity of the factors that determine the final price, that is to say the series of final prices which the consumer may be charged for the same product (and/or brand) by different shops in different countries.

The above analyses have given practical form to the idea of a monographic approach to the product, since, working from a large number of items of information (prices and mark-ups) relating to a large number of products, the ultimate aim should be to narrow our attention down to a number of selected products, each studied separately by a kind of monograph and subjected to the most detailed analysis possible with the information available.

The point now is to complete this monographic approach by product along two lines:

(a) detecting and analysing excessive prices[1];

(b) analysing the causes of excessive prices, with particular reference to:
- the existence of a distribution circuit involving too many stages;
- the existence of excessive mark-ups;
- the existence of particularly heavy taxes.

But this analysis of the causes of excessive prices is bound to involve completion of the monographic approach by firm if excessive prices are caused by:
- the existence of dominance, caused in its turn by:
- the existence of an excessive degree of concentration, nationally or locally.

2.8.2. The chain of excessive prices

Section 2.7. highlighted certain phenomena of price formation, the analysis being based on the relations between firms and the two ends of the distribution chain:

- producers;

- retailers.

The study of excessive prices means that the analysis must be extended to:

- the other links in the distribution chain between producer and retailer[2];

- factors conditioning the producers prices.

---

1. The detection and analysis of excessive prices are essential to the Commission's activities in relation to Community competition policy. The judgment given by the Court of Justice on 14 February 1978 in Case 27/76, Chiquita (United Brands Company v. Commission) confirms the need for systematic, detailed analysis of excessive pricing.

2. As regards the retail trade, it will be remembered that a distinction is made between integrated distribution - firms buying direct from the producers - and independent distribution - buying through wholesalers.

One might imagine the existence of a chain of excessive prices since these can be charged:

- at the retail level (final consumer price);

- at the producer level;

- at any intervening level.

Any excessive price at any stage in the distribution chain obviously affects downstream levels of distribution, the full cumulative effect being manifested, of course, at the consumer stage. An example of the formation and development of prices is given in Table VII.

2.8.3. The detection of excessive prices

One practical consequence flows from the foregoing:

In the detection of excessive prices, the basic, primary point of observation is the consumer price. The retail selling price is a transparent datum easily accessible to all. This final price is the point of departure for any specific operational enquiry. We therefore have every reason for regarding it as a kind of thermometer.

An excessive price can be detected in the following ways:

I) IN STATIC TERMS, by studying the relevant structure at a given point in time:
   a) Comparison of retail selling prices;
      - between different shops in the same region or town;
      - between different countries or regions.
   b) Breakdown of the retail selling price into its various components.

II) IN DYNAMIC TERMS, by studying the evolution of this structure with reference to the two above aspects (comparison in prices and breakdown of the final price). The two keys with which we are now familiar will be used:
   - key one: analysis of the evolution of the different prices (selling price, buying price, producers' price) for the same sample of shops in the same country;
   - key two: analysis of the comparative international evolution, between shops in different countries.

   But with particular reference to breakdown of the retail selling price (aspect (b)), key three - comparison between products - may be of precious assistance.

In questions 85 to 91[1] we described the instruments that can be used to highlight the countries, products and shops of which it can be said that prices are probably excessive.

Since an excessive price is the most flagrant example of an anomaly of competition, the point now is to seek out the cause of the excessive prices, and the result of our search may be:

- proof that the prices are really excessive;

- description of the causes behind these excessive prices;

- in certain cases, an operational conclusion as to means of attenuating or even eliminating these excessive prices.

---

1. Points 2.7.19. to 2.7.21.

TABLE VII

FORMATION AND EVOLUTION OF PRICES FOR CERTAIN SELECTED PRODUCTS

PRODUCT: Nescafé Instant Coffee (10 bags: 18 grammes) — made by Nestlé (Switzerland)

Number and date of survey	PRICE (in national currency) PRICE VARIATIONS (%) (*)									
	PRODUCER'S PRICE (**)					WHOLESALE PRICE = RETAIL BUYING PRICE (**)				
	Maximum		Minimum		Average	Maximum		Minimum		Average (***)
	Price and % ±	Name or No	Price and % ±	Name or No	Price and % ±	Price and % ±	Name or No	Price and % ±	Name or No	Price and % ±
I) January 77										
II) July 77										
VARIATION AND DIFFERENCE	/////		/////			/////		/////		
III) ...										
VARIATION AND DIFFERENCE										
IV) ...										
VARIATION AND DIFFERENCE										
V) ...										
VARIATION AND DIFFERENCE										

N.B. The figures in this example relate to Italy and prices are in Lit.

*   A distinction must be made between price variations (the percentage increase or decrease over the original price) and differences in mark-ups (calculated between the new rate of mark-up and the old rate of mark-up). This example seeks to highlight the distinction between the two concepts.

**   Where integrated trade is concerned, producers price = retail buying price.

*** The average price is always calculated from all available prices. It does not therefore constitute the midway point between the maximum and the minimum.

TABLE VII

FORMATION AND EVOLUTION OF PRICES FOR CERTAIN SELECTED PRODUCTS

PRODUCT: Nescafé Instant Coffee (10 bags: 18 grammes) — made by Nestlé (Switzerland)

Number and date of survey	PRICE (in national currency) PRICE VARIATIONS (%) (*)										
	RETAIL PRICE										
	M a x i m a								Minimum		Average (***)
	I		II		III		IV				
	Price and % ±	Name or No	Price and % ±	Name or No	Price and % ±	Name or No	Price and % ±	Name or No	Price and % ±	Name or No	Price and % ±
I) Jan. 77	700								490		572
II) Jul. 77	850								540		635
VARIATION AND DIFFERENCE	+21.4%								+10.2%		+11,0%
III) ...											
VAR. AND DIFF.											
IV) ...											
VAR. AND DIFF.											
V) ...											
VAR. AND DIFF.											

N.B. The figures in this example relate to Italy and prices are in Lit.

* A distinction must be made between price variations (the percentage increase or decrease over the original price) and differences in mark-ups (calculated between the new rate of mark-up and the old rate of mark-up). This example seeks to highlight the distinction between the two concepts.

** Where integrated trade is concerned, producers price = retail buying price.

*** The average price is always calculated from all available prices. It does not therefore constitute the midway point between the maximum and the minimum.

TABLE VII

FORMATION AND EVOLUTION OF PRICES FOR CERTAIN SELECTED PRODUCTS

PRODUCT: Nescafé Instant Coffee (10 bags: 18 grammes) – made by Nestlé (Switzerland)

Number and date of survey	RETAIL MARK–UPS AND DIFFERENCES (*) (%)								Minima		Average
	Maxima										
	I		II		III		IV		Rate and Diff.	Name or No	Rate and Diff.
	Rate and Diff.	Name or No	Rate and Diff.	Name or No	Rate and Diff.	Name or No	Rate and Diff.	Name or No			
I) Jan. 77	44.9		34.6		30.4		24.2		1.4		18.4
II) Jul. 77	53.4		35.4		26.4		22.7		−2.5		14.7
VAR. AND DIFF.	+8.5		+0.8		−4.0		−1.5		−3.9		−3.7
III) ...											
VAR. AND DIFF.											
IV) ...											
VAR. AND DIFF.											
V) ...											
VAR. AND DIFF.											

N.B. The figures in this example relate to Italy and prices are in Lit.

*   A distinction must be made between price variations (the percentage increase or decrease over the original price) and differences in mark–ups (calculated between the new rate of mark–up and the old rate of mark–up). This example seeks to highlight the distinction between the two concepts.

**   Where integrated trade is concerned, producers price = retail buying price.

*** The average price is always calculated from all available prices. It does not therefore constitute the midway point between the maximum and the minimum.

2.8.4. The concept of the excessive price – Proposal for an operational definition – QQ. 116 and 117

The following working hypotheses are proposed:

(a) An excessive price could be regarded as being the exact opposite of the price of a loss leader, considered at section 2.6.;

(b) thus, just as reference could be made to the lowest prices and mark-ups brought out by the fourth, fifth and sixth tables in order to establish a guide list of products and shops that might be surveyed for the existence of loss-leading, likewise reference could be made to the highest figures in those tables to establish a guide list of products and shops that it might be worth examining for excessive pricing;

(c) at a later stage in the survey, possibly taking account of the various qualitative factors, the two guide lists (loss leaders and excessive prices) could be restricted to products and shops where the values of the degree of dispersion of prices and mark-ups are highest (and particularly the co-efficients εR_p and εA_s).

On this basis an attempt must then be made to answer the following questions:

CXVI) Referring to questions 85 to 88 (in section 2.7.19. and 2.7.20.), is it possible,
(116) in each country surveyed and in all the countries surveyed and compared, to establish a guide list of suspect products and firms as regards the question of excessive pricing? Do the suspect firms include sole distributors? It goes without saying that initially it will be the quantitative criterion of maximum prices, mark-ups and differences and increases in them that will be used for establishing this list.

CXVII) Can the list of products and firms suspected of excessive pricing be broken into
(117) three categories:

(a) certainty or great probability of excessive pricing;

(b) probability or reasonable presumption;

(c) abstract possibility still to be checked and proved.

2.8.5. Excessive prices and the speed at which retail prices react to change in producers' prices – Q. 118

CXVIII) Can the suspect products and firms be ranked according to the following criteria:
(118)
(a) speed at which a downstream price (retail buying or selling price) reacts to an increase in the producers price;

(b) speed at which a downstream price reacts to a fall in the producers price?

What role is played by exclusive agreements? And by the type of trading?

Products and firms can then be ranked, by reference to two extreme cases:

– anticipation (highest speed): downstream prices rise or fall before the producer's price rises or falls;

– impermeability (zero): downstream prices do not change when producers' prices do.

It goes without saying that the speed at which final prices react to change in producers' prices constitutes a significant pointer to the practical functioning of competition – or alternately of restrictive practices.

2.8.6. Selection and analysis of suspect products — Table VII

The search for the causes of excessive prices entails, among other things, analysis of price formation and trends. This is the first stage of the operational phase of the survey, aiming to analyse the real scope of competitive anomalies.

Here it will be worth establishing a comparative summary table by means of which the formation and evolution of the prices of certain products can be brought out (Table VII).

It should be noted that the table distinguishes between the wholesaler (or trade) price and the producers' price, though these two prices will of course coincide where integrated trade is involved. As regards the currency in which prices are expressed, this will be the national currency of the country where the relevant products are retailed. Conversion of producers' prices where products are imported will have to be based on the nearest exchange rate to that actually paid by the importer (dealer or major retailer).

The importance of Table VII lies in the fact that it combines a dynamic approach (or the comparative statics approach) over what may turn out to be quite a long period with a vertical section of price structure from production to the retail stage.

By studying this table we can immediately detect certain competitive anomalies. Indication of the percentages to be added to the producer's price in order to obtain the retail selling price and the wholesale price respectively enables comparisons to be drawn between the various tendencies affecting "crucial" products.

In practical terms a distinction has to be made between:

— the selection of products whose prices are to be broken down;

— the object of this breakdown.

On the first point, it is obvious that the operation is so complex and costly that very strict limits have to be accepted. We shall confine ourselves to selecting two or three products where the operation would at first sight seem to be realistic and fruitful.

The list of criteria to be applied in selecting products for analysis in itself highlights the orientations and objectives of our research, as can be seen from the following:

(a) Size of the mark-up

The answers to question 91 will highlight those products for which excessive mark-ups are observed at whatever level of distribution (wholesale or retail).

(b) Upward trend of mark-ups

This will be observed from the answers to question 87.

(c) Existence of dominant positions on national and/or local markets

This is a decisive point, for as a rule it is precisely the existence of dominance that enables producers, retailers or other intermediaries to set excessive prices. The criterion was already emphasized at point 2.2.3., and we shall return to it.

2.8.7. Analysis of the comparative evolution of various cost and price components — The search for explanations → QQ. 119-121

The following points will have to be considered for suspect products:

CXIX) Referring to the answers to questions 85 to 87, is it possible to establish a table
(119) of comparative statics, highlighting the following factors:

    — producers' prices in the main countries of origin, expressed in national currency
      at the various times t, t+1, t+2, etc;

- series of variations in producers' prices (average, maximum and minimum) at any given moment, expressed as percentages of the price at time t;

- percentage of the producers' price accounted for at a given time t+i (i=0, 1, 2, ..) by transport, insurance and storage costs, distinguishing the average, maximum and minimum, from each producer country to each town or region covered by the retail selling price surveys;

- other specific cost components (taxes, duties, etc);

- the mark-up taken by the wholesaler or importer, as a percentage of the producers' price, and the evolution of the mark-up over the reference period, specifying the proportion accounted for by taxes[1];

- buying price paid by each retailer at each time t, distinguishing the average, maximum and minimum, the price being expressed in several different monetary units (price in the producing country, price in the buyer's country, price in European units of account);

- series of variations in buying prices (according to country of origin) for each retailer at each time t+i, as a percentage of the price at time t;

- retail mark-up as a percentage of:

  (a) the producer's price; and

  (b) the buying price,

  specifying the average, maximum and minimum and the proportion accounted for by taxes;

- retail selling price for each retailer, converted into the currency of the producer's country and into the European unit of account;

- series of variations in retail selling prices (according to country of origin) for each retailer at each time t+i, as a percentage of the price at time t.

CXX) What conclusions can be drawn from the answers to question 119? Can a divergent
(120) evolution of the various prices, costs and cost components for certain products be observed according to producing and/or buying country? What causes are suggested for the divergent evolution?

CXXI) Is it possible to estimate the net gains (or losses) to certain retailers, producers
(121) (or manufacturers) or dealers as a result of changes in the above prices and costs? Are the net gains, if any, linked to dominance or even monopoly, to restrictive agreements or to restrictive practices? Do exclusive agreements have the effect of raising prices and mark-ups?

2.8.8. The breakdown of mark-ups - Q. 122

The answers to the foregoing questions should make it possible to break down the various variable cost components that constitute the mark-up. But the problem of fixed costs cannot be overlooked.

CXXII) Can the mark-up for certain products or categories of products be broken down for
(122) certain firms (answer to question 91), with a distinction being made, among other things, between wages and salaries, interest on capital, rent, insurance and costs affecting processing plant in general, storage and marketing? Can this be done again for certain retailers and for certain wholesalers and/or importers? The proportion accounted for by taxes should be specified particularly.

---

1. It is obvious that where the integrated trade is involved - particularly where the retailer imports direct - this item will not apply.

The answer to question 122 raises highly complex problems. Very often estimates will have to be made, taking account of the cost structure of the various types of firm (retailers, dealers, importers). In some cases it will not be possible to break down mark-ups for a given product but only for a category of products and possibly only for the whole business of the relevant firm.

2.8.9. Breakdown of the producer's price - Q. 123

The analyses may reveal that the causes of the excessive price lie at the first link of the chain, that is to say with the producer. In this case an attempt must be made to answer the following question:

CXXIII) Can the producer's price be broken down for a given product or category of products
(123) whose producer's price at first sight seems excessive or has risen considerably during the reference period? The point here is to take the producer's price for each of the various firms studied and break it down into its components:

- taxes;

- energy used in processing or manufacturing the products;

- raw materials purchased (before processing);

- wages and salaries;

- interests on capital;

- rent and insurance;

- storage and transport.

The Institute will also estimate R & D expenditure, and especially expenditure on advertising either for a specific product or for a group of products.

It is clear that serious problems will arise in such an operation as regards:

- high-technology products requiring highly capital-intensive production plant;

- firms with a high degree of diversification or of vertical integration;

all these factors thus constitute a serious barrier to the breakdown of fixed costs, though this would be the only way of highlighting the cost structure of a given period. Even so it must be borne in mind:

I) costs could be broken down per group of related products;

II) the use of alternative bases for estimation might throw up certain conclusions as to the comparative evolution of company and group structures over a given period;

III) the cost breakdown will have the greatest chance of success for fairly simple products manufactured by single product firms.

In this connection, it is worth noting what the Court of Justice of the European Communities said in its Chiquita judgment of 14 February 1978 in Case 27/76 (United Brands Company v Commission), grounds of judgment 254 and 255:

"While appreciating the considerable and at times very great difficulties in working out production costs which may sometimes include a discretionary apportionment of indirect costs and general expenditure and which may vary significantly according to the size of the undertaking, its object, the complex nature of its set up, its territorial area of operations, whether it manufactures one or several products, the number of its subsidiaries and their relationship with each other, the production costs of the banana do not seem to present any insuperable problems.

In this case it emerges from a study by the United Nations Conference on trade and development of 10 February 1975 that the pattern of the production, packaging, transportation, marketing and distribution of bananas could have made it possible to compute the approximate production cost of this fruit and accordingly to calculate whether its selling price to ripener/distributors was excessive."

2.9. COMPLETION OF THE FIRM-BY-FIRM MONOGRAPHIC APPROACH: NATIONAL AND LOCAL CONCENTRATION

2.9.1. Dominance as an explanation of excessive prices - Table VIII

Dominance may appear:

- on the producer's market;

- on the distributor's (or retailer's) market.

In the first case it is "product dominance" - that is to say dominance exerted by the manufacturer of the product - that has repercussions on the purchasing retailer and, as a consequence, on the final consumer.

In the second case it is dominance by the large retailer which has repercussions both upstream on the producer and downstream on the consumer.

Studies by the Commission have already revealed the existence of a great many producer's markets which exercise a considerable power of dominance in several EEC Member States. Table VIII gives a series of examples of national markets of which the leading firm holds more than 25%.[1] Most of the products to be covered by the detailed survey envisaged at this stage of the investigation can be found in the list in Table VIII for at least one Member State.

The following are the products involved:

- instant coffee and possibly coffee grounds or beans;

- sugar;

- pure chocolate, in powder and solid form, and/or cocoa;

- margarine and/or other edible oils (groundnut oil, corn oil, etc.);

- tinned peas (natural);

- tinned and packet soups (vegetable - minestrone, vermicelli - chicken, tomato, pea, mushroom);

- homogenized baby foods: (a) desserts (fruit), (b) mixed vegetables with meat, fish, chicken;

- beer (bottled and in cans);

- mineral water;

- cola beverages.

---

1. This table is taken from the Seventh Annual Report on Competition Policy, point 287 (Table 12), published by the Commission in April 1978.
   The definition of dominance used for the table is independent of the interpretation of the Treaty rules on competition.

TABLE VIII

LIST OF PRODUCT MARKETS IN WHICH THE LEADING FIRM
HOLDS MORE THAN 25% OF THE TOTAL NATIONAL MARKET

(based on a limited sample of products and countries
covered by sectoral surveys)

Rank-ing	c_1 (in %)	Market	Sector	Coun-try	Year	Leading brand and/or firm
1	86	Sugar	ALI	DK	1975	De danske sukker-fabrikker
2	>85	Cola beverages	ALI	B	1976	Coca Cola
2	>85	Spirits	ALI	DK	1976	
2	85	Beer	ALI	DK	1975	United Breweries[1]
2	85	Needlework threads	TEX	F	1973	Dollfus Mieg
2	85	Chewing gum	ALI	F	1972	General Foods
7	84	Electric coffee-makers	ELE	F	1975	Moulinex
8	82	Unworked filter paper	PAP	B	1975	Intermills
9	>80	Refrigerators and freezers	ELE	F	1974	Thomson – Brandt
9	80	Dishwashers	ELE	F	1974	Thomson – Brandt
9	80	Hairdryers	ELE	F	1975	Moulinex
9	80	Sewing threads, haberdashery	TEX	F	1973	Dollfus Mieg
9	80	Automobile ignition systems	TRA	D	1974	Bosch
9	80	Floor detergent powders	CHI	I	1976	Spic-Span (Procter & Gamble)
9	80	White rum	ALI	GB	1974	Bacardi – Bass Charrington
16	75	Jute yarn and fabrics	TEX	F	1972	Agache-Willot
16	75	Unsweetened condensed milk	ALI	F	1972	Gloria (Carnation)
16	75	Baby foods	ALI	DK	1975	Nestlé
16	75	Sparking plugs (as originally fitted)	TRA	I	1974	Marelli
20	74	Coffee grinders	ELE	F	1975	Moulinex
21	73	Frozen foods	ALI	I	1973	Sages[2]
22	72	Ciné film (8, Super 8, etc.)	CHI	GB	1973	Kodak
23	71	Still films	CHI	GB	1973	Kodak
24	>70	Non-barbiturate sedatives	PHA	GB	1973	Roche
24	70	Chocolate powder	ALI	F	1972	Poulain
24	70	Cereals (flakes)	ALI	F	1972	Kellogg
24	70	Milk powder	ALI	GB	1973	Cadbury Schweppes
24	70	Dog and cat food	ALI	F	1972	Mars (Unisabi)
24	70	Instant coffee	ALI	F	1972	Nestlé
24	70	Sweetened condensed milk	ALI	F	1972	Lait Mont-Blanc[3]
24	70	Tranquillizers	PHA	NL	1973	
24	70	Sulphite paper	PAP	B	1974	Denayer

TABLE VIII

LIST OF PRODUCT MARKETS IN WHICH THE LEADING FIRM
HOLDS MORE THAN 25% OF THE TOTAL NATIONAL MARKET

(based on a limited sample of products and countries
covered by sectoral surveys)

Rank-ing	c_1 (in %)	Market	Sector	Country	Year	Leading brand and/or firm
33	69	Detergent for dishwashers	CHI	I	1976	Finish (Soilax)[4]
34	67	Margarine	ALI	GB	1973	Van der Bergh & Jurgens[2]
34	67	Detergent powders	CHI	GB	1975	Unilever
36	66	Tinned spaghetti, etc.	ALI	GB	1973	H.J. Heinz
37	65	Kraft paper or similar	PAP	I	1972	Import
37	65	Newsprint	PAP	B	1975	Import
37	65	Vermouth	ALI	GB	1974	Martini
37	65	Corrugated board	PAP	B	1974	Import
37	65	Sparking plugs (replacement market)	TRA	GB	1975	Champion
42	63	Batteries (as originally fitted)	TRA	I	1972	Marelli
43	61	Frozen foods	ALI	GB	1973	Unilever
44	>60	Stationery	PAP	GB	1972	Dickinson Robinson Group
44	>60	Other hypertensive drugs	PHA	GB	1973	MSD
44	60	Bulbs and lamps for motor vehicles	TRA	D	1974	Osram
44	60	Margarines and edible oils and fats	ALI	D	1974	Unilever
44	60	Puffed cereals	ALI	F	1972	Kellogg
44	60	Whisky	ALI	GB	1974	Distillers
44	60	Tinned soups	ALI	GB	1973	H.J. Heinz
44	60	Dietetic products and baby foods	ALI	F	1972	Fali[5]
44	60	Dehydrated potato powder	ALI	F	1972	Nestlé
44	60	Margarine	ALI	F	1972	Astra-Calvé
44	60	Tinned meat	ALI	I	1973	Simmenthal
44	60	Sparking plugs	TRA	D	1974	Bosch
44	60	Malted beverages	ALI	F	1972	Sopad – Nestlé
57	58	Edible oils	ALI	F	1972	Groupe Lesieur
57	58	Processed cheese	ALI	F	1972	Bel
59	57	Prepared potatoes	ALI	D	1974	Pfanni-Werk
59	57	Car tyres	TRA	F	1975	Michelin
59	57	Analgesics	PHA	DK	1972	The Danish Pharmacies
59	57	Powered scythes	MAC	I	1974	BCS
63	56	Board from recycled paper	PAP	B	1975	Import

TABLE VIII

LIST OF PRODUCT MARKETS IN WHICH THE LEADING FIRM
HOLDS MORE THAN 25% OF THE TOTAL NATIONAL MARKET

(based on a limited sample of products and countries
covered by sectoral surveys)

Rank-ing	c_1 (in %)	Market	Sector	Coun-try	Year	Leading brand and/or firm
63	56	General-purpose computers	MAC	I	1973	IBM
65	55	Soups	ALI	D	1974	Maggi[3]
65	55	Milk powder	ALI	F	1972	France-Lait
65	55	Instant chocolate drinks	ALI	F	1972	Nestlé
65	55	Tinned soups	ALI	F	1972	Liebig
65	55	Mustards and condiments	ALI	F	1972	Générale Alimentaire (Cavenham – GB)
65	55	Mopeds and scooters 50 cc	TRA	I	1972	Piaggio
65	55	Tinned baked beans	ALI	GB	1973	Heinz
65	55	Lining materials	TEX	F	1972	Dollfus, Mieg & Cie
65	55	Newsprint	PAP	F	1974	Import
74	54	Sugar	ALI	GB	1973	Tate & Lyle
75	53	Tranquillizers	PHA	DM	1972	Dumex
76	> 52	General-purpose computers	MAC	GB	1973	IBM
76	> 52	General-purpose computers	MAC	D	1973	IBM
76	52	Batteries (as originally fitted)	TRA	GB	1975	Lucas
79	51	Electric cookers	ELE	DK	1973	Ernst Voss
80	> 50	Cola beverages	ALI	NL	1974	Coca Cola
80	> 50	Slimming preparations	PHA	GB	1973	
80	> 50	Refrigerators	ELE	I	1973	Zanussi
80	> 50	Anti-angina drugs	PHA	GB	1973	ICI
80	> 50	"Plain skin" hormones	PHA	GB	1973	Glaxo
80	> 50	Tranquillizers	PHA	GB	1973	Roche
80	50	Tinned salmon	ALI	GB	1973	John West[2]
80	50	Flax yarn	TEX	F	1972	Agache-Willot
80	50	Dietetic preparations	ALI	I	1973	Plasmon[6]
80	50	Precooked meals	ALI	F	1972	Buitoni-Perugina
80	50	Chocolate biscuits	ALI	GB	1973	United Biscuits
80	50	Crisps	ALI	F	1972	Flodor
80	50	Ice cream	ALI	D	1974	Langnese-Iglo[2]
80	50	Printing paper and stationery	PAP	B	1975	Import
80	50	Electric vacuum cleaners	ELE	F	1975	Moulinex
80	50	Rice	ALI	F	1972	Cofariz

TABLE VIII

LIST OF PRODUCT MARKETS IN WHICH THE LEADING FIRM
HOLDS MORE THAN 25% OF THE TOTAL NATIONAL MARKET

(based on a limited sample of products and countries
covered by sectoral surveys)

Rank-ing	C_1 (in %)	Market	Sector	Coun-try	Year	Leading brand and/or firm
96	49	Condensed and evaporated milks, sterilized creams	ALI	GB	1973	Carnation Foods
96	49	Vacuum cleaners	ELE	GB	1975	Hoover
98	48	General-purpose computers	MAC	B	1973	IBM
99	47	Dry-cleaning machines	ELE	DK	1973	Fisker og Nielsen
99	47	Biscuits	ALI	F	1972	Aliment Essentiel
99	47	Synthetic detergents	CHI	GB	1975	Unilever
102	46	Ice cream	ALI	DK	1975	Frisko[2]
102	46	Corned beef	ALI	GB	1973	Fray Bentos
102	46	General-purpose computers	MAC	F	1973	IBM
105	45	Dehydrated soups	ALI	F	1972	Maggi (Nestlé)
105	45	Mineral water	ALI	F	1972	Groupe Perrier
105	45	Special soups	ALI	GB	1973	Baxters
105	45	Cocoa (butter and powder)	ALI	NL	1973	De Zaan (Grace Cy.)
105	45	Motor vehicle lighting systems	TRA	D	1974	Westfälische Metallindustrie
105	45	Frozen foods	ALI	F	1972	Findus
105	45	Beer	ALI	F	1972	BSN
105	45	Sedatives and hypnotics	PHA	NL	1973	Hoffmann-La Roche
113	44	Colour television sets	ELE	I	1973	Germany (FR)
113	44	Cardio-vascular drugs (non reserpinic)	PHA	F	1972	
113	44	Tinned fish	ALI	GB	1974	Unilever
116	43	Ice cream	ALI	GB	1973	J. Lyons & Co.
116	43	Pasta	ALI	F	1972	Panzani-Milliat[4]
116	43	Mayonnaise	ALI	F	1972	Mayolande
119	42	Colour television sets	ELE	DK	1973	Philips Pope
119	42	School and students' exercise books	PAP	B	1975	Papeterie de Belgique
121	40	Kraft paper for large-capacity sacks	PAP	F	1975	Import
121	40	Washing machines	ELE	GB	1975	Hoover
121	40	Condensed milk	ALI	GB	1973	Carnation Foods
121	40	Tinned tuna	ALI	GB	1973	John West[2]
121	40	Sauces	ALI	F	1972	Générale Alimentaire (Cavenham - GB)
121	40	Washing machines	ELE	I	1973	Zanussi
121	> 40	Medium-sized and large EDP systems	MAC	I	1974	

TABLE VIII

LIST OF PRODUCT MARKETS IN WHICH THE LEADING FIRM
HOLDS MORE THAN 25% OF THE TOTAL NATIONAL MARKET

(based on a limited sample of products and countries
covered by sectoral surveys)

Ranking	C_1 (in %)	Market	Sector	Country	Year	Leading brand and/or firm
121	>40	Vodka	ALI	GB	1974	Grand Metropolitan Ltd.
121	>40	Electric cookers	ELE	I	1973	Zanussi
121	>40	Bottled beer	ALI	NL	1974	Heineken
121	>40	Computer terminals	MAC	I	1974	IBM
121	>40	Beer	ALI	NL	1974	Heineken
121	>40	Other vitamins	PHA	GB	1973	Ciba
121	>40	Professional calculating machines	MAC	I	1974	
121	>40	Scientific micro-calculators	MAC	I	1974	
121	>40	Ladies' stockings	TEX	GB	1974	Courtaulds
121	>40	Cold-cure preparations	PHA	GB	1973	B. Wellcome
121	40	General-purpose computers	MAC	NL	1973	IBM
121	40	Tomato ketchup	ALI	F	1972	Générale Alimentaire (Cavenham GB)
121	>40	Bronchial dilators	PHA	GB	1973	
121	40	Tufted carpets	TEX	F	1972	Agache-Willot
121	40	Industrial sewing threads	TEX	F	1973	Dollfus Mieg & Cie
121	40	Dehydrated and powdered soups	ALI	GB	1973	Unilever
121	>40	Cough medicines	PHA	GB	1973	Parke Davis
121	40	Cognac	ALI	GB	1974	Martell
121	40	Psychotropics	PHA	NL	1973	Hoffmann-La Roche
121	>40	Baby foods (vegetables, meat, fruit)	ALI	D	1975	Hipp
121	>40	Woven yarn	TEX	GB	1968	Carrington
121	40	Car batteries	TRA	D	1974	Bosch
150	39	Cereals (flakes)	ALI	GB	1973	Kellogg
151	38	Sewing thread	TEX	GB	1972	Coats-Paton
151	38	Yoghurt	ALI	GB	1973	Express Diary Co.
151	38	Knitting machines	MAC	I	1973	Germany (FR)
151	38	Television sets (all types)	ELE	F	1974	
151	38	Agricultural tractors	MAC	I	1974	Fiat
156	37	Anti-diabetic preparations	PHA	NL	1973	Hoechst
156	37	Sound recording equipment	ELE	DK	1973	Philips
158	36	Washing machines	ELE	F	1975	
158	36	Vitamins	PHA	DK	1972	The Danish Pharmacies

TABLE VIII

LIST OF PRODUCT MARKETS IN WHICH THE LEADING FIRM
HOLDS MORE THAN 25% OF THE TOTAL NATIONAL MARKET

(based on a limited sample of products and countries
covered by sectoral surveys)

Ranking	c_1 (in %)	Market	Sector	Country	Year	Leading brand and/or firm
158	36	Hyper-cholesterolaemic drugs	PHA	F	1972	
158	36	Fruit and vegetable condiments	ALI	F	1972	Générale Alimentaire (Cavenham – GB)
158	36	Colour television sets	ELE	F	1974	
163	35	Cardboard	PAP	I	1972	Verona
163	35	Batteries (replacement market)	TRA	GB	1975	Chloride
163	35	Crackers and sandwich biscuits	ALI	GB	1973	ABM (Ass. Biscuits Man. Ltd.)
163	35	Sparking plugs (replacement market)	TRA	I	1973	Marelli
163	35	Diuretic drugs	PHA	NL	1973	Hoechst
163	35	Cotton velvet	TEX	F	1972	Agache-Willot
163	35	Fishing nets	TEX	F	1972	Agache-Willot
163	35	Canadian tents	TEX	F	1972	Agache-Willot
163	35	Bed linen	TEX	F	1973	Dollfus Mieg & Cie
163	35	Antibiotics	PHA	NL	1973	Beecham
163	35	Envelopes	PAP	B	1975	Enveleo (Intermills)
163	35	Sanitary and household paper	PAP	F	1975	Béghin-Say
175	34	Tyres (as originally fitted)	TRA	I	1974	Michelin
175	34	Gynaecological drugs	PHA	NL	1973	Organon
175	34	Baby foods	ALI	GB	1973	H.J. Heinz
175	34	Black and white television sets	ELE	GB	1975	Thorn
179	33	Electric cookers	ELE	GB	1975	Thorn
179	33	Snack foods	ALI	F	1972	Générale Alimentaire (Cavenham – GB)
179	33	Oral diabetic drugs	PHA	DK	1972	Hoechst
179	33	Ice cream	ALI	F	1972	Ortiz
179	33	Psychotropic drugs	PHA	F	1972	
179	33	Sugar	ALI	I	1973	Eridania
179	33	Spinning machines	MAC	I	1973	Germany (FR)
179	33	Mineral water	ALI	DK	1976	
179	33	Pepper and spices	ALI	F	1972	Générale Alimentaire (Cavenham – GB)
188	32	Tinned meat	ALI	DK	1974	Jaka
188	32	Weaving machines	MAC	I	1973	Suisse
188	32	Newsprint	PAP	I	1972	Timavo/Arbatax
188	32	Cardboard	PAP	F	1975	Import

TABLE VIII

LIST OF PRODUCT MARKETS IN WHICH THE LEADING FIRM
HOLDS MORE THAN 25% OF THE TOTAL NATIONAL MARKET

(based on a limited sample of products and countries
covered by sectoral surveys)

Rank-ing	c_1 (in %)	Market	Sector	Coun-try	Year	Leading brand and/or firm
192	31	Refrigerators and freezers	ELE	GB	1975	Thorn
192	31	Liquid detergents	CHI	I	1976	Sole Piatti
192	31	Combine harvesters	MAC	I	1974	Laverda
192	31	Knitting wool	TEX	F	1974	Lainière de Roubaix
192	31	Worsted goods	TEX	F	1974	Peignage Amédée
192	31	Sulfonamides	PHA	DK	1972	Hoffmann-La Roche
198	>30	Cardboard	PAP	GB	1972	Unilever
198	>30	Anti-tuberculosis preparations	PHA	GB	1973	
198	>30	Oral diabetic drugs	PHA	GB	1973	Pfizer
198	>30	Systemic antibiotics	PHA	GB	1973	
198	>30	Parkinson anticonvulsants	PHA	GB	1973	Geigy
198	>30	Systemic anti-inflammatory drugs	PHA	GB	1973	MSD
198	>30	Dishwashers	ELE	D	1972	Miele
198	>30	Draught beer	ALI	NL	1974	Heineken
198	30	Cocoa powder	ALI	F	1972	Nestlé
198	>30	Non-board packaging materials	PAP	GB	1972	DRG
198	30	Contraceptives	PHA	DK	1972	Schering
198	>30	Broad-spectrum antibiotics	PHA	GB	1973	Beecham
198	>30	Haematinic drugs	PHA	GB	1973	
198	>30	Diuretic drugs	PHA	GB	1973	Hoechst
198	>30	Contraceptives	PHA	GB	1973	
198	>30	Anti-nauseants	PHA	GB	1973	
198	>30	Record players	ELE	DK	1973	Bang & Olufsen
198	30	Lemonades	ALI	NL	1974	Heineken
198	30	Batteries (replacement market)	TRA	I	1972	FAR
198	>30	General analgesics	PHA	F	1972	
198	>30	Non-narcotic analgesics	PHA	GB	1973	
198	30	Laxatives	PHA	GB	1973	
198	30	Radios	ELE	DK	1973	Bang & Olufsen
198	30	Peripheral vasodilators	PHA	F	1972	
198	>30	Plain antacids	PHA	GB	1973	Boehringer
198	>30	Knitwear	TEX	GB	1968	Courtaulds
198	30	Antibiotics (pencillin and derivatives)	PHA	F	1972	

TABLE VIII

LIST OF PRODUCT MARKETS IN WHICH THE LEADING FIRM
HOLDS MORE THAN 25% OF THE TOTAL NATIONAL MARKET

(based on a limited sample of products and countries
covered by sectoral surveys)

Ranking	C_1 (in %)	Market	Sector	Country	Year	Leading brand and/or firm
198	30	Jonge Genever (Holland's gin)	ALI	NL	1974	Bols
226	29	Motorcycles	TRA	D	1974	BMW
227	28	Detergents for washing machines	CHI	I	1976	Dash (Procter & Gamble)
227	28	Mushrooms	ALI	F	1972	Euro-conserves
227	28	Sugar	ALI	F	1972	Béghin-Say
227	28	Frozen foods	ALI	DK	1974	FDB
227	28	Lager beer	ALI	GB	1974	Bass Charrington
227	28	Margarine	ALI	DK	1974	Unilever
227	28	Psychopharmacological drugs	PHA	DK	1972	Dumex
234	27	Tinned meats for hot meals	ALI	GB	1973	Fray Bentos
234	27	Black and white television sets	ELE	DK	1973	Bang & Olufsen
234	27	Non-alcoholic beverages	ALI	F	1974	Perrier
234	27	Fishing industry	ALI	D	1974	Nordsee[2]
234	27	Tyres (as originally fitted)	TRA	GB	1975	Dunlop - Pirelli
234	27	Rotary cultivators	MAC	I	1974	MPM - Sicilia
240	26	Tyres (replacement market)	TRA	GB	1976	Dunlop - Pirelli
240	26	Colour television sets	ELE	GB	1975	Thorn
240	26	Anti-rhumatismatic drops	PHA	F	1972	
240	26	Fruits in syrup	ALI	F	1972	Roussillon Alimentaire
244	25	Car tyres (replacement market)	TRA	I	1974	Michelin
244	25	Ice cream	ALI	I	1973	Algel-Findus[2]

1. Tuborg-Carlsberg
2. Controlling group: Unilever
3. Controlling group: Nestlé
4. Economics Laboratory Inc., Delaware (USA)
5. Controlling group: BSN - Gervais - Danone
6. Controlling group: Heinz - USA

Key to abbreviations

a) Sector or industry

ALI = Food and beverages
CHI = Chemicals
ELE = Electrical appliances (radio and TV sets, record players, tape decks, etc;
    household electrical appliances)
MAC = Non-electrical machinery (agricultural, office, textile, building, hoisting and
    handling machines)
PAP = Paper manufacturing and processing
PHA = Pharmaceuticals
TEX = Textiles
TRA = Vehicles, aircraft, etc.

Key to abbreviations (cont.)

b) Country

    B = Belgium
    D = Germany (Federal Republic)
    DK = Denmark
    F = France
    GB = United Kingdom
    I = Italy
    NL = Netherlands

In the case of certain markets dominated by imports it has only been possible to state "Import" or the country of origin instead of the leading firm.

2.9.2. Correlation between dominance and price levels and increases – QQ. 124–126

The data in Table VIII constitute a basis for a dynamic table along the following lines, for each of the above-mentioned products in each Member State, the example being taken from the French model:

No.	Product market	Country	Year	Market shares of the four main brands and/or firms			
				I	II	III	IV
1	Instant coffee	F	1970 1972 1974 1976	70% Nestlé	....	....	....
2	Sugar	F	1970 1972 1974 1976	28% Béghin–Say	....	....	....
3	Powdered chocolate	F	1970 1972 1974 1976	70% Poulain	....	....	....
4	Cocoa powders	F	1970 1972 1974 1976	30% Nestlé	....	....	....
5	Margarine		1970 1972 1974 1976	60% Astra–Calvé (Unilever)	....	....	....

and so on, for each "critical" product and for each Member State in question.

170

The questions arising are of great practical interest.

CXXIV) Is there a correlation between the dominance enjoyed by producers on national
 (124) markets for a given product – measured by the market shares of the dominant firms
shown in Table VIII – and the prices of the products in question? Is it possible,
by comparing price divergences between different countries, to conclude that prices
are higher in precisely those countries in which the relevant firms have greater
market power? Can one be certain that these price divergences are not caused by
differing tax rates?

CXXV) Is the increase in the price of a product greater in countries and/or regions where
 (125) dominance – ie. the market share of the leading brands and/or firms – is greater
than in countries and/or regions where oligopolistic concentration is less great
and competition is keener?

CXXVI) Is there a correlation between the degree of dominance enjoyed by producers on a
 (126) national market for a given product and the existence:

- of uniform or identical producer prices;

- of uniform or identical retail prices at the sample sales points;

- of uniform or identical variations in prices at the sample sales points?

Can such uniformity be explained by the existence of agreements or concerted
practices among producers, between producers and distributor-retailers or among
distributor-retailers?

2.9.3. Dominance and profitability of the leading producer firms – Tables IX and X – Q. 127

An increase in market power ought in theory to be accompanied by monopoly rents, ie. it ought
to lead to an increase in the profitability of the firm itself. But the structural
complexity of the modern firm is such that an automatic correlation between market power
and profitability cannot always be established. Indeed, the contrary may prove to be the
case.

As the Court of Justice pointed out in its judgment of 14 February 1978 (United Brands
Company – "Chiquita" bananas), the existence of "excessive prices", resulting from the
existence of a dominant market position, need not necessarily be accompanied by the
realization of large profits.

The Court commented in particular:

"An undertaking's economic strength is not measured by its profitability; a reduced
profit margin or even losses for a time are not incompatible with a dominant position,
just as large profits may be compatible with a situation where there is effective
competition" (Ground of Judgment 126).

It is appropriate to note at this point that the two sources of a firm's profitability
are (a) the efficiency of management and labour in the broad sense (a socially positive
phenomenon) and (b) exploitation of a dominant market position (a socially negative
phenomenon).

Only by analysing a firm's structure and the markets in which it operates is it possible
to compute the share attributable to each factor (efficiency and dominance).

Because of this view taken by the Court, we too must analyse profitability – from several
angles and with many different tools, approaches and methods – in order to find out if the
products manufactured by dominant firms are sold at "excessive" or "unfair" prices on
certain markets.

171

Here it will be necessary to use the various methods which are commonly employed for measuring the profitability of firms. In particular, we shall use the method which consists in bringing out the comparative profitability of the different firms operating in a given sector, a method which has already been used in our "Methodology".[1]

Under this method the firms in the sample are graded by juxtaposing their ranking in each of the four profitability ratios in order to obtain a "profitability score" for each firm (a "final ranking").

These ratios may be defined briefly as follows:

$$r_1 = \frac{\text{net profit}}{\text{sales}} \times 100$$

$$r_2 = \frac{\text{net profit}}{\text{own capital}} \times 100$$

$$r_3 = \frac{\text{cash flow}}{\text{sales}} \times 100$$

$$r_4 = \frac{\text{cash flow}}{\text{own capital}} \times 100$$

With regard to the definition of the above variables, it will be necessary to indicate for each individual case:

- whether the definitions set out in the Methodology have been used (eg. net pre-tax profit plus cash flow = gross income); or, on the contrary,

- whether only data complying with other definitions were available.

Table IX covers the top 100 firms in the agri-foodstuffs sector. For 64 of these firms it was possible to use the method of ranking according to comparative profitability, as outlined above[2]. Table X brings out the relationship between profitability and "disequilibrium of size" for each of the 64 firms which it has been possible to subject to the complete analysis.

In this connection, the following fundamental question must be asked:

CXXVII) What are the dominant brands and the dominant positions on each national product
(127) market owned by each of the 100 firms in the world agri-foodstuffs industry covered by Table IX? The worldwide character of the structure, and consequently of our investigation, is merely confirmed by this Table IX.

2.9.4. Approaches to and correlation of profitability - QQ. 128-131

A series of questions, connected with the analysis of profitability, must be posed:

CXXVIII) Is there any significant relationship between the degree of dominance exerted on
(128) certain product markets and the level of comparative profitability enjoyed by the dominant firm? Is it possible to discover any increase in that profitability (of a given firm) subsequent to an increase in its power and its market share on certain product markets?

---

1. See R. Linda, Methodology of concentration analysis applied to the study of industries and markets, Commission of the European Communities, September 1976 (Catalague No 8756), pages 49 to 67.

2. The ratios in Table IX are based on net profit and cash flow after tax, which, with a few exceptions, correspond approximately to the average of the value of the same ratios which would be calculated - as provided for by the Commission's research programme - from net profit and cash flow before tax.

TABLE IX

THE TOP 100 GROUPS IN THE WORLD FOOD INDUSTRY *
(in 1974)

A) The 64 world groups graded according to comparative profitability

Size ranking		Profitability score		Ratios								Variable value (US $ '000)				Firm	Country
Among the 64 firms	Among the 100 firms	Ranking	Score	$R_1 = \frac{04}{01}$ Ranking	Rate (%)	$R_2 = \frac{04}{07}$ Ranking	Rate (%)	$R_3 = \frac{05}{01}$ Ranking	Rate (%)	$R_4 = \frac{05}{07}$ Ranking	Rate (%)	01 Sales	04 Net profit	05 Cash flow	07 Own capital		
10	12	1	23	5	7.77	4	19.18	7	10.10	7	24.94	2522150	195972	254828	1021572	Coca Cola	USA
34	49	2	26	8	7.13	3	20.40	9	8.85	6	25.31	1009818	72031	89345	353030	Kellogg	USA
33	46	3	28	6	7.52	6	18.70	8	9.99	8	24.86	1035053	77795	103410	416034	Beecham	GB
29	41	4	44	3	8.24	9	15.88	4	10.71	28	20.64	1088557	89677	116559	564849	National Distillers	USA
36	53	5	47	15	5.59	5	18.80	17	7.22	10	24.31	967700	54052	69906	287503	Heublien Inc.	USA
46	65	6	51	11	6.01	13	15.54	10	8.68	17	22.42	814524	48982	70674	315260	Jos Schlitz Brewing Co.	USA
48	68	7	61	14	5.66	12	15.57	14	7.88	21	21.66	753131	42661	59332	273968	Castle & Cook	USA
12	16	8	64	23	4.20	11	15.70	21	6.51	9	24.32	2080759	87414	135420	556926	Pepsico	USA
8	10	9	76	25	3.86	8	16.65	31	5.46	12	23.55	2570273	99153	140229	595565	CPC International	USA
64	100	10	77	1	14.82	27	12.69	1	17.88	48	15.32	455269	67469	81414	531482	Hiram Walker—Gooderham	CAN
14	18	11	81	26	3.76	13	15.54	28	5.57	14	23.06	2000103	75137	111486	483438	General Mills	USA
15	19	12	82	22	4.22	10	15.85	27	5.70	23	21.39	1886828	79661	107512	502632	Carnation	USA

*Sources: AGRODATA — Institut Agronomique Méditerranéen de Montpellier (I.A.M.), Commission, Seventh Report on Competition Policy, Part III, Point 296, Brussels–Luxembourg, April 1978

TABLE IX

THE TOP 100 GROUPS IN THE WORLD FOOD INDUSTRY
(in 1974)

A) The 64 world groups graded according to comparative profitability

| Country | Firm | Variable value (US $ '000) | | | | Ratios | | | | | | | | Profitability score | | Size ranking | |
		07 Own capital	05 Cash flow	04 Net profit	01 Sales	R4 = 05/07 Rate (%)	Ranking	R3 = 05/01 Rate (%)	Ranking	R2 = 04/07 Rate (%)	Ranking	R1 = 04/01 Rate (%)	Ranking	Score	Ranking	Among the 100 firms	Among the 64 firms
USA	Campbell Soup	625367	118678	85365	1468199	18.98	37	8.08	13	13.65	25	5.81	13	88	13	30	23
GB	Scottish New-castle Brew.	219575	40573	28575	484264	18.48	38	8.38	12	13.01	26	5.90	12	88	13	93	59
USA	Anheuser-Busch	537762	109061	64019	1413091	20.28	31	7.72	15	11.90	32	4.53	17	95	15	34	25
USA	Oscar Mayer & Co.	173668	40811	29791	972438	23.50	13	4.20	41	17.15	7	3.06	34	95	15	51	35
GB	Allied Breweries	672200	103714	68175	840068	15.43	47	12.35	3	10.14	41	8.12	4	95	15	64	45
USA	Standard Brands	388866	88569	55932	1647939	22.78	16	5.37	33	14.38	19	3.39	29	97	18	24	18
USA	Heinz	447434	86855	64320	1438251	19.41	36	6.04	25	14.38	19	4.47	19	99	19	31	24
GB	Arthur Guinness	225874	44390	28128	641492	19.65	34	6.92	20	12.45	29	4.38	21	104	20	79	53
USA	Del Monte	273437	57173	39136	1042608	20.91	27	5.48	30	14.31	21	3.75	27	105	21	45	32
GB	Whitbread	346199	49862	34740	484032	14.40	51	10.03	5	10.03	42	7.18	7	105	21	94	60
USA	Beatrice Foods	767737	163762	116991	3541216	21.33	24	4.62	35	15.24	16	3.30	31	106	23	5	5
USA	General Foods	873204	174544	119480	2986692	19.99	32	5.84	26	13.68	24	4.00	24	106	23	9	7
CAN	Seagram	866703	110212	81575	885678	12.72	57	12.44	2	9.41	48	9.21	2	109	25	59	41

TABLE IX

THE TOP 100 GROUPS IN THE WORLD FOOD INDUSTRY
(in 1974)

A) The 64 world groups graded according to comparative profitability

Country	Firm	Variable value (US $ '000)				Ratios								Profitability score		Size ranking	
		07 Own capital	05 Cash flow	04 Net profit	01 Sales	$R_1 = \frac{04}{01}$ Rate (%)	Ranking	$R_2 = \frac{04}{07}$ Rate (%)	Ranking	$R_3 = \frac{05}{01}$ Rate (%)	Ranking	$R_4 = \frac{05}{07}$ Rate (%)	Ranking	Ranking	Score	Among the 100 firms	Among the 64 firms
USA	Ralston Purina	602576	131063	90691	3073210	2.95	36	15.05	17	4.26	40	21.75	20	26	113	8	6
USA	Amstar Corporation	202822	43667	31411	1046820	3.00	35	15.49	15	4.17	42	21.53	22	27	114	43	31
GB	Associated British Foods	346290	90504	48227	2525521	1.91	47	13.93	22	3.58	46	26.14	5	28	120	11	9
USA	Norton Simon	662483	103935	72327	1599831	4.52	18	10.92	35	6.50	22	15.69	46	29	121	25	19
USA	Iowa Beef Processors	77617	21464	16538	1537198	1.08	56	21.31	2	1.40	61	27.65	4	30	123	28	21
CH	Nestlé Alimentana	2541560	410222	250093	5603155	4.46	20	9.84	46	7.32	16	16.14	43	31	125	2	2
USA	American Beef Packers	22558	7359	4861	896904	0.54	61	21.55	1	0.82	63	32.62	3	32	128	57	39
GB	Tate and Lyle	217625	51664	30261	1551876	1.95	46	13.91	23	3.33	49	23.74	11	33	129	26	20
USA	Quaker Oats	338441	66048	39878	1227345	3.25	32	11.78	33	5.38	32	19.52	35	34	132	39	28
GB	Bass Charrington	876837	87574	59487	851634	6.99	9	6.78	57	10.28	6	9.99	63	35	135	63	44
GB/NL	Unilever	2979817	610991	362807	13666667	2.65	40	12.18	31	4.47	37	20.50	29	36	137	1	1
F	Pernod Ricard	202771	36818	17132	514737	3.33	30	8.45	50	7.15	18	18.16	39	36	137	89	57

TABLE IX

THE TOP 100 GROUPS IN THE WORLD FOOD INDUSTRY
(in 1974)

A) The 64 world groups graded according to comparative profitability

| Size ranking | | Profitability score | | $R_1 = \frac{04}{01}$ | | $R_2 = \frac{04}{07}$ | | $R_3 = \frac{05}{01}$ | | $R_4 = \frac{05}{07}$ | | Variable value (US $ '000) | | | | Firm | Country |
Among the 64 firms	Among the 100 firms	Ranking	Score	Ranking	Rate (%)	Ranking	Rate (%)	Ranking	Rate (%)	Ranking	Rate (%)	01 Sales	04 Net profit	05 Cash flow	07 Own capital		
40	58	38	139	10	6.54	54	7.53	11	8.41	64	9.67	888570	58128	74700	772166	Distillers	GB
47	66	38	139	28	3.70	37	10.66	29	5.51	45	15.86	781965	28959	43106	271720	Reckitt & Colman	GB
51	71	40	141	39	2.66	30	12.19	39	4.30	33	19.72	708000	18800	30418	154238	Molson Industries	CAN
37	54	41	145	48	1.84	18	14.73	54	2.65	54	2.65	943163	17369	25036	117932	Geo A. Hormel and Co.	USA
52	73	42	146	63	0.33	63	3.00	19	7.06	1	64.67	688176	2252	48596	75140	Beghin Say	F
55	84	42	146	42	2.33	38	10.55	36	4.48	30	20.31	592090	13790	26550	130736	Rowntree Mackintosh	GB
16	22	44	147	33	3.07	40	10.52	34	5.26	40	18.01	1679855	51632	88443	491022	CSR — Colonial Sugar Ref.	AUS
54	80	45	152	16	4.54	52	7.86	23	6.39	61	11.06	627348	28495	40118	362683	Liggett & Myers	USA
3	3	46	161	52	1.47	28	12.68	55	2.45	26	21.04	4615715	68066	112952	536934	Swift (Esmark)	USA
13	17	47	162	59	0.66	64	2.43	24	6.26	15	22.91	2035037	13524	127292	555568	Gervais Danone	F
62	98	48	168	54	1.20	58	6.16	38	4.35	18	22.35	465901	5589	20275	90702	Perrier	F
4	4	49	170	44	2.12	34	11.13	51	3.22	41	16.91	4471427	94627	143777	850011	Kraftco	USA

TABLE IX

THE TOP 100 GROUPS IN THE WORLD FOOD INDUSTRY
(in 1974)

A) The 64 world groups graded according to comparative profitability

Size ranking		Profit-ability score		Ratios								Variable value (US $ '000)				Firm	Country
Among the 64 firms	Among the 100 firms	Rank-ing	Score	$R_1 = \frac{04}{01}$ Rank-ing	Rate (%)	$R_2 = \frac{04}{07}$ Rank-ing	Rate (%)	$R_3 = \frac{05}{01}$ Rank-ing	Rate (%)	$R_4 = \frac{05}{07}$ Rank-ing	Rate (%)	01 Sales	04 Net profit	05 Cash flow	07 Own capital		
56	86	50	180	57	0.79	45	9.85	59	1.78	19	22.04	581777	4624	10345	46928	Burns Foods	CAN
63	99	51	182	37	2.91	47	9.49	43	4.07	55	13.27	464710	13520	18902	142447	Libby McNeill and Libby	USA
61	96	52	183	64	0.26	55	7.24	62	1.22	2	34.59	472820	1207	5768	16677	Ward Foods	USA
11	15	53	186	45	1.96	49	9.25	48	3.38	44	16.01	2230106	43607	75484	471547	United Brands (AMK)	USA
42	61	54	189	42	2.33	51	8.33	44	4.00	52	14.31	883238	20577	35352	246989	PET	USA
22	29	55	193	55	1.12	36	10.77	60	1.75	42	16.90	1479492	16530	25941	153525	Canada Packers	CAN
49	69	56	196	51	1.59	39	10.54	56	2.25	50	14.93	751926	11960	16945	113519	International Multifoods	USA
43	62	57	197	38	2.82	44	9.86	53	3.08	62	10.78	878999	24771	27081	251242	Anderson Clayton Co.	USA
38	56	58	201	41	2.35	53	7.62	47	3.54	60	11.48	904847	21232	31993	278633	Brooke Bond	GB
17	23	59	211	50	1.61	56	7.03	52	3.13	53	13.69	1652112	26587	51763	377994	Rank Hovis McDougall	GB
27	38	60	212	49	1.66	60	5.41	45	3.88	58	12.64	1299088	21574	50442	398974	Cadbury Schweppes	GB

TABLE IX

THE TOP 100 GROUPS IN THE WORLD FOOD INDUSTRY
(in 1974)

A) The 64 world groups graded according to comparative profitability

Size ranking		Profit-ability score		Ratios								Variable value (US $ '000)				Firm	Country
Among the 64 firms	Among the 100 firms	Ranking	Score	$R_1 = \frac{04}{01}$ Ranking	Rate (%)	$R_2 = \frac{04}{07}$ Ranking	Rate (%)	$R_3 = \frac{05}{01}$ Ranking	Rate (%)	$R_4 = \frac{05}{07}$ Ranking	Rate (%)	01 Sales	04 Net profit	05 Cash flow	07 Own capital		
26	37	61	216	53	1.46	59	6.02	50	3.25	54	13.34	1366004	20005	44328	332339	J. Lyons	GB
50	70	61	216	61	0.54	43	9.89	63	0.82	49	14.94	727051	3960	5985	40049	Missouri Beef Packers	USA
30	42	63	232	58	0.73	61	4.49	57	2.13	56	13.19	1057828	7675	22548	170901	Spillers	GB
58	91	64	239	60	0.60	62	3.94	58	1.85	59	12.15	507986	3042	9382	77235	Di Giorgio Corp.	USA

TABLE IX

B) The other 36 world groups graded according to size
(owing to lack of complete data it was not possible to include these 36 groups in the
grading based on comparative profitability)

Size ranking		Ratios				Variable value (in US $ '000s)				Firm	Country
Among the 36 firms	Among the 100 firms	R$_1$	R$_2$	R$_3$	R$_4$	01 Sales	04 Net Profit	05 Cash flow	07 Own Capital		
1	6	1.68	10.14	-	-	3 458 336	57 995	-	571 822	Greyhound (Armour)	USA
2	7	2.57	10.35	-	-	3 264 502	83 845	-	810 431	Borden	USA
3	13	0.18	4.84	-	-	2 489 517	4 599	-	95 028	Taiyo Fishery	JAP
4	14	3.01	11.86	-	-	2 379 862	71 581	-	603 750	Consolidated Foods	USA
5	20	2.54	11.81	-	-	1 793 049	45 458	-	384 804	Nabisco	USA
6	21	1.80	16.26	-	-	1 749 304	31 572	-	194 157	Central Soya	USA
7	27	1.90	16.62	-	-	1 551 289	29 410	-	176 923	Archer - Daniels Midland	USA
8	32	-	-	-	-	1 423 630	-	-	173 340	Oetker Grupp	BRD
9	33	-	-	-	-	1 416 298	-	-	55 817	Ass. Milk Producers	USA
10	35	1.13	11.38	-	-	1 405 392	15 825	-	139 028	Union International	GB
11	36	-	-	-	-	1 390 000	-	-	-	Cavenham	GB
12	40	1.67	6.00	-	-	1 145 308	19 092	-	318 282	Unigate	GB

179

TABLE IX

B) The other 36 world groups graded according to size
(owing to lack of complete data it was not possible to include these 36 groups in the grading based on comparative profitability)

Size ranking		Ratios				Variable value (in US $ '000s)				Firm	Country
Among the 36 firms	Among the 100 firms	R_1	R_2	R_3	R_4	01 Sales	04 Net Profit	05 Cash flow	07 Own Capital		
13	44	-	-	-	-	1 046 120	-	-	-	Groupe Coop. Gama	F
14	47	-	-	-	-	1 029 160	-	-	130 930	Svenska M. Riskforering	SW
15	48	0.67	8.43	-	-	1 012 339	6 828	-	81 012	Snow Brand Milk Products	JAP
16	50	2.82	14.04	-	-	1 004 231	28 309	-	201 617	Pillsbury	USA
17	52	0.60	23.02	-	-	970 424	5 868	-	25 488	Groupe Coop. MacMahon	F
18	55	3.52	11.12	-	-	934 707	32 894	-	295 744	Kirin Brewery	JAP
19	60	2.03	9.48	-	-	885 366	17 939	-	189 327	Ajinomoto	JAP
20	67	2.04	14.78	-	-	765 620	15 640	-	105 640	United Biscuits	GB
21	72	-2.00	-11.29	-	-	691 270	13 827	-	122 472	Cie Financière Lesieur	F
22	74	1.03	12.11	-	-	677 569	6 966	-	57 532	Nisshin Flour	JAP
23	75	5.99	37.18	-	-	671 261	40 221	-	108 190	Booker McConnell	GB
24	76	0.60	15.57	-	-	661 526	3 947	-	25 345	Meiji Milk Products	JAP

B) The other 36 world groups graded according to size
(owing to lack of complete data it was not possible to include these 36 groups in the grading based on comparative profitability)

| Size ranking | | Ratios | | | | Variable value (in US $ '000s) | | | | | Firm | Country |
Among the 36 firms	Among the 100 firms	R_1	R_2	R_3	R_4	01 Sales	04 Net Profit	05 Cash flow	07 Own Capital			
25	77	1.52	14.09	–	–	690 901	10 040	–	71 232		Kane Miller Corp.	USA
26	78	0.18	2.70	–	–	650 690	1 140	–	42 210		Union Laitière Normande	F
27	81	0.52	4.97	–	–	621 620	3 230	–	65 040		Koninklijke Wessanen	NL
28	82	–	–	–	–	620 828	–	–	–		Sodima – Yoplait	F
29	83	–	–	–	–	607 420	–	–	–		Rumasma	ESP
30	85	2.61	14.51	–	–	590 171	15 406	–	106 406		Campbell Taggart	USA
31	87	0.16	1.09	–	–	549 840	890	–	82 020		Mjolkcentralen	SW
32	88	0.36	3.45	–	–	523 804	1 898	–	54 941		Morinaga Milk Industry	JAP
33	90	4.30	12.76	–	–	513 999	22 094	–	173 173		Hershey Foods Corp.	USA
34	92	6.58	12.33	–	–	491 460	32 330	–	262 100		Heineken N.V.	NL
35	95	3.28	28.85	–	–	475 820	15 630	–	54 180		Mars	GB
36	97	1.30	15.92	–	–	471 497	6 136	–	38 552		Hygrade Food	USA

181

TABLE X

WORLD (the West)				
FOOD INDUSTRY (including beverages) Year: 1974			Sample: $n^* = 64$	
Profitability ranking	Firm	Size ranking	$\dfrac{_{01}x_i}{_{01}x_1} \times 100$	$\dfrac{_{07}x_i}{_{07}x_1} \times 100$
– Top "01" firm (turnover) US $ 13 667 million UNILEVER				
– Top "07" firm (own capital) US $ 2980 million UNILEVER				
1	Coca–Cola (USA)	5	18.45	34.28
2	Kellogg (USA)	31	7.39	11.84
3	Beecham (GB)	28	7.57	13.96
4	National Distillers (USA)	29	7.97	18.95
5	Heublein (USA)	35	7.08	9.64
6	Jos. Schlitz – Brewing (USA)	42	5.96	10.57
7	Castle & Cook (USA)	38	5.51	9.19
8	Pepsico (USA)	10	15.23	10.68
9	CPC International (USA)	8	18.81	19.98
10	Hiram Walker – Gooderham (CAN)	43	3.33	17.83
11	General Mills (USA)	16	14.63	16.22
12	Carnation (USA)	15	13.81	16.86
13	Campbell Soup (USA)	13	10.74	20.98
13	Scottish & Newcastle Breweries (GB)	54	3.34	7.36
15	Oscar Mayer (USA)	43	7.12	5.82
15	Allied Breweries (GB)	27	6.15	22.55
15	Anheuser – Busch (USA)	19	10.34	18.04
18	Standard Brands (USA)	21	12.26	13.04
19	Heinz (USA)	26	10.52	15.01
20	Arthur Guinness (GB)	51	4.69	7.58
21	Del Monte (USA)	34	7.63	9.17
21	Whitbread (GB)	50	3.54	11.61
23	Beatrice Foods (USA)	6	25.91	25.76
23	General Foods (USA)	4	21.85	29.30
25	Seagram (CAN)	23	6.48	29.08
26	Ralston Purina (USA)	7	22.49	20.22
27	Amstar Corporation (USA)	39	7.66	6.80
28	Associated British Foods (GB)	18	18.48	11.62
29	Norton Simon (USA)	11	11.71	22.23
30	Iowa Beef Processors (USA)	40	11.25	2.60
31	Nestlé Alimentana (CH)	2	41.00	85.29

TABLE X

Profitability ranking	Firm	Size ranking	$\frac{O_1 x_i}{O_1 x_1} \times 100$	$\frac{O_7 x_i}{O_7 x_1} \times 100$
32	American Beef Packers (USA)	52	6.56	0.75
33	Tate and Lyle (GB)	33	11.36	7.30
34	Quaker Oats (USA)	30	8.98	11.35
35	Bass Charrington (GB)	24	6.23	29.42
36	Unilever (GB/NL)	1	100.00	100.00
36	Pernod − Ricard (F)	54	3.77	6.80
38	Reckitt & Colman (GB)	48	5.72	9.11
38	Distillers (GB)	24	6.50	25.91
40	Molson Industries (CAN)	52	5.18	5.17
41	Geo A. Hormel (USA)	49	6.90	5.97
42	Béghin Say (F)	58	5.04	2.52
42	Rowntree Mackintosh (GB)	57	4.33	4.38
44	CSR − Colonial Sugar Ref. (AUS)	17	12.29	16.47
45	Liggett & Myers (USA)	43	4.59	12.17
46	Swift (Esmark) (USA)	8	33.77	18.09
47	Gervais Danone (F)	11	14.89	18.64
48	Perrier (F)	63	3.41	3.04
49	Kraftco (USA)	3	32.72	28.52
50	Burns Foods (CAN)	61	4.26	1.57
51	Libby McNeill (Libby's) (USA)	60	3.40	4.78
52	Ward Foods (USA)	64	3.46	0.55
53	United Brands (AMK) (USA)	13	16.32	15.82
54	Pet (USA)	46	6.46	8.28
55	Canada Packers (CAN)	36	10.83	5.15
56	International Multifoods (USA)	54	5.50	3.80
57	Anderson − Clayton (USA)	46	6.43	8.43
58	Brooke Bond Liebig (GB)	37	6.62	9.35
59	Rank Hovis McDougall (GB)	21	12.09	12.68
60	Cadbury Schweppes (GB)	31	9.51	13.38
61	Missouri Beef Packers (USA)	58	5.32	1.34
61	Lyons (GB)	58	10.00	11.15
63	Spillers	41	7.74	5.73
64	Di Giorgio (USA)	61	3.72	2.59

Clearly the existence of such a correlation:

- would have to be established by several alternative methods of measuring profitability, in order to leave no doubt as to the validity of the results obtained;

- would be easier to establish for firms that were more or less single-product firms compared with the large diversified firms the multiplicity of whose activities and products enables them to offset profits and losses flowing from these different activities.

CXXIX) Is it possible to discover a correlation between price levels — on certain
(129)   national product markets — and the profitability of a given firm? What role is played by exclusive-rights agreements?

CXXX)   Does an increase in the price of a given product have any repercussions — and
(130)   if so, to what extent — on the degree of profitability of a given firm?

CXXXI) Can it be established that the existence either of uniform or identical producer
(131)   prices or of uniform or identical retail prices or of uniform or identical changes in prices is capable of positively (or even negatively) influencing the profitability of the producer firms concerned?

2.9.5. Concentration of demand — questions put to producers: the share of the ten leading customers — Table XI — Q. 132

There arises the problem of finding out to what extent the power of domination exercised by the manufacturer through his own brand is matched by the countervailing power of the distributor-buyer, who takes the form — in the case of integrated trade — of the large retailer. The answer to this problem might explain why the large multinational firms, holding a whole series of powerful positions on several markets, are not necessarily the most profitable concerns, their profitability being eroded by the bargaining power enjoyed by the large retailers who buy from them.

The concentration and power of distributor-retailers must be considered from the following two aspects:

a) concentration and power in relation to suppliers, ie. manufacturers who make food products and beverages, together with wholesalers or dealers;

b) concentration and power in relation to consumers, who buy the relevant products in the shops.

The increase in the power of the large retailers as buyers over the past ten years is shown by Table XI, which reproduces the results of a survey organized by the European Association of Branded Goods Industries (AIM). The results have been classified in such a way as to bring out the countervailing power with which each of these six national producers is faced in its own country. Thus, for example, in 1976 a German producer (described by the code number "I") derived 54% of its national turnover from only ten national customers (as opposed to 40% in 1967). The producer indicated by the code number "X" has had the advantage of being faced by the least concentrated demand[1].

Table XI gives only a very general view of the situation. Subsequent investigation will have to produce a more thorough analysis and answer the following questions:

---

1. Commission, Seventh Report on Competition Policy, Part III, Points 303-304, April 1978.

CXXXII) Is it possible to obtain the following information from the ten principal
(132) manufacturers of food products and beverages in each country:

- the movement in the percentage share, for each year from 1970 to 1977, of the
purchases made by each of the ten largest national customers from each
manufacturer taking part in the survey, in relation to the total turnover
achieved by each of these manufacturers:

a) on its domestic market;

b) on its total market (both domestic and foreign);

- an analysis of these sales over each of the ten national customers and over
product groups, following the classification into 22 groups used in Chapter One
(1.1: for example, tinned meat, tinned fish, baby foods, etc.);

- the names of these ten largest national customers.

Among these ten largest national customers we shall distinguish between
independent wholesalers (or dealers) and distributor-retailers in order to
show how their role has evolved and how their market shares and trading margins
have moved in relation to integral traders. We shall also ask these producers
to state the name, nationality and relative power of their actually and/or
potentially most formidable competitors.

2.9.6. Concentration of demand — questions put to distributor-retailers: share of the ten leading suppliers — Q. 133

To confirm the information received from different sources, a question similar to question
132 will have to be put to the ten principal groups of distributor-retailers in each country,
viz:

CXXXIII) Can the following information be obtained from the ten principal groups of
(133) distributor-retailers operating in each country:

- the movement in the percentage share, for each year from 1970 to 1977, of the
purchases made by each of these distributors from their ten principal national
suppliers in relation to the total purchases made by each of these distributor-
retailers:

a) on its domestic market,

b) on its total market;

- a breakdown of these purchases by national supplier and by product group
following the classification into 22 groups established in Chapter One (1.1.);

- the names of these ten largest national suppliers;

- the names of alternative or potential suppliers, even foreign ones.

Can the same information be obtained from a few large wholesalers or dealers?

It will be necessary to record negative as well as affirmative answers, and in particular
to record the reasons given by the firms questioned.

2.9.7. Relation between the development of demand-concentration and the movement of producer prices — QQ. 134-135

At this point two kinds of formulation and approach ought to be established:

a) from the angle of the price of the product;

b) from the angle of the firm: b1) producer; b2) wholesaler or dealers; b3) retailer.

On the basis of the answers to questions 132-133 and also to questions 85-91, it would be very useful to consider the following points:

CXXXIV) Is there any relation between the movement in the producer's selling prices for
(134) certain specific products and for certain groups of products and the movement in the proportions of the products in question purchased from the manufacturers by:

    a) the wholesalers or dealers,

    b) the distributor-retailers?

What conclusions can be drawn from such an analysis?

In particular, do exclusive-rights contracts have any special influence?

CXXXV) Is it possible to analyse the contractual advantages other than price reductions
(135) (such as special conditions for delivery and storage, credit, finance, contribution to advertising expenditure, exclusive rights and exclusive-rights premiums, etc.) which producers may be prompted to grant:

    a) to wholesalers or dealers,

    b) to distributor-retailers,

by reason of changes in total purchases?

Is there any correlation between the sum of these advantages and an increase in the concentration and power of the large purchasers?

2.9.8. Individual information sheets for each responding firm

It should be possible, on the basis of the replies to the questions above, to draw up a series of individual information sheets for each:

- producer;

- wholesaler (or dealer);

- distributor-retailer,

covered by the limited selected sample.

With regard to the distributor-retailers, however, further details will be needed.

2.9.9. Natural size of the market and analysis of local concentration

One problem which will have to be considered is the power of the distributor-retailer vis-à-vis the consumer, which will entail examining local concentration.

The phenomenon of concentration must be analysed by considering the "natural size" of each unit, in this case the size of each geographical market. For producers of industrial food products and beverages the "natural size" coincides with the size of the country, whereas in the case of the distribution of those same products the "natural size" is the size of the town in question, including its suburbs if any.

When determining the natural size we must have regard to operational and practical criteria inherent in the functioning of competition, which entails determining the geographical area in which supply and demand come together, or, in more concrete terms, the number and identity of the shops between which consumers in a given town or conurbation may choose when making their purchases.

Since the number and identity of the shops (and distributing firms) involved will vary from one town to the next there would be no sense in simply measuring the degree of concentration at the national level.

Data gathered in this way (at national level) would give misleading net results: various local dominant positions would balance each other out because the strength of each distributing-retailing group varies very greatly from town to town and from region to region.

TABLE XI

DEGREE OF DEPENDENCE OF PRODUCER-SELLERS ON DEMAND
FROM LARGE DISTRIBUTOR-PURCHASERS OF FOOD PRODUCTS

(In decreasing order, 1976 position)

Shares of the FIVE leading purchasers in the total sales of the producer-seller

Producer-seller	Federal Republic of Germany		France		Italy		Belgium	
	1967	1976	1967	1976	1967	1976	1967	1976
I	29	54	14	34	7	12	22	47
II	33	44	16	23	-	12	13	45
III	20	43	8	22	6	12	15	44
IV	6	36	11	21	6	11	13	44
V	-	23	9	20	-	10	17	43
VI	6	15	18	19	7	10	11	43
VII	5	15	16	18	-	8	10	39
VIII	6	14	1	18	5	7	15	37
IX	7	14	12	16	3	7	17	36
X	5.4	11.4	8	12	3	6	25	35

Shares of the TEN leading purchasers

Producer-seller	Federal Republic of Germany		France		Italy		Belgium	
	1967	1976	1967	1976	1967	1976	1967	1976
I	40	72	26	48	10	18	29	57
II	49	66	26	36	9	16	31	56
III	25	65	11	35	-	16	21	56
IV	-	34	18	33	-	15	18	54
V	9	22	16	32	8	14	20	53
VI	10	20	22	30	11	13	25	52
VII	8	20	21	29	8	12	35	51
VIII	9	20	3	27	-	12	20	50
IX	12	19	18	25	6	10	15	20
X	8	17	11	17	4	10	26	45

Source: Based on a sample of 10 producers per country who took part in a survey organized by the European Association of Branded Goods Industries (AIM).

187

Concentration and power on the distributive side (vis-à-vis the final consumer) must therefore be measured and analysed at local level.

With this aim in mind, we shall consider a series of typical indicators of the concentration of distribution, comparing the data calculated at national level with those calculated for a few major conurbations in each country.

The following indicators in particular are relevant[1]:

1) The number of "large shops" (distinguishing the six size categories – hypermarkets, superstores, large supermarkets, supermarkets, large self-service shops, small self-service shops – mentioned as criterion No 15 in paragraph 1.1.22):

   - either in a given country or conurbation (absolute figure),

   - or per segment of 10 000 inhabitants (relative figure).

2) Total floor area (in square metres or square feet) of "large shops" exceeding 4000 sq. ft. in area (hypermarkets, superstores, large supermarkets, supermarkets):

   - either in a given country or conurbation (absolute figure),

   - or per segment of 10 000 inhabitants.

3) Total floor area (in square metres or square feet) of all shops (distinguishing between "large shops" and "small shops") used by each of the 10 principal groups of retailers:

   - operating in the country in question,

   - operating in the conurbation in question,

     indicating separately:

     - the absolute figure for the country or conurbation in question,

     - the relative figure calculated per segment of 10 000 inhabitants.

4) The movement over the past ten years of the indicators mentioned under 1), 2) and 3) above.

2.9.10. The concentration of distribution on the supply side – difference between national concentration and local concentration – QQ. 136-138

The starting-point for studying concentration in distribution is to be found in some of the reports already published by the Commission (November 1976 to October 1977, relating to the United Kingdom, France, the Federal Republic of Germany, Denmark and Italy). These results will be used along with the findings of a wider investigation in order to obtain answers to the following questions:

CXXXVI) What are the 10 principal groups of distributor-retailers of food products and
(136) beverages:

   - in the country as a whole,

   - in several large conurbations in the country?

   Is it possible to calculate the share of total sales of the products concerned accounted for by each of these groups, both at national level and in the sample conurbations?

   What is the value of the six concentration indicators set out in para. 2.9.9. both in the country as a whole and in the sample conurbations?

---

1. We would draw readers' attention to the paper presented by Mr W.N. Barnes, of the Middlesex Polytechnic, London, to the International Symposium on "Distribution: Structure and Management" under the title "The Urgent Need for Specific and Realistic International Marketing and Distribution Indicators". The symposium, organized by the European Institute for Advanced Studies in Management, was held in Brussels on 29 and 30 May 1978.

TABLE XII

SURVEYS ON PRICES AND MARK-UPS

Table of actual prices and price deviations (in %)
for each brand or "own label"[1]

SURVEY NO: Month/Year (Month/Year)
(Figures in parentheses are for a
previous survey, No ....)

COUNTRY: .....
TOWN: .....
CURRENCY: .....

Name of owner:

Sales point No: .....

Product group	Detailed description of product	Identity code				Origin	Manufacturer		Purchase price		Sale price			
		n*	Size/ brand	Product No	Brand No		Name and/or code No	Nation-ality	This shop	Average	Average retail price	Actual price in this shop	Deviation from average price (+/−)	Deviation (in %) from average price (+/− %)
1	2	3	4	5	6	7	8	9	10	11	12	13	14	15
				0006	006						9.06	9.50	+ 0.44	+ 4.80
				..	..						..	..	..	..
												Total for branded products	→∑+/−	∑+/−
				0006	000						8.6	8.5	− 0.1	− 1.2
				..	..						..	..	..	..
												Total for branded products	→∑+/−	∑+/−
				..	..						..	..	..	..
												Total for 'own label' products	→∑+/−	∑+/−

1. One table per sales point.

This table was suggested by Development Analysts Ltd. (DAL) - Croydon, UK.

189

CXXXVII) What movement has there been, in the past ten years, in the market shares both
(137) at national level and in the sample conurbations considered in the previous
question?

Do these ten groups include any producers who have extended their vertical
integration downstream as far as the level of retail trading?

What is the trend in the values of the six concentration indicators mentioned
above (2.9.9.) during the past ten years?

CXXXVIII) What conclusions can be drawn from a comparison between the level and the trend
(138) in the degree of concentration of distribution (of food products and beverages)
on the national scale and on the local scale?

Do local surveys reveal that the large distributors have been acquiring shops
to any considerable extent?

2.9.11. Price levels and pricing policies of selected shops and groups of distributors – Table XII – Q. 139

The problem of reconciling the results of analyses at national level with the results of
detailed surveys of prices and mark-ups at local level now arises in acute form. In what
way and to what extent does an increase in local concentration – in a given town or
conurbation – react upon the level and trend of prices and mark-ups? That point will be
considered in our last question (No 140) in the present research programme. But first we
must find out how, and by what approach, an answer to a question of such complexity and
scope can be arrived at. We must initially use the results obtained in the first phase
(Chapter One) and the second phase (this chapter) of the study to try to find an
exhaustive answer to the following questions:

CXXXIX) Is it possible to draw up for each shop selected – not for all the shops in the
(139) local sample – a series of Tables XII showing both the selling price and the
purchase price of each product at each shop selected, in relation to the average
prices for all the shops in the local sample?

In this way Table XII would show the relative position of each sales point and
of each selected group of distributor-retailers with regard to its pricing
policy for each product (item sold) in the context of the pricing system (selling
prices as well as purchase prices) characterizing the local sample of sales points
as a whole. A few explanations on Table XII are called for. Table XII was
suggested, in more concise form, by Development Analysts Ltd. (DAL) of Croydon
(R.W. Evely and A.J. MacNeary).

Table XII must be drawn up for each sales point in the local sample belonging to
one of the groups of distributor-retailers chosen for more detailed analysis by
means of questions 132 and 133.

Table XII gives other information, viz:

- the manufacturer and his nationality;

- the purchase price, the object of the exercise being to compare, firstly, the
individual purchase price at the shop in question with average purchase prices
(despite the difficulty of finding out the individual purchase price) and,
secondly, selling prices with purchase prices (both average prices and
individual prices at each shop).

In addition, for the products bearing a brand name or trade mark and for the
products bearing the distributor's own label, the table shows aggregate deviations
from the average price (+/-) and the same deviations (+/-) expressed as percentages.
In this way it will be possible to use all the Tables XII (one for each sales
point selected) to rank the different shops selected from the most expensive (with
the highest positive % deviation from the average selling price) to the cheapest
(with the highest negative % deviation from the average selling price). See also
paragraphs 2.5.11. to 2.5.17. (section 2.5. of this chapter).

2.9.12. <u>Transition to the dynamic operational phase – market power and level of prices and mark-ups – Q. 140</u>

It is now time to pass directly to the <u>dynamic</u> phase of the analysis, proceeding to two essential operations:

I) comparing a series of Tables XII over a period that is long enough to be significant, for each selected shop or group and dealing, as we have seen, with all the products sold in the shops concerned;

II) integrating the Table XII for <u>each</u> distributor-retailer with a series of individual tables analysing specific products, as follows:

   a) the tables of the two examples of para. 1.1.25 ("pathological" and "concerted" price variations),

   b) the additional tables (fourth A, fifth A, sixth A) of para. 2.5.20, limited to the "critical" products used, in conjunction with the other paragraphs of section 2.5. (notably para. 2.5.19.),

   c) the tables in the examples of paras. 2.6.6. (analysis of the pricing policy of a selected retailer – shop A – in regard to a given product) and 2.6.7. (positive mark-up, and "loss-leader" strategy in times of inflation).

All the results obtained should together enable us to answer our question, the final one in the research programme:

CXL) Do the overall results of the surveys give us answers to the following points:
(140)
   a) Is there a significant positive relationship between the local <u>market power</u> of the large distributor-retailers and the <u>relative level of prices and mark-ups</u>?

   b) Are the towns and/or countries where the concentration of distribution is greatest also those where prices and mark-ups are the greatest?

   c) Is an increase in local concentration accompanied by an increase in prices and mark-ups?

   d) Should <u>excessive</u> or <u>unfair</u> retail prices be regarded as originating from an increase in concentration of distribution at local level or from the existence of restrictive practices?

   e) Is it possible to ascertain that <u>excessive or unfair prices are charged by the producers</u> of certain brands or items who hold dominant positions on certain local and/or national markets?

   f) Is it possible to detect any concrete cases where consumers in given towns, regions or countries have **been forced to accept** the dominance or even the monopoly of certain articles or brands, or excessive or unfair prices for such monopolistic or dominant products? And if such cases do exist are they caused by:

      – the dominance enjoyed by either the producer or the relevant distributor-retailers or by both together;

      – the terms of anticompetitive agreements;

      – in particular, the existence or the introduction of exclusive dealing or supply agreements?

   g) Is it considered that, in order to obtain more reliable and unequivocal results, a higher number of towns or regions should be included in each country for detailed surveys on prices and mark-ups in the shops constituting each local sample?

   h) What results could be expected from extending the surveys to non-EEC countries?

The replies to the various parts of this question could provide valuable reference points for a new direction and further development of the research.

2.10. CRUCIAL POINTS OF THE RESEARCH

2.10.1. Reformulation of the ultimate objectives of the research

The foregoing analysis gives us a view of the crucial points of the research.

We shall now emphasize once again, and demonstrate point by point, that there is a direct logical and functional link between the ultimate objectives of the research and the philosophy, aspects and sequences of our research programme.

With this aim in mind, it is necessary to reformulate the ultimate objectives of the research in the following terms:

 I) to inform the European Parliament, public opinion, interested circles and the Commission of developments in concentration, competition and prices, this being a general objective within the limits of the area laid down for investigation;

II) to obtain practical results which will enable "anomalies of competition" to be tracked down.
It is this second ultimate objective, which is nevertheless a quite specific objective, that gives direction and purpose to the philosophy and the sequences of the research.

Two types of conclusion might be reached in the research:

— either anomalies of competition do in fact exist on certain specific markets,

— or it is neither proven nor even probable that such anomalies exist.

In the first case, proof that such anomalies exist may be followed by different forms of action depending whether:

— they fall within the scope of Article 85 and 86 of the Treaty of Rome so that the Commission is obliged to initiate specific investigations;

— they fall outside the scope of Community law.

It is, moreover, a good thing that public opinion — and of course the European Parliament — should be kept informed of the existence and growth of such anomalies and of their impact on economic life in general and of their effect on consumers, firms and the inflationary process in particular.

2.10.2. Definition and pinpointing of anomalies of competition

The crucial point is clearly to define and pinpoint an "anomaly of competition".

An anomaly of competition may for practical purposes be defined as follows: it is a variance or deviation in the actual functioning of the mechanisms of competition from a given — perhaps ideal — "competitive model". This in turn entails the empirical solution of two problems:

— definition of the "competitive model";

— definition of the magnitude of the variance or deviation, so that by the mere fact of exceeding a certain "ceiling" or level the variance or deviation will be regarded as a per se anomaly.

---

1. See the introduction to Chapter One: "Aims and stages of the research programme".

2.10.3. Definition of "competitive models": market structures

The "competitive model" may be defined in concrete terms by reference to:

 I) market structures,

II) prices.

The Commission has considered all these levels in its investigations and several elements needed for the definition of some of these competitive models have already been obtained.

The competitive model based on market structures

This model is characterized by the following conditions:

a) an adequate number of suitably balanced brands and producer groups (for example, eight producer firms – all present at any given moment – on a specific market, each with an identical size of 12.5%, the L index thus being $1/8 = 0.125$);

b) constant variations in the market shares of each producer firm (in 1970 firm A has 15% and firm B 3%, whereas in 1975 both firms have 7%). The degree of dynamism of each market must therefore be considered[1].

Thus Table VIII, which deals with 250 or so national product markets where the leading firm holds over 25% of the total (of which about a hundred are dominated by one firm which has more than 50% of the total) gives a series of concrete and eloquent examples of deviations from the competitive model[2]. As we note in our report, the research programme will be developed in several different directions, with the aim of tracking down and quantifying the deviations from the competitive model. Such deviations appear:

- in the movement or evolution of the national producers' market, seen by reference to two opposite patterns: dynamism (as in the competitive model) and rigidity; rigidity is an example of deviation from the model – see section 2.9., especially paras. 2.9.1. and 2.9.2.;

- in the movement or evolution in the national balance of power between producers and retailers; growing and excessive concentration of retailers may also be considered an example of deviation (see section 2.9., especially paras. 2.9.5. and 2.9.6., Table XI, questions 132 and 133);

- in the movement or evolution of the local concentration of distributor-retailers; this movement, in that it may entail a reduction in the number of different shops (among which the consumer may choose when making purchases), is another example of deviation from the competitive model (see section 2.9., especially paras. 2.9.9. and 2.9.10., questions 136 to 138).

---

1. The degree of dynamism may be measured by the indices d and F. See our Methodology, points 51, 52 and 54–61.

2. François Perroux, in his well-known works, has illustrated the aspects and effects of dominance. See in particular:
    "Esquisse d'une théorie de l'économie dominante", Economie Appliquée, Archives de l'I.S.E.A., No 2–3, 1948.
    "L'effet de domination dans les relations économiques", Hommes et Techniques, January 1949.
    "Les comptes de la Nation", P.U.F., pp. 8 et seq., 1949
    "Note sur la dynamique de la domination de la domination", Economie Appliquée, Archives de l'I.S.E.A., no 2, 1950.
    "La concurrence et l'effet de domination", Banque, May 1952.
    "L'économie dominante", in "L'Economie du XXe siècle", P.U.F., Paris, 3e édition, 1969, pp. 61–144.
    "Pouvoir et économie", Etudes Economiques, Dunod, Paris 1974.

2.10.4. Competitive models based on prices

Both the research carried out this far and the research to be undertaken in the present programme is aimed at establishing a series of competitive models based on prices.

The practical utility of this is obvious. Application of Articles 85 and 86 calls for proof, or at least sound evidence, that the firms concerned have **engaged** in conduct forbidden by the Treaty. The most striking manifestation of such behaviour is to be found in prices. It is by analysing and comparing price levels and changes that the existence of competitive anomalies can be tracked down; this is the first step on the road to proving that the conduct giving rise to such anomalies may be contrary to those Articles.

Therefore the competitive model will be defined by reference to:

- retail prices;
- purchase prices paid by retailers;
- producer prices;
- retailers' and possibly wholesalers' mark-ups,

and three basic indicators will be used to characterize and quantify the structure of competition:

a) from the static angle
   - dispersion (or disparity) of retail prices between sales points (local dispersion);
   - difference in retail prices between the different countries or regions concerned (international differentiation);
   - size of mark-ups: both their absolute level and also their local dispersion (or disparity) and international differentiation;

b) from the dynamic angle

   the three indicators considered in their linked movement or evolution.

   In this connection it is worth recalling the practical usefulness of our three "magic keys" (see section 5 of this chapter):
   - first key: analysis, over the different sales points, of the movement that has taken place;
   - second key: international comparisons of that movement;
   - third key: multiple comparisons between products, particularly useful with regard to mark-ups and the various cost components.

Having said this, we shall now briefly restate the essential stages to be gone through in tracking down competitive anomalies and in proving their perverse or illicit nature.

The "thermometer" used in the investigations is provided, as already noted, by retail prices, that is to say by:

- the local dispersion (or disparity) of prices,
- the international differentiation of prices.

2.10.5. Competitive model based on the dispersion of retail prices between the sales points of a single town or region (local dispersion)

A certain degree of dispersion of prices and price variations is a symptom of imperfect, though still effective, competition. On the other hand if prices and price variations were identical this would be a symptom of competition so perfect or abstract that it amounted virtually to collusion or the abuse of a monopoly.

194

We have therefore postulated, on the basis of the findings of our empirical surveys, a "competitive platform" which is characterized by a "reasonable" degree of dispersion of prices. This competitive platform corresponds to a difference of between 10% and 40% above the minimum price for an identical product found in the local sample shops.

Within the platform the dispersion of prices is justified by differences in operating costs between sample shops as a result of their location, size, organizational form, degree of specialization and diversification, and so on (see Chapter One, para. 1.1.28., point II: "Special position of price controls").

So when the degree of dispersion – measured by the index of relative difference, εR_p – exceeds 40% or is lower than 10%, there can be said to be a deviation from the competitive model.

A series of comments can be made on the causes of the deviation from the relevant competitive model or competitive platform.

2.10.6. Dispersion of and discrimination in prices

Two extreme hypothetical cases may be distinguished:

 I) excessively high dispersion of prices,

II) excessively low dispersion of prices.

In the case of an upward deviation, ie. a relative difference in retail prices exceeding the minimum price by more than 40%, there must be either very strong bargaining power on the part of some retailers vis-à-vis the producers or suppliers (they can sell very low because they have enjoyed exceptional buying terms), or a predatory policy pursued by some large retailers (selling goods below cost in order to increase their share of the local market), or local dominant positions exploited by some retailers who impose much higher prices than those charged in another district of the same town or region, or other reasons about which it would be very interesting to have precise knowledge. These are all phenomena which would in principle justify more thorough investigation of causes[1].

For example, where very large differences in the prices charged and in the terms granted to some large retailers by their suppliers are found, this might be an instance of the application of "dissimilar conditions to equivalent transactions with other trading parties, thereby placing them at a competitive disadvantage".

If such practices were capable of affecting trade between Member States, the Commission would have to start specific and comprehensive investigations into the products and firms involved.

The usefulness of highlighting the dispersion of prices at local level (ie. between sales points in the same town or region) does not stop here.

Quantification of the dispersion of selling prices at local level is an essential preliminary to international comparisons of prices (buying prices and selling prices) for the same product in the different EEC Member States.

It is necessary to clear the ground of the problem of the local dispersion of prices before one can usefully examine the problem of price differences – and price discrimination – between different countries. It is therefore necessary:

- to know the maximum and minimum prices observed at several shops (and not merely average prices; these are liable to be far too deceptive or fallacious) before it is possible to state that a certain product is much more expensive in one country than in another;

---

1. See para. 2.5.5. and Table IV of this chapter.

- to apply several conversion rates — we have listed two different rates in Chapter One (1.3.)[1] — before we can judge whether the real magnitude of the differences in price between different countries for the same product is great enough to warrant speaking of "discriminatory prices".

In practice, of course, there will be found to be straightforward cases and more complicated cases.

A straightforward case: according to all the calculation criteria the maximum price of a product as recorded in country A is found to be at least 50% lower than the minimum price for an identical product recorded in country B. Unless it can be shown that there are very high transport costs or particularly heavy tax rates in country B, there is no doubt that this case can be investigated from the angle of discriminatory prices.

For the more complicated cases a whole series of examples could be given:

- the results of the comparisons might vary according to the conversion rates used;

- the minimum prices found in country A might be higher than the minimum prices in country B but lower than the maximum prices in that country;

- the products might not be absolutely identical and there would therefore be a problem of comparability.

In several such cases it would be necessary to deepen and widen the analysis of the "critical" products, ie:

- either to step up the frequency with which retail prices were surveyed in the various shops covered (recording them every month or every other month);

- or to increase the number of regions and towns covered in each country (eg. to prepare a sample of shops in Hamburg, Frankfurt, etc., rather than limiting the survey to the Greater Munich conurbation);

- or to combine several such operations.

We have therefore proposed that we should confine ourselves to basing our investigations on a "mobile or variable sample" related either to the products, or to the countries, regions or towns, or to the firms (producers as well as retailers), for it goes without saying that to intensify some aspects of the research would entail greater specialization and concentration to the detriment of continuing the overall research on a routine basis over the whole field of investigation at the six-monthly intervals originally envisaged — for obvious reasons of economies in the costs of the research itself. The mobile (or variable) sample could even be set up, if necessary, in a few non-EEC countries.

2.10.7. "Lightning surveys" and the setting up of "local waiting-list samples"

Establishment of the mobile sample would make it possible to supplement the periodical surveys (half-yearly or monthly) with "lightning surveys" to be carried out on the spot without any warning. The idea would then be that, for all products or for certain critical products:

- a "waiting-list" or temporary list of local or regional samples would be drawn up in each country covered by the study (eg. in France: Bordeaux, Nice, Limoges, Metz, Lille, Marseilles, Le Havre, Calais, Strasbourg, Rheims), each local sample consisting of not more than about ten shops controlled by given retail groups or chains;

- simultaneous lightning surveys would take place in one or several towns or regions (eg. Bordeaux, Metz, Rheims) on an unannounced date (eg. 17 May, 5 October, 13 November in all the shops, in all the towns and in all the countries).

---

1. Experience with several surveys and with processing the results of such surveys might eventually lead us to prefer one conversion rate to the others.

Obviously, the waiting list and the date of each lightning survey would have to be kept secret in order to enhance the practical usefulness of this kind of survey. It would be left to the Commission's Directorate-General for Competition alone to trigger off the surveys of selected, specified "local waiting-list samples" in the different countries, giving notice by telephone or telegram no more than a week or ten days in advance. Lightning surveys could even be carried out in a few non-EEC countries as well.

The lightning surveys would of course record the prices at which the goods were offered for sale to the public but they ought also to record additional information if possible on:

- producer prices;

- wholesalers' or importers' prices, if relevant (in the case of independent trade);

- purchase dates;

- storage period;

- incidence of taxes and duties.

All the information obtained in this way would be used to confirm the data obtained through the regular periodical surveys and for international comparisons, later confirming the entire series of data for analysis.

2.10.8. <u>Existence of uniform prices at sales points in the same town or region</u>

We shall now examine the other hypothetical case of deviation from the competitive model or platform, namely the case where the differences in retail prices of the same **product** as between sales points do not exceed 10%.

In this case it would seem much easier to carry out international comparisons, which are more significant when the degree of dispersion at local level is very small. Of course, not only the average prices but also the maximum and minimum prices found in each country must be compared. If it is found that all <u>these</u> prices, in a given country, are at least 40% higher than in another country one is entitled to consider whether there is discriminatory pricing. It would then be necessary to seek evidence and to ascertain the causes. High taxation on the product in question in a given country? Dominance of one brand and/or one firm on the market of a given country? International agreement between producers to keep the price of a certain product at an excessively high level in a given country? Or an excessively costly distribution system in a country? Or, again, dominance of the distributor-retailers?

It goes without saying that the existence of relatively uniform retail prices in a given country always gives rise to the suspicion that price-fixing agreements are in operation between producers or between distributor-retailers or between producers and retailers.

In section 2.8. and 2.9. we formulated a series of questions designed to evoke practical and direct replies indicating whether either Article 85 or, especially, Article 86 of the Treaty applies (<u>Questions 116-140</u>).

With regard more especially to proof of abuse of a dominant position, we would draw attention to the following example:

- existence of a dominant position exceeding, say, 40% of the total national market of country A; 1

---

1. This "ceiling" is related directly to the criteria propounded by the Court of Justice in the United Brands case already mentioned (27/26).
   A market share of between 40% and 45% is sufficient to constitute power of domination on the part of the firm concerned — in this case United Brands — because:
   - the percentage "must be determined having regard to the strength and number of the competitors" (Ground of Judgment 110);
   - a firm "does not have to have eliminated all opportunity for competition in order to be in a dominant position" (Ground of Judgment 113).

- existence of relatively <u>uniform</u> retail prices in country A exceeding by at least 40% the retail prices charged in country B for the same or a reasonably comparable product;

- objective and well-documented evidence that this price difference is not due to higher tax in country A nor to the higher mark-ups commonly taken by the trade in country A than in country B.

If these conditions are all fulfilled and are verified on the basis of a comprehensive analysis of the economic chain and of the structure of prices, particularly with regard to the level and evolution of <u>producer prices</u>, one can envisage a fairly clear, straightforward case under Article 86 (abuse of a dominant position).

2.10.9. Competitive models based on mark-ups

These models and the relevant deviations can only be determined with any accuracy actually on the ground. A series of questions (39 to 50 and 54 to 64) have been designed to bring out the main aspects of the problems connected with mark-ups. Experience gained to date enables us to note the following "focal points":

I) <u>Dispersion and uniformity</u>,

II) <u>Maxima</u> (very high mark-ups) and <u>minima</u> (excessively low mark-ups).

An important comment may be made at this point: the <u>competitive platform</u> or model is, by its very nature, situated <u>in the middle</u> of the interval between the two hypothetical extremes (respectively: I. dispersion and uniformity, and II. maxima and minima), whereas the "<u>pathological</u>" <u>deviations</u> tend to lie close to one of the extremes.

I) Thus, on the first point, an excessive dispersion of mark-ups denotes the existence of an <u>excessively large difference</u> in the concrete competitive situations in which the survey shops find themselves.

On the other hand the existence of excessively <u>uniform</u> mark-ups, or <u>identical</u> mark-ups, may be a symptom of the existence either of an <u>agreement</u> between retailers, or of a pricing policy imposed by producers, or of prices fixed officially by the authorities. In this connection it will be the tables of Chapter One – and in particular Tables 5 and 6 and Tables 10 and 11 – which will indicate the reference points for detecting anomalies and analysing deviations from the competitive model.

II) The problems connected with the <u>level</u> of mark-ups involve consideration of a number of important points.

a) In the first place, there is no automatic link between the <u>level</u> of the mark-up and the existence of dominance or a monopoly because a <u>high mark-up</u> may be caused **not** only by the existence of market power but also by the existence of a wide <u>disparity</u> in the efficiency and profitability of the survey shops. Subject to this reservation, we may use the criterion of comparison between products underlying the ranking in Table 6 in Chapter One, in the sense that the products and shops appearing in the upper quarter of Table 6 probably represent cases of deviation from the competitive platform since their mark-up is higher than that of the other products and shops appearing lower down.

b) However, comparison of mark-ups on different products and at different shops calls for two kinds of comment.

With regard to <u>products</u>, it must be borne in mind that all things being equal <u>the mark-up will be much higher</u> on perishable, delicate or bulky goods which cost more to keep and store (eg. frozen foods) than on products whose keeping and storing only pose problems of space (eg. tinned vegetables, tinned meat, tinned fish) and higher still than on high-value, non-perishable products with long shelf-life and easy to handle (eg. instant coffee, tea).

With regard to <u>shops</u>, account must also be taken of the stock turnover rate because the length and cost of the stocking period clearly tend to be correlated with the level of mark-up. The first, second and third tables of Chapter Two all show the importance of the length of the product stocking period (Tj); see section 2.3.[1]

---

1. The incidence of different tax rates on different products must also be taken into account.

c) It must also be remembered that there are two types of deviation from the competitive model:

- one consists of an upward deviation, which we have just considered, ie. mark-ups that are excessive in relation to the normal average margin found on most products and in most shops;

- the second type consists of downward deviation in relation to the normal average margin corresponding to the competitive platform.

We shall therefore have to consider as well the mark-ups on products and in shops that fall in the lower quarter of the above-mentioned Table 6. This quarter will include all the "loss leaders" (fully discussed in section 2.4. and especially in section 2.6.). Nil mark-ups or negative mark-ups are often a worrying symptom of an unhealthy or pathological state of competition, that is to say a state of competition that leaves the door wide open to concentration and dominance. It is neither normal nor desirable nor even possible for firms to operate at a loss over the long term. Such nil or negative mark-ups are therefore a deviation from the competitive platform.

2.10.10. Distinction between formal mark-ups and actual mark-ups - Determination of purchase date and purchase price - Analysis of cost structures

We have already pointed out that nil or negative mark-ups may be fictitious or misleading, ie. they may be based on an overstated buying price. In other words large distributor-retailers may obtain from producers discounts, rebates or other special terms that are not available to every purchaser and may thus enjoy a very low buying price - one which is naturally meant to be kept secret. Since in the workings in Chapter One the buying prices are estimated on the basis of official scales there is a resultant overestimation of these prices (in the case of the distributor-retailers enjoying the special privileges just described) and consequently an underestimation of their mark-ups. An attempt at a reply to questions 92 to 94 should enable us to get close to reality; see section 2.7. ("Retailers' buying prices and power interplay").

In any case an attempted reply to the questions on the actual purchase prices and purchase dates of a given product bought by the large distributor-retailers forms the first stage in establishing the analysis of costs which is the only way that proof of the existence of an "unfair price" within the meaning of Article 86 of the Treaty is going to be obtainable See also section 2.8. ("Completion of the monographic approach by individual product: excessive prices and the search for causes - in particular the breakdown of the price").

Clearly, unless there is accurate information on the price actually charged and paid one can abandon any hope of ever being able to prove that this price - or another price lower down in the chain - is "unfair".

2.10.11. Transition to the conclusive and practical dynamic analysis - Aims and object

Aims

A series of questions (26 to 38 for selling prices, and 75 to 84 for buying prices) concerning in particular the main aspects of the movements of prices.

A study of price variations, of divergences between these variations and hence of the different mark-ups must have the following aims:

 I) to confirm and reinforce (or weaken) the significance of the practical conclusions resulting from the correlations brought out by the static analysis;

II) to uncover new competitive anomalies which by their nature escaped detection under the static analysis method.

In both cases dynamic analysis is the culmination and conclusion, both scientific and practical, of the research.

<u>Object</u>

Comparison of the movements taking place in prices and mark-ups has a multiple significance:

I) <u>Structural comparison</u>: movements in prices and mark-ups <u>according to the position in the chain</u>, ie:

   a) retail prices;

   b) purchase prices paid by retailers;

   c) producer prices;

   d) retailers' and, if relevant, wholesalers' mark-ups showing the comparative incidence of taxes and duties.

   In this connection the reader should recall the replies given to questions 85 to 91 and Tables VI and VII of Chapter Two.

II) <u>Local comparison</u>: movements in retail prices according to the identity of the shop in the local sample, thus showing the value of the index εAs (absolute difference in price variations: see Tables 2, 3 and 4 of Chapter One).

III) <u>International comparison</u>: movements in prices and mark-ups by country concerned, <u>taking account of the incidence of taxes and duties</u>.

IV) <u>Inter-product comparison</u>: movements in prices and mark-ups by item concerned, taking account of the incidence of taxes and duties.

In this connection the reader's attention is drawn to the three "magic keys" (see section 2.5.) and in particular to:

- key one: paras. 2.5.5. et seq;

- key two: paras. 2.5.18. and 2.6.5.;

- key three: paras. 2.7.14. et seq.

2.10.12. <u>The results expected</u>

In connection with the dynamic analysis the establishment of competitive models — and determination of deviations from those models — obviously ought to be carried out "on the ground", ie. after the event. It is not possible — at the present stage of our knowledge and empirical research — to fix strict and specific criteria in advance. It is possible, however, to lay down a few guidelines, bearing in mind the <u>starting-points</u> from which we developed our dynamic analysis (Tables 4, 10 and 11 of Chapter One).

Table 4 of Chapter One classifies, in decreasing order, the price variations which took place in the period in question, for each item and for each shop.

Thus Table 4 highlights:

a) price variations that are <u>so high</u> that they may be considered <u>pathological</u>, a phenomenon which is also brought out by Tables 10 of Chapter One;

b) <u>identical</u> price variations which lead one to suspect the existence of <u>concerted action</u>, a phenomenon which is also brought out by Tables 11 of Chapter One.

In either case one can envisage that the detailed analysis based on the methodology of Chapter Two could be used, in order to obtain an answer to the question:

- with regard to a), whether Article 86 (provisions on "<u>unfair prices</u>") applies, because certain price changes are exaggerated and not justifiable on economic grounds and therefore the prices resulting from these unfair changes may also be considered unfair;

- with regard to b), whether Article 85 (on price-fixing agreements and practices) applies, the other conditions for the application of the article being fulfilled and proven.

In particular, all the elements and analyses which can bring out the magnitude and impact of market dominance must be noted: see section 2.9.

There will be an exploratory attempt to obtain information about any correlation that might exist between market dominance, price levels and the level of profitability as disclosed by firms' accounts; this will be done by analysing the trend of earnings (as shown by their accounts) of the principal firms holding dominant positions on product markets. If no positive correlation is found, the causes will have to be sought; these might be: the existence of countervailing power and a constant low-price policy; social initiatives and social expenditure by the firm; promotion of research; diseconomies of scale and high cost of domination; and, finally, possible divergence between the information disclosed by the accounts and the information obtained through a subsequent thorough analysis of the true "economic" profitability of the firms concerned.

Such an analysis could be supplemented, in specific cases, by a detailed analysis of the various cost components and, especially, of comparative movements in them, and this could be done for the various countries and industries involved.

Together, the criteria set out in Chapters One and Two and the body of replies obtained to the 140 questions put in Chapter Two are capable of achieving the two objectives of the research:

- providing general information for the European Parliament, public opinion, interested parties and the Commission, in order to secure a certain degree of "transparency" of structures and, in particular, to ensure that there is systematic and thorough knowledge of market structures and changes in them;

- providing a collection of specific economic analyses which will enable the Commission to take concrete practical initiatives under Articles 85 and 86 of the Treaty.

2.10.3. Basis for discussion: long-term prospects of the research

It can be said with certainty, at the current stage of our factual knowledge, that it will be several years before the research programme is completed and that complete results will come only in stages, market by market, product by product and country by country. The difficulties and constraints to which the investigations will be subject cannot be over-estimated. On the other hand, if we persevere with the steady completion and expansion of the research, it should be possible to set up a semi-automatic and continuous apparatus for observing and analysing structures and prices world-wide. It is still difficult at the present juncture to describe the whole range of concrete actions open to the EEC in the field of competition policy and in the fight against inflation as a result of the findings of the studies. Besides the specific results expected in the short term, the research programme provides a basis for discussion of future developments.

Collection and comparison of prices of identical and/or comparable products - retail prices, mark-ups and producer prices - should make it possible to substantiate the existence or non-existence of competitive anomalies at world level. If, for example, the studies described in the research programme reveal that in one or more EEC Member States retail prices and producer prices are being charged that are excessively high or excessively low in relation to prices in non-Community countries or in another Member State, it would be necessary to analyse both the causes and the resultant concrete effects on production and marketing structures in the EEC as a whole and, especially, to analyse the harm which may be suffered from this by consumers and/or producer firms in one or more Member States in comparison with consumers and/or producer firms in a non-Community country or in another EEC Member State. Among other things the findings, even interim and partial, of the studies could provide the Community authorities with a series of objective, systematic and continuous reference points to guide them in their attitude to the strategies employed by the large multinational firms and/or by certain producer countries.

There is no doubt that the level and structure of international prices play a decisive role in influencing the trends which will in future characterize a new worldwide division of productive economic activities. This means that it is necessary to collect, compare and analyse those prices.

The aims of the research programme thus go beyond the sphere of food products and beverages. The same model can be applied and adapted to other markets and products.

APPENDIX ONE

DOMINANCE STRUCTURE IN 150
SELECTED PRODUCT MARKETS

INTRODUCTORY AND EXPLANATORY REMARKS

1. As it has already pointed out recent developments in research into concentration, competition and prices in individual industries and markets reflect
the economic principles affirmed by the Court of Justice on 14 February 1978
in Case 27/76 (United Brands). The following are the seven main principles
that can be deduced from the judgment since they have considerable influence
on the orientation and objectives of the economic research and analysis
undertaken under the Commission's programme :

(1) the existence of a dominant position derives in general from a combination
of several factors which, taken separately, would not necessarily be
determinant   (Ground of Judgment 66) ;

(2) one of the factors which point to dominance is the market share of a
given company compared with the shares of its competitors (Ground 58).
This market share must exceed 40 % ;

(3) a company with a market share in excess of 40 % does not automatically
control the market, for its market share must be assessed in the light
of the strength and number of its competitors (Grounds 108 to 110) ;

(4) the fact that the market leader has twice the sales of its most strongly
placed competitor and that there is no appreciable decline in its sales,
even when new competitors enter the market, would tend to confirm the
dominant positions (Grounds 120 to 129) ;

(5) where a given firm has a dominant position on a specific product market,
Article 86 comes into play where discriminatory or unfair pricing is
practised, provided all the requirements of the Article are met ;

(6) a policy of price differentiation enabling the dominant firm to
apply dissimilar conditions to equivalent transactions with its
various trading partners, thereby placing them at a competitive
disadvantage, constitutes abuse of dominance (Ground 234, relating to
discriminatory prices) ;

(7) the existence of excessive differences between the highest and lowest prices (Ground 237) can constitute an indicium of excessive disproportion between costs actually born and prices actually charged (Ground 252), so that the Commission must :

(a) retrace the process of retail price formation ;

(b) either in absolute terms or in comparison with competing products ;

(c) in order to evaluate the mark-up.

Where the conclusions reached upon this analysis indicate that excessive prices are being charged out of all reasonable proportion to the economic value of the service or product supplied, it may be concluded that a dominant position is being abused (Grounds 250 to 259, relating to unfair pricing).

2. From the principles set forth by the Court of Justice it is helpful to draw up conclusions as regards the research analysis development on :

(a) market structure and the analysis of dominance ;

(b) price structures.

The latter are considered in Chapter Two of the present volume.

As regards market structure, the industries and specific product markets which may be under the influence of a dominant firm must be ascertained and analysed.

In the VIIth Report on the Competition Policy, referring to 1977, the Commission has published a table outlining the share and the name of the dominant firms in 245 national markets for certain products (see Table VIII of the Chapter Two, n° 2.9.1., pages 162 to 169 of the present volume).

Research of the Commission into the development of concentration in national product markets continued during 1978 and the structure of dominance power has been analysed in depth by considering not only the strength or share of the top firm, but the share as well as the rank of each of the top 4 firms, operating in each product market.

The purpose of this Appendix is, therefore, to present these detailed data referring to 150 selected product markets, these products coinciding only partially with markets considered in the above mentioned Table VIII of Chapter Two.

The table 1 of this Appendix has been established in French, but table 2 gives the English translation for each of the 150 selected product markets, designated by a code number.

These markets are ranked in decreasing order of the coefficient 2L, expressing in % the relation between the absolute figure for the first firm and the absolute figure for the second. The interpretation of coefficient 2L is very easy.

If 2L = 100 %, the two largest firms have identical shares of the industry or market considered.

If 2L = 200 %, the first firm has twice the second firm's share of the relevant industry or market and this, according to the economic principles affirmed by the Court of Justice of European Communities on 14 February 1978, Judgment in Case 27/76 (United Brands) raises a suspicion of individual potential dominance.

If 2L = 400 %, the largest firm is four times the second firm and so on.

Table 1 is not limited to only one indicator of dominance power (i,e. : 2L), since for the assesment of the position of a company in relation to the strength and number of its competitors (as required by the Court of Justice in the above quoted case 27/76), more indicators are needed.

So, three coefficients of inequality (or disparity) are used - 2L (as we have seen) and, moreover, 3L and 4L - in combination with the ratios C_1, C_2, C_3, C_4, that is the shares, in %, of the first firm (C_1), of the two top firms (C_2), of the three top firms (C_3), of the top 4 firms (C_4).

The coefficients 2L, 3L and 4L give a percentage measurement of the relative strength of the four largest firms so as to give a quantitative picture of the degree of dominance enjoyed by the leading firm(s).

5. These coefficients are interpreted and calculated immediately. Firstly, firms are ranked in decreasing order of their share of the relevant industry or market. The coefficients are then calculated rapidly :

(1) only the absolute figures for the two top firms (K = 2) are considered. Coefficient 2L gives the relation between the absolute figure for the first firm and the absolute figure for the second ;

(2) figures for the first three firms are taken (K = 3).
Coefficient 3L is the arithmetic mean between two relations :

(a) relation between the size of the first firm and the average size of the next two firms ;

(b) relation between the average size of the first two firms and the size of the third ;

(3) figures for the first four firms are taken (K = 4).
Coefficient 4L is the arithmetic mean between three relations :

(a) relation between the size of the first firm and the average size of the next three firms ;

(b) relation between the average size of the first two firms and the average size of the second two firms ;

(c) relation between the average size of the first three firms and the size of the fourth.

All these relations are expressed in percentages, being multiplied by 100.

$$\text{F O R M U L A}$$

$$DO_i = \frac{A_i}{i} \ / \ \frac{A_K - A_i}{K-i}$$

$$DO_i = \frac{K-i}{i} \ \frac{A_i}{A_K - A_i}$$

$$KL = \frac{\displaystyle\sum_{i=1}^{K-1} DO_i}{K-1}$$

$$A_K = C_K = a_1 + a_2 + \ldots a_K = \sum_{i=1}^{K} = a_i \quad \begin{array}{l}\text{(cumulative share}\\ \text{(or size of the top}\\ \text{(K firms}\end{array}$$

$$A_1 = a_1 = x_1$$

$$A_2 = a_1 + a_2 = x_1 + x_2$$

$$A_3 = a_1 + a_2 + a_3 = x_1 + x_2 + x_3$$

$$x_i = a_i = \text{absolute size or individual share of firm } \underline{i}$$

PRACTICAL APPLICATIONS

I) STRUCTURE CONSTITUTED BY 3 FIRMS :

$$x_1 = 60 \ ; \quad x_2 = 30 \ ; \quad x_3 = 10.$$

I.I) K = 2 ; i = K - 1 = 1

$$DO_1 = \frac{2-1}{1} \ \frac{A_1}{A_K - A_1}$$

$$2L = \frac{\displaystyle\sum_{i=1}^{1} DO_i = 1}{1}$$

Exemple : $A_1 = 60$; $A_2 = 90$

$$\underline{\underline{COEFFICIENT\ \ 2L}} = \frac{60}{90-60} = \frac{60}{30} = 2 = 200\ \%$$

I.II) K = 3 ; i = 1   Exemple : $A_1 = 60$
             i = 2 $A_2 = 90$
                                  $A_3 = 100$

i = 1

$$DO_1 = \frac{3-1}{1}\ \frac{A_1}{A_3 - A_1} = 2\ \frac{60}{100-60} = 2.\ \frac{60}{40} = 300\ \%$$

i = 2

$$DO_2 = \frac{3-2}{2}\ \frac{A_2}{A_3 - A_2} = \frac{1}{2}\ \frac{90}{100-90} = \frac{1}{2}.\ \frac{90}{10} = 450\ \%$$

$$\underline{\underline{COEFFICIENT\ \ 3L}} = \frac{\sum\limits_{i=1}^{2} DO_i}{2} = \frac{300\% + 450\%}{2} = 375\ \%$$

II) STRUCTURE CONSTITUTED BY 4 FIRMS :

$x_1 = 40$; $x_2 = 20$; $x_3 = 20$; $x_4 = 20$ (See hypothesis 5 in the Graph)

II.I) K = 2 ; i = K-1 = 1

$$\underline{\underline{COEFFICIENT\ \ 2L}} = \frac{40}{60-40} = \frac{40}{20} = 200\ \%$$

II.II) K = 3 ; i = 1   Exemple : $A_1 = 40$
             i = 2 $A_2 = 60$
                                  $A_3 = 80$

i = 1

$$DO_1 = \frac{3-1}{1}\ \frac{40}{80-40} = 2\ .\ \frac{40}{40} = 200\ \%$$

$\underline{i = 2}$

$$DO_2 = \frac{3-2}{2} \quad \frac{60}{80-60} = \frac{1}{2} \cdot \frac{60}{20} = 150\ \%$$

$\underline{\underline{COEFFICIENT\ \ 3L}} = \frac{200\% + 150\%}{2} = 175\ \%$

II.III) K = 4 ; i = 1   Exemple : $A_1 = 40$
          i = 2 $A_2 = 60$
          i = 3 $A_3 = 80$
                                $A_4 = 100$

$$DO_1 = \frac{4-1}{1} \quad \frac{40}{100-40} = 3 \cdot \frac{40}{60} = 200\ \%$$

$$DO_2 = \frac{4-2}{2} \quad \frac{60}{100-60} = 1 \cdot \frac{60}{40} = 150\ \%$$

$$DO_3 = \frac{4-3}{3} \quad \frac{80}{100-80} = \frac{1}{3} \cdot \frac{80}{20} = 133\ \%$$

$\underline{\underline{COEFFICIENT\ \ 4L}} = \frac{200\% + 150\% + 133\%}{3} = \underline{\underline{161\ \%}}$

It is helpful to point out the economic meaning of indexes K L, by presenting the Graph 1 :

"Range of power relations between the Top 4 firms. Sample of 13 basic structure hypotheses".

This graph aims to compare each of 13 basic hypotheses of "summit structures" :

- the individual shares of each of Top 4 firms (section below of the graph) x_1, x_2, x_3, x_4 ;

- the corresponding values thus resulting for each of the following indexes : 2L, 3L and 4L, in %, (upper section of the graph).

2L   3L   4L

The graph outlines, thanks to the bulk of the 13 basic structure hypotheses taken into account, the great "sensitivity" of these indexes to quantitative changes in "Power Relations" between the Top 4 firms, according to multiple but coherent rates of interlocking variations

*

*   *

I) Analysing the "value connections" between the indexes 2L, 3L and 4L, referring to any given power structure, it is possible to draw up the fundamental quantitative picture relative to the structure considered.

II) In this way, it is possible to compare, through time and in the space, several structures, their degree of dominance and inequality being measured, not by only one index (as is the usually done too simplistically) but by a set of three logically connected indexes (2L, 3L and 4L) jointly outlining all relevant and comparable quantitative aspects of the structures compared.

III) Accordingly, it is "reasonably" possible to relate the given values of the subsequent coefficients 3L and 4L to the yardistick constituted by the basic coefficient 2L (which is transparent and meaningful since it represents the ratio of the size of the top firm to that of the second firm), in order to outline, on this basis, the "equivalent" degrees of inequality emerging from the 3L and 4L coefficients. Thus, the 2L value is the new quantitative lightening milestone for other coefficients (2L, 3L, ... KL).

*

*   *

212

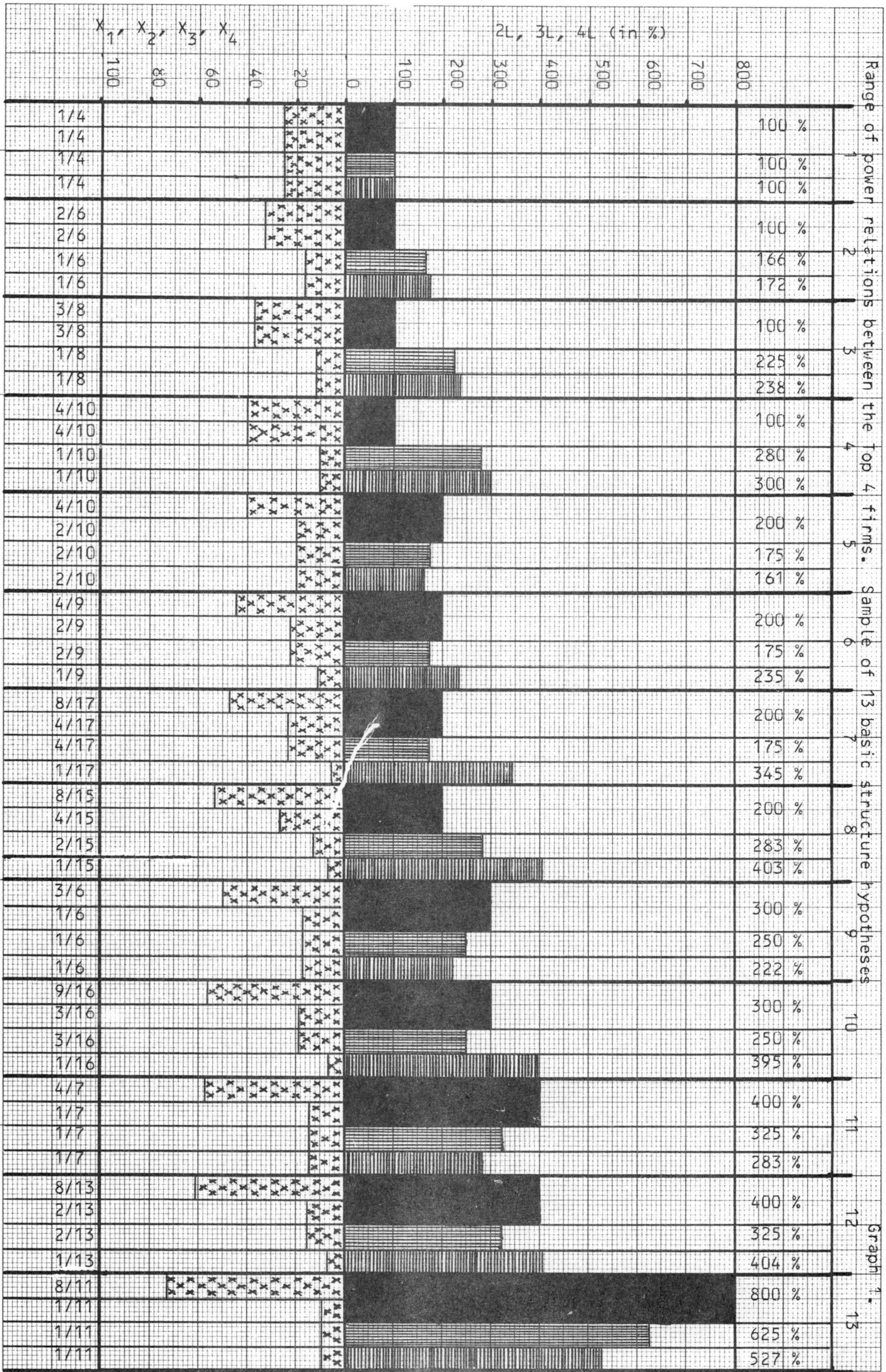

Range of power relations between the top 4 firms. Sample of 13 basic structure hypotheses

Graph 1.

X₁, X₂, X₃, X₄ — X_1, X_2, X_3, X_4

2L, 3L, 4L (in %)

Scale: 100 80 60 40 20 0 100 200 300 400 500 600 700 800

Group	Ratio	Value
1	1/4	100 %
	1/4	100 %
	1/4	100 %
	1/4	100 %
2	2/6	100 %
	2/6	
	1/6	166 %
	1/6	172 %
3	3/8	100 %
	3/8	
	1/8	225 %
	1/8	238 %
4	4/10	100 %
	4/10	
	1/10	280 %
	1/10	300 %
5	4/10	200 %
	2/10	
	2/10	175 %
	2/10	161 %
6	4/9	200 %
	2/9	
	2/9	175 %
	1/9	235 %
7	8/17	200 %
	4/17	
	4/17	175 %
	1/17	345 %
8	8/15	200 %
	4/15	
	2/15	283 %
	1/15	403 %
9	3/6	300 %
	1/6	
	1/6	250 %
	1/6	222 %
10	9/16	300 %
	3/16	
	3/16	250 %
	1/16	395 %
11	4/7	400 %
	1/7	
	1/7	325 %
	1/7	283 %
12	8/13	400 %
	2/13	
	2/13	325 %
	1/13	404 %
13	8/11	800 %
	1/11	
	1/11	625 %
	1/11	527 %

213

6. The dominance power is very high on the product markets considered, as results from the following figures drawn up from Table 1 (markets sample including 150 cases of C_2, 115 cases of C_3 and 78 cases of C_4) :

- $C_2 \geqslant 80 \%$:   31 cases

- $C_2 \geqslant 50 \%$:   120 cases

- $C_3 \geqslant 80 \%$:   49 cases

- $C_3 \geqslant 50 \%$:   103 cases

- $C_4 \geqslant 80 \%$:   32 cases

- $C_4 \geqslant 50 \%$:   70 cases

- $C_4 < 50 \%$:   8 cases

7. Having recourse to a new "Model of Econometric X-ray" founded on the Linda system of indexes and applied to the selected 150 national product markets, it is possible to outline the structure of Power Relations between the Top 4 (or less) firms dominating these product markets. See Table 3.

The major size gap lies between the third and fourth largest firms, for it is the 4L coefficient that has the highest values :

- in 78 % of cases it exceeds the 200 % threshold (as against only 40 % of cases for the 2L coefficient and 60 % of cases for the 3L coefficient) ;

- in 87% of cases 4L is greater than 2L and in 82 % of cases it is greater than 3L.

One important automatic conclusion from the samples studied is that the normal form of market dominance on the national markets forming the Community is the tricpoly, which is to say that three firms dominate most national product markets.

8. The reality is that in most national product markets, the fourth firm is not provided at all with any market power, owing to its negligeable market share, while the third firm has this market power.

In fact, a glance to the sample of 150 product markets (Table 1) shows that :

- in 34 cases the third firm has a market share equal or superior to
  15 % of the total market size ;

- while only in 2 cases the <u>fourth firm</u> has such a share of the product
  market;

- in 17 cases the third firm has even 20 % or more of the total product
  market, against zero case as regards the fourth firm;

- on the other side, the fourth firm has 10 % or more of the total product
  market only in 15 cases, while the third firm has 10 % or more in 73 cases.

It seems reasonable to suppose that one firm having less than 10 % of the total
market is indeniably not provided with market power, while this market power
might exist in principle when market share of one given firm is equal to 15 %
or more.

9. Within the tricpolistic arena there is a clear superdominant duopoly with
   two very powerful firms of often comparable size. As we have seen, in 120
   cases, out of the sample of 150 product markets (i.e. in 80 % of cases), the
   cumulative share of the top two firms (C_2) is equal or superior to 50 %, while
   in 31 cases C_2 is equal or superior to 80 %.

   The intensity of the triopolistic and duopolistic dominance is very high,
   which creates a formidable barrier to entry into the same arena by other firms.
   The existence of this barrier is confirmed by the rigidity of market shares
   over time on most of the 150 markets studied.

10. On the other hand, monopoly situations, as where 2L is greater than 400 %, would
    seem to be less frequent, though their impact on competition should neither be
    overlooked nor underestimated. Only in 16 % of cases does 2L exceed 400 %
    (where the largest firm is more than 4 times larger than the second), whereas
    3L exceeds 400 % in 25 % of cases and 4L in 27 %.

    It is also worth adding that in 9 % of cases the 2L coefficient exceeds 600 %,
    which is to say that monopolistic dominance has reached such a high level as
    virtually to eliminate any possibility of competition by other firms (margarine
    in France and Great Britain, biscuits in Ireland, beer in Denmark, certain baby
    foods in Great Britain, aniseed-based beverages in France, sparking plugs and
    frozen foods in Italy, coffee substitutes in Germany, and so on).

215

TABLE 1

MODELE D'ANALYSE DE LA DOMINANCE SUR LES MARCHES DES PRODUITS

CODE MARCHE PRODUIT	DESCRIPTION MARCHE DU PRODUIT	ANNEES	PAYS	COEFFICIENTS L 2L	3L	4L	C_1	C_2	C_3	C_4	ENTREPRISES
001	Margarine	1974	F	2000	-	-	60	63	-	-	1) ASTRA-CALVE (UNILEVER) 2) EXCEL-SOPRODEL (LESIEUR)
002	Biscuiterie	1974	IRL	1540	1368	1187	77	82	86	89	1) IRISH BISCUITS 2) UNITED BISCUITS 3) ASSOCIATED BISCUITS 4) CADBURY
003	Bières	1974	DK	1383	1386	-	83	89	93	-	1) DE FORENEDE BRUGGERIER 2) FAXE 3) ALBANI
004	Succédanés de café (boissons)	1974	D	1143	-	-	80	87	-	-	1) UNIFRANK (NESTLE) 2) QUIETA-WERKE
005	Aliments surgelés en général	1973	I	900	1065	785	73	81	88	93	1) SAGES (UNILEVER) 2) SURGELA (IRI-SME) 3) FRIGODAUNIA (EFIM) 4) BRINA
006	Aliments pour enfants (biscottes et céréales)	1973	GB	870			87	97			1) GLAXO 2) RECKITT COLMAN 3) WANDER (SANDOZ)
007	Matières adhésives	1974	NL	852	724	621	68	76	83	90	
008	Confiserie (gomme à macher)	1972	F	850	-	-	85	95	-	-	1) GENERAL FOODS 2) CHICLETS
009	Apéritifs anisés (boissons)	1974	F	822	-	-	74	83	-	-	1) PERNOD-RICARD 2) MARTINI-ST.RAPHAEL
010	Bougies pour voitures	1973	I	750	588	-	75	85	95	-	1) MARELLI 2) CHAMPION 3) LODGE

(INDICATEURS)

MODELE D'ANALYSE DE LA DOMINANCE SUR LES MARCHES DES PRODUITS

CODE MARCHE PRODUIT	DESCRIPTION MARCHE DU PRODUIT	ANNEES	PAYS	INDICATEURS							ENTREPRISES
				COEFFICIENTS L			RATIOS				
				2L	3L	4L	c_1	c_2	c_3	c_4	
011	Lait concentré	1972	F	700	770	-	70	80	86	-	1) LAIT MONT-BLANC (NESTLE) 2) FRANCE LAIT 3) PREVAL (PERRIER)
012	Soupes (bouillons solides)	1972	F	700	550	1040	70	80	90	92	1) SOPAD (NESTLE) 2) SPN (CPC) 3) LIEBIG (BROOKE BOND) 4) ASTRA-CALVE (UNILEVER)
013	Margarine	1973/76	GB	670	1216	1217	67	77	82	84	1) VANDENBERGH & JURGENS (UNILEVER) 2) KRAFT 3) CWS 4) SAINSBURY
014	Fromages fondus	1972	F	644	665	-	58	67	73	-	1) BEL 2) PISON 3) ROUSTANG
015	Biscottes	1972	F	587	509	631	47	55	62	67	1) ALIMENTS ESSENTIELS 2) PICARD 3) CLEMENT 4) LU BRUN ET ASSOCIES
016	Lait en poudre	1973	GB	583	661	1131	70	82	89	91	1) CADBURY SCHWEPPES 2) CARNATION FOODS 3) SAINSBURY 4) NESTLE
017	Sucre	1973	DK	567	-	-	85	100	-	-	DDS : DE DANSKE SUKKENFABRIKKER SUKKERFABRIK. NYKØBING
018	Sédatifs et hypnotiques	1973	NL	500	400	349	45	54	63	65	1) HOFFMANN-LA ROCHE 2) UNION CHIMIQUE BELGE 3) KALICHEMIE 4) CIBA
019	Potages en boîtes (canned soups)	1973	GB	500	525	-	60	72	80	-	1) H.J. HEINZ 2) CAMPBELL 3) CROSS & BLACKWEL
020	Desserts frais	1972	F	500	400	-	55	66	77	-	1) GERVAIS-DANONE 2) SODIMA 3) CHAMBOURCY

CODE MARCHE PRODUIT	DESCRIPTION MARCHE DU PRODUIT	ANNEES	PAYS	COEFFICIENTS L			RATIOS				ENTREPRISES
				2L	3L	4L	C_1	C_2	C_3	C_4	
021	Aliments surgelés en général	1974	D	500	466		51	62	65		1) LANGNESE-IGLO (UNILEVER-NESTLE) 2) OETKER 3) TIKO (GEG) 4) TIEFKÜHLUNION
022	Batteries pour voitures	1973	I	450	575	-	63	77	84	-	1) MARELLI 2) F.A.R. 3) VARTA
023	Conserves de poisson	1974	GB	443			58	76			1) UNILEVER 2) CUCUMBER
024	Ordinateurs "General Purpose"	1972	D	433	350	401	52	64	76	83	1) IBM 2) HONEYWELL 3) UNIDATA 4) UNIVAC
025	Conserves de viande	1973	I	400	427	453	60	75	85	93	1) SIMMENTHAL 2) ACSAL 3) TRINITY 4) STAR
026	Matières grasses en général	1974	D	400	598	638	60	75	81	86	1) UNION DEUTSCHE LEBENSMITTELWERKE 2) FRITZ HOMANN 3) WALTER RAU 4) ELITE MARGARINE FEINKOST
027	Lait condensé non sucré	1972	F	375			75	95			1) GLORIA 2) FRANCE LAIT
028	Fromages frais	1972	F	372	460		36	47	52		1) GERVAIS DANONE 2) SODIMA 3) CHAMBOURCY
029	Moutardes	1972	F	367			55	70			1) GEN.ALIMENTAIRES (GEN.OCCIDENTALE) 2) SEGMA (POULAIN)
030	Matières grasses en général	1973	GR	367	361	301	29	37	42	49	1) ELAÏS SA 2) HUILERIES DE LA GRECE DU NORD 3) HUILERIES DE GRECE 4) ELEDURGIKI S.A.

Note: INDICATEURS regroupe COEFFICIENTS L et RATIOS.

MODELE D'ANALYSE DE LA DOMINANCE SUR LES MARCHES DES PRODUITS

CODE MARCHE PRODUIT	DESCRIPTION MARCHE DU PRODUIT	ANNEES	PAYS	INDICATEURS								ENTREPRISES
				COEFFICIENTS L			RATIOS					
				2L	3L	4L	C_1	C_2	C_3	C_4		
031	Succédanés de café soluble (boissons)	1974	D	350	854		70	90	94			1) UNIFRANK (NESTLE) 2) GÜNZBURGER NAHRUNGSMITTEL FABRIK 3) MELITTA BENTZ
032	Aliments pour enfants à base laitière	1972	F	350			70	90				1) GERVAIS-DANONE (BSN + G.D.) 2) GUIGOZ (NESTLE)
033	Poissons surgelés	1973	GB	350	541		63	81	88			1) BIRD'S EYE (UNILEVER) 2) FINDUS (NESTLE) 3) ROSS (IMPERIAL)
034	Aliments surgelés en général	1973	GB	339	481		61	79	87			1) UNILEVER 2) NESTLE 3) IMPERIAL
035	Soupes en boîtes (canned soups)	1973	F	333	650	742	60	78	83	87		1) LIEBIG (BROOKE-BOND-LIEBIG) 2) BARBIER-DAUPHIN 3) SOPAD (NESTLE) 4) SPM/CPC
036	Bières	1975	F	333	420		50	65	73			1) B.S.N. BIERES 2) UNION DES BRASSERIES 3) ALBRA (HEINEKEN NL) 4) PELFORTH
037	Aliments pour enfants en boîtes et en flocons	1973	GB	331	452		63	82	91			1) H.J. HEINZ 2) GERBER (CPI) 3) UNIGATE
038	Huiles alimentaires	1972	F	317	634		57	75	80			1) LESIEUR 2) G.I.E. INTERHUILES 3) ASTRA-CALVE (UNILEVER)
039	Antirheumatics	1972	NL	300	304	494	48	64	76	80		1) MSD 2) BOOTS 3) GEIGY 4) MIDY
040	Aliments pour enfants en général	1972	F	300	462		60	81	94			1) FALI (BSN + GERVAIS-DANONE) 2) GUIGOZ (NESTLE) 3) S.P.M. (CPC) 4) GERVAIS-DANONE

MODELE D'ANALYSE DE LA DOMINANCE SUR LES MARCHES DES PRODUITS

CODE MARCHE PRODUIT	DESCRIPTION MARCHE DU PRODUIT	ANNEES	PAYS	COEFFICIENTS L			RATIOS				ENTREPRISES
				2L	3L	4L	c_1	c_2	c_3	c_4	
041	Yoghurt	1973	IRL	300			60	80			1) EDEN VALE (EXPRESS DAIRIES) 2) GOLDEN VALE
042	Biscuits	1973	NL	300	330	303	45	60	70	76	1) DE ZAAN (GRACE, USA) 2) WESSANEN 3) BENSDORP/CACAO 4) GERKENS
043	Thé noir	1974	D	294	267	244	50	67	82	97	1) TEEKANNE 2) MESSMER 3) JACOBS 4) BÜNTING
044	Psychotérapiques	1973	NL	285	480	477	40	54	59	64	1) HOFFMANN-LA ROCHE 2) WEITH 3) CIBA-GEIGY 4) MSD
045	Produits à base de pommes de terre	1974	D	285	312		57	70	90		1) PFANNI 2) MAGGI (NESTLE) 3) KNORR (Groupe Maïzena : CPC-USA)
046	Cuisinières électriques	1973	DK	283	282	294	51	69	83	94	1) ERNST VOLL 2) AEG & BBC 3) HUSQUARNA-KOCKUMS 4) SCAN ATLAS
047	Boissons alcoolisées (rhum)	1972	F	250	405	402	45	63	70	77	1) BARDINET 2) CIE METROPOLE DES RHUMS (MARTINI-ST.RAPHAEL) 3) DUQUESNE 4) ST.JAMES (COINTREAU-REMY MARTIN)
048	Fruits et légumes condimentaires	1972	F	240			36	51			1) GEN.ALIMENTAIRE (GEN.OCCIDENTALE) 2) SEGMA (POULAIN)
049	Hormones	1973	NL	237	223	225	19	27	34	39	1) ORGANON 2) PHILIPS DUPHAR 3) SCHERING 4) AYERST
050	Aliments surgelés en général	1972	F	237	295	429	45	64	75	80	1) FRANCE-GLACE FINDUS 2) COFRALIM 3) ORTIZ 4) SERVIFRAIS

MODELE D'ANALYSE DE LA DOMINANCE SUR LES MARCHES DES PRODUITS

CODE MARCHE PRODUIT	DESCRIPTION MARCHE DU PRODUIT	ANNEES	PAYS	COEFFICIENTS L			RATIOS				ENTREPRISES
				2L	3L	4L	c_1	c_2	c_3	c_4	
051	Moissonneuses - batteuses	1972	D	235	220	219	40	57	72	85	1) GEBRÜDER CLAAS 2) MASSEY FERGUSON 3) JOHN DEERE LANZ 4) KLÖCKNER-HUMBOLDT-DEUTZ
052	Lait condensé	1974	D	233	265		35	50	60		1) ALLGÄUER ALPENMILCH (NESTLE) 2) GLÜCKS-KLEE GmbH (CARNATION & Co USA) 3) DEUTSCHE LIBBY
053	Aliments pour enfants et diététiques	1973	I	227	291	349	50	72	85	93	1) PLASMON (HEINZ) 2) GERBER (CPI, USA) 3) IPB BUITONI-PERUGINA 4) CARLO ERBA (MONTEDISON)
054	Boissons non alcoolisées en général	1974	F	225	206	325	27	39	50	54	1) PERRIER 2) VITTEL 3) AVIAN 4) J.F.A.
055	Poudres de savon	1974	GB	223	-	-	67	97			
056	Lait en poudre	1972	F	220	270		55	80	95		1) FRANCE LAIT 2) GLORIA 3) LAIT MONT-BLANC (NESTLE)
057	Biscuiterie	1973	GB	217		264	50	73			1) UNITED BISCUITS 2) CADBURY SCHWEPPES
058	Meunerie	1973	GR	216	225	264	17	25	31	35	1) ST.GEORGES HILLS SA 2) ALLATINI SA 3) MELISSARIS, NACEO MILLS 4) CRETE FLOUR MILLS SA
059	Yoghurt	1974	GB	211	225	294	38	56	67	75	1) EXPRESS DAIRY 2) UNIGATE 3) VANDENBERGH'S (UNILEVER) 4) MARKS & SPENCER
060	Crèmes glacées	1974	D	206	260	264	33	49	58	67	1) LANGNESE-IGLO (UNILEVER-NESTLE) 2) SCHOLLER 3) SÜDMILCH 4) OETKER

221

MODELE D'ANALYSE DE LA DOMINANCE SUR LES MARCHES DES PRODUITS

CODE MARCHE PRODUIT	DESCRIPTION MARCHE DU PRODUIT	ANNEES	PAYS	COEFFICIENTS L			RATIOS				ENTREPRISES
				2L	3L	4L	C_1	C_2	C_3	C_4	
061	Aliments pour enfants en général	1974	DK	200	439		60	90	98		NESTLE / PLUMROSE / IRMA
062	Café soluble	1974	D	200	175	196	40	60	80	94	1) NESTLE 2) DEK 3) JACOBS 4) GENERAL FOODS
063	Potages déshydratés	1973	GB	200	175		40	60	80		1) UNILEVER 2) CORN PRODUCT 3) NESTLE 4) CADBURY
064	Boissons alcoolisées (calvados)	1972	F	194			33	50			1) DEBRISE DULAC (gpe Vve Clicot-Ponsardin) 2) BUSNEL ET LANCELOT (PERNOT-RICARD)
065	Poivre (industrie condimentaire)	1972	F	194			33	50			1) GEN.ALIMENTAIRE 2) DUCROS
066	Machines à laver	1973 1974	GB	189	262	373	36	55	65	70	1) HOOVER 2) GEC 3) SERVIS 4) PHILIPS
067	T.V. Couleurs	1973 1974 1975	GB	188	200	199	32	49	62	74	1) THORN 2) PHILIPS 3) GEC 4) RANK 1) THORN 2) PHILIPS 3) RANK 4) GEC 1) THORN 2) PHILIPS 3) GEC 4) RANK
068	Sucre	1977	GB	184			59	91			1) TATE & LYLE + MANBRE & GARTON 2) BRITISH SUGAR CORP.
069	App. pour la reprod.du son autres que radios et TV	1973 1974 1975	GB	183	185	212	22	34	44	51	1) THORN 2) RANK 3) PHILIPS 4) BSR 1) THORN 2) BSR 3) PHILIPS 4) RANK 1) THORN 2) BSR 3) RANK 4) PHILIPS
070	Réfrigérateurs et congélateurs	(1973) (1974)	GB	182	235	301	31	48	58	64	1) THORN 2) LEC 3) ELECTROLUX 4) GENERAL MOTORS FRIGIDAIRE (G.M.F.)

MODELE D'ANALYSE DE LA DOMINANCE SUR LES MARCHES DES PRODUITS

CODE MARCHE PRODUIT	DESCRIPTION MARCHE DU PRODUIT	ANNEES	PAYS	INDICATEURS							ENTREPRISES
				COEFFICIENTS L			RATIOS				
				$2L$	$3L$	$4L$	c_1	c_2	c_3	c_4	
071	Ordinateurs "General Purpose"	1973	NL	181	246	253	40	62	74	85	1) IBM 2) HONEYWELL 3) DIGITAL EQUIMENT 4) UNIDATA
072	Eaux minérales (boissons)	1976	F	180	181	723	47	73	95	97	1) PERRIER 2) EVIAN 3) VITTEL 4) VOLVIC
073	Ordinateurs "General Purpose"	1973	B	178	279	407	48	75	87	93	1) IBM 2) HONEYWELL 3) UNIDATA 4) UNIVAC
074	Antidiabétiques	1973	NL	176	284	**327**	37	58	67	74	1) HOECHST 2) NOVO 3) ORGANON 4) WINTHROP
075	Soft drinks (limonades, etc)	1976	DK	176	267	343	30	47	55	60	1) DE FORENEDE BRUGGERIER 2) COCA-COLA 3) FAXE 4) ALBANI
076	Diurétiques	1973	NL	175	**182**	254	35	55	71	79	1) HOECHST 2) RIT 3) CIBA-GEIGY 4) SEARLE
077	Machines à laver	1973	DK	174	-	-	47	75	-	-	1) FISKER 2) HOOVER
078	Sucre	1974	D	172	218		31	49	61		1) SÜDDEUTSCHE ZUCKER 2) PFEIFFER & LANGE 3) ZUCKERFAB. FRANCKEN 4) ZUCKERFAB. VELZEN
079	Ordinateurs "General Purpose"	1973	I	170	415	432	56	89	97	100	1) IBM 2) HONEYWELL 3) UNIVAC 4) UNIDATA
080	Aliments pour enfants en général	1973	GB	170	179		34	54	70		1) H.J. HEINZ 2) GLAXO 3) UNIGATE 4) GERBER

MODELE D'ANALYSE DE LA DOMINANCE SUR LES MARCHES DES PRODUITS

CODE MARCHE PRODUIT	DESCRIPTION MARCHE DU PRODUIT	ANNEES	PAYS	INDICATEURS							ENTREPRISES
				COEFFICIENTS L			RATIOS				
				2L	3L	4L	c_1	c_2	c_3	c_4	
081	T.V. Noir/Blanc	1974	GB	168	198	292	32	51	64	70	1) THORN 2) PHILIPS 3) RANK 4) GENERAL ELECTRIC
082	Antibiotiques	1973	NL	166	362	553	35	56	62	65	1) BEECHAM 2) PFIZER 3) MYCOFARM 4) HOFFMANN-LA ROCHE
083	Entremets	1972	F	165	214		33	53	65		1) GEN.ALIMENTAIRE 2) S.P.M. 3) ANCEL
084	Crèmes glacées	1974	DK	164	211		46	74	91		FRISKO (UNILEVER / PREMIER (BEATRICE FOOD) / EVENTYR
085	Bières	1974	I	162	209	218	29	46	57	66	1) PERONI 2) DREHER (gr. LUCIANI) 3) Gr. WÜHRER 4) PORETTI (gr. BASSETTI)
086	Pâtes alimentaires plats cuisinés	1972	F	161	648		50	81	85		1) IBP (BUITONI-PERUGINA) 2) PANZANI-MILLIAT 3) RIVOIRE-CARRE-LUSTUCRU
087	Mayonnaise (industrie condimentaire)	1972	F	160	191		40	65	82		1) MAYOLANDE 2) LESIEUR 3) GEN.ALIMENTAIRE
088	Conserves de poisson	1972	F	160	200	214	15	24	30	35	
089	Gynécologiques	1973	NL	154	150	316	34	56	76	81	1) ORGANON 2) SCHERING 3) WYETH 4) NOURY PHARMA
090	Chocolaterie, confiserie et biscuiterie	1973	GR	152	143	209	27	45	62	70	1) ION SA 2) LOUMIOIS SA 3) PAVLIDIS SA 4) MELO SA

MODELE D'ANALYSE DE LA DOMINANCE SUR LES MARCHES DES PRODUITS

CODE MARCHE PRODUIT	DESCRIPTION MARCHE DU PRODUIT	ANNEES	PAYS	COEFFICIENTS L			RATIOS				ENTREPRISES
				2L	3L	4L	C_1	C_2	C_3	C_4	
091	Pneumatiques de remplacement	1975	GB	150	135	186	32	47	66	76	1) DUNLOP-PIRELLI 2) GOODYEAR 3) MICHELIN 4) FIRESTONE 5) UNIROYAL 6) AVON
092	Eclairages pour véhicules à moteur	1974	D	150	248	-	45	75	88	-	1) WESTFÄLISCHE METALLINDUSTRIE 2) BOSCH 3) SWF
093	Dermatologiques	1973	NL	150	201	241	18	30	37	42	1) SCHERING 2) CIBA-GEIGY 3) LABAZ-LEDERLE 4) GLAXO
094	Grues industrielles	1973	GB	150	138	-	30	50	70	-	1) CLARK CHAPMAN 2) HERBERT MORRIS 3) DEMAG
095	Aspirateurs de poussière	1974	GB	144	396	-	46	78	85	-	1) HOOVER 2) ELECTROLUX 3) BSR
096	Ordinateurs "General Purpose"	1973	F	144	340	493	46	78	86	91	1) IBM 2) HONEYWELL 3) UNIDATA 4) DIGITAL EQUIPMENT
097	Lait condensé et concentré	1973	GB	144	319	443	49	83	93	99	1) CARNATION 2) NESTLE 3) LIBBY 4) CWS
098	Pâtes alimentaires	1972	F	143	367	647	43	73	80	83	1) PANZANI-MILLIAT 2) RIVOIRE ET CARRE-LUSTUCRU 3) BERTRAND 4) IBP (BUITONI-PERUGINA)
099	Cardio-vasculaires	1973	NL	141	139	161	17	29	40	48	1) MSD 2)SANDOZ 3) ICU 4) ASTRA CHEMIE EN PHARMA
100	Bas pour dames	1973	GB	140	-	-	35	60	-	-	1) COURTAULDS 2) PRETTY POLLY

MODELE D'ANALYSE DE LA DOMINANCE SUR LES MARCHES DES PRODUITS

CODE MARCHE PRODUIT	DESCRIPTION MARCHE DU PRODUIT	ANNEES	PAYS	INDICATEURS							ENTREPRISES
				COEFFICIENTS L			RATIOS				
				2L	3L	4L	C_1	C_2	C_3	C_4	
101	Batteries de rem-placement	1972	I	136	223	227	30	52	62	72	1) FAR 2) MARELLI 3) VARTA 4) FIAMM
102	Articles de pa-piers et enve-loppes	1974	NL	134	142	137	19	34		58	
103	Conserves végé-tales	1973	GR	133	167	165	4	7	9	11	1) KYKNOS SA 2) SEKOBE SA 3) VEKO SA 4) KOPAÏS SA
104	Batteries pour voitures	1974	D	133	-	-	40	70	-	-	1) BOSCH 2) VARTA
105	Sauces (industrie condimentaire)	1972	F	133			40	70			1) GEN.ALIMENTAIRE (GEN.OCCIDENTALE) 2) SALINS DU MIDI (GEN.OCCIDENTALE - CIE DU NORD)
106	Sucre	1973	I	132	198		33	58	71		1) ERIDANIA (MONTI) 2) ITALIANA ZUCCHERI (MONTESI) 3) AIE (MARALDI)
107	Aliments pour en-fants en général	1974	D	131	212	257	42	74	89	100	1) HIPP-WERK 2) ALLGÄUER ALPENMILCH (NESTLE) 3) MAIZENA (C.P.C. USA) 4) GLÜCKS KLEE (CARNATION) SA
108	Industrie du lait	1973	GR	130	371	392	18	31	35	37	1) EVGA SA 2) DELTA SA 3) RODOPI SA 4) DODONI SA
109	Farines	1973	GB	129	182		45	80	100		1) ASSOCIATED BISCUITS MANUFACT. 2) UNITED BISCUITS 3) NABISCO
110	Margarine	1974	DK	127	129	252	28	50	70	76	UNILEVER / ALFA / FDB / IRMA

CODE MARCHE PRODUIT	DESCRIPTION MARCHE DU PRODUIT	ANNEES	PAYS	COEFFICIENTS L			RATIOS				ENTREPRISES
				2L	3L	4L	c_1	c_2	c_3	c_4	
111	Spasmolitiques	1973	NL	125	146	161	20	36		58	1) BROCADES 2) HOFFMANN-LA ROCHE 3) PHILIPS DUPHAR 4) BOEHRINGER
112	Bières	1974	GB	125	131	140	20	36	50	62	1) BASS CHARRINGTON 2) ALLIED BREWERIES 3) GRAND METROPOLITAN (WATNEY) 4) WHITBREAD
113	Potages déshydratés	1972	F	125			40	72			1) SOPAD (NESTLE) 2) SPM (CPC) 3) LIEBIG (BROOKE-BOND) 4) ASTRA-CALVE (UNILEVER)
114	Fils à tricoter (de laine)	1974	F	124	-	-	31	56	-	-	1) LAINIERE DE ROUBAIX 2) FILS DE L. MULLIEZ
115	Conserves de viande	1973	GB	123			27	49			1) BROOKE BOND LIEBIG 2) SPILLERS 3) MARKS & SPENCER
116	Moissonneuses - batteuses	1972) 1974)	GB	122	120	197	28	51	73	82	1) NEW HOLLAND 2) CLAAS 3) MASSEY FERGUSON } 1) CLAAS 2) NEW HOLLAND 3)MASSEY FERGUSON } 4) JOHN DEERE
117	Radiateurs	1973) 1974) 1975)	GB	122	127	186	22	40	56	64	1) BELLING 2) GEC 3) TUBE INVESTMENTS 4) UNITED GAS
118	Ordinateurs "General Purpose"	1973	GB	120	223	262	30	55	65	73	1) ICL 2) IBM 3) HONEYWELL 4) NCR
119	Produits de la Meunerie	1973	NL	119	-	-	43	79	-	-	1) MANEBA 2) WESSANEN 3) K.S.H. 4) VAN DEN VENNE (WESSANEN)
120	Détergents liquides	1974	GB	117	-	-	27	50	-	-	1) PROCTER & GAMBLE 2) UNILEVER

227

MODELE D'ANALYSE DE LA DOMINANCE SUR LES MARCHES DES PRODUITS

CODE MARCHE PRODUIT	DESCRIPTION MARCHE DU PRODUIT	ANNEES	PAYS	COEFFICIENTS L			RATIOS				ENTREPRISES
				$2L$	$3L$	$4L$	c_1	c_2	c_3	c_4	
121	Cuisinières électriques	1973 1974 1975	GB	117	145	162	28	52	69	83	1) TUBE INVESTMENTS 2) GEC 3) THORN 4) BELLING 1) TUBE INVESTMENTS 2) THORN 3) BELLING 4) GEC 1) THORN 2) TUBE INVESTMENTS 3) BELLING 4) GEC
122	Yoghurt	1972	F	116	139	192	22	41	55	63	1) GERVAIS-DANONE 2) SODIMA-YOPLAIT 3) CHAMBOURCY 4) GAMA NOVA
123	Conserves de viande	1973	GR	115			24	44			1) VOKTAS SA 2) MIMICOS BROS. SA
124	Aliments pour enfants à base de lait	1973	GB	114	166		40	75	95		1) UNIGATE 2) GLAXO 3) J. WYETH
125	Lait condensé	1973	GB	114			40	75			1) CARNATION FOODS 2) NESTLE 3) UNIGATE 4) CADBURY SCHWEPPES
126	Boissons alcoolisées (gin)	1972	F	114	131		33	62	85		1) MARIE BRIZARD 2) SIMON FRERES 3) CDC
127	Papier pour journaux quotidiens	1972	I	113	146	276	35	66	87	94	1) TIMAVO-ARBATAX 2) BURGO 3) S.I.C. 4) CARTIERE RIUNITE DONZELLIE MERIDIONALI (CRDM)
128	Tracteurs agricoles	1972 1973 1974	GB	112	182	214	27	51	61	71	1) FORD 2) MASSEY-FERGUSON 3) DAVID BROWN 4) INTERNATIONAL HARVESTER
129	Carton ondulé et boîtes en carton	1974	NL	112	117	120	21	39		71	
130	Aliments surgélés en général	1974	DK	112	128	235	28	53	73	80	BOUVAIS-PLUMROSE / DYBFROST / IRMA

INDICATEURS

228

MODELE D'ANALYSE DE LA DOMINANCE SUR LES MARCHES DES PRODUITS

CODE MARCHE PRODUIT	DESCRIPTION MARCHE DU PRODUIT	ANNEES	PAYS	INDICATEURS							ENTREPRISES
				COEFFICIENTS L			RATIOS				
				2L	3L	4L	c_1	c_2	c_3	c_4	
131	Carton et papier (à usage sanitaire et ménager)	1974	NL	111	115	235	29	55	79	86	
132	Pneumatiques de première monte	1975	GB	111	109	171	27	52	76	87	1) DUNLOP-PIRELLI 2) GOODYEAR 3) FIRESTONE 4) MICHELIN 5) UNIROYAL 6) AVON
133	Papier pour journaux quotidiens et presse périodique	1972	I	110	174	256	32	61	76	84	1) TIMAVO-ARBATAX 2) BURGO ET FILIALES 3) MARZA-BOTTO 4) ASCOLI ET VALCERUSO
134	Café en grain	1974	D	110	156	120	22	42	54	66	1) JACOBS 2) TCHIBO 3) EDUSCHO 4) HAG
135	Aliments surgelés et congelés	1973	IRL	109	308		46	88	98		1) BIRD'S EYE (UNILEVER) 2) FINDUS (NESTLE) 3) FRIONOR
136	Sucre	1972	F	108	106		27	52	77		1) BEGHIN-SAY 2) GENERALE SUCRIERE 3) SUCRE-UNION
137	Pneumatiques de remplacement pour voitures	1974	I	107	139	209	25	48	64	72	1) MICHELIN 2) PIRELLI 3) CEAT 4) FIRESTONE 5) CONTINENTAL 6) UNIROYAL 7) KLEBER-COLOMBES 8) METZELER
138	Motocycles	1974	D	107	111	153	30	58	84	99	1) BMW 2) HERKULES 3) ZÜNDAPP 4) KREIDLER
139	Conserves de viande	1974	DK	107	278	296	32	62	70	78	1) JAKA 2) PLUMROSE 3) DAK 4) FAABORG
140	Crèmes glacées	1973	GB	105			43	84			1) J. LYONS 2) T. WALLS (UNILEVER)

MODELE D'ANALYSE DE LA DOMINANCE SUR LES MARCHES DES PRODUITS

CODE MARCHE PRODUIT	DESCRIPTION MARCHE DU PRODUIT	ANNEES	PAYS	INDICATEURS							ENTREPRISES
				COEFFICIENTS L			RATIOS				
				2L	3L	4L	C_1	C_2	C_3	C_4	
141	Céréales en flocons	1972	GB	105	363	427	39	78	85	92	1) KELLOGG 2) WEETABIX 3) NABISCO 4) QUAKER OATS
142	Tracteurs agricoles	1972	D	105	142	179	21	41	54	63	1) INTERNATIONAL HARVESTER 2) KLÖCKNER-HUMBOLDT-DEUTZ 3) FENDT 4) MASSEY FERGUSON
143	Conserves de fruits au sirop	1972	F	104	187	-	26	51	62	-	1) ROUSSILLON-ALIMENTAIRE 2) CONSERVES GARD 3) LENZBOURG
144	Fils à coudre	1972	GB	103	-	-	38	75	-	-	1) COATS-PATON 2) TOOTAL
145	Crèmes glacées	1972	F	103	210	231	33	65	77	88	1) ORTIZ 2) FRANCE GLACES 3) MOTTA 4) STE CREMIERE NANTAISE
146	Conserves de champignons	1972	F	103	117	-	29	55	77	-	1) EUROCONSERVES 2) CHAMPI-FRANCE 3) BLANCHAUD
147	Biscuits	1973	GR	102	-	-	17	34	-	-	1) PAPADOPOULOS E.P. SA 2) ALLATINI SA
148	Poudres synthétiques	1974	GB	100	-	-	47	94	-	-	1) PROCTER AND GAMBLE 2) UNILEVER
149	Aliments surgelés en général	1976	IRL	100	208	-	44	84	99	-	1) FINDUS (NESTLE) 2) BIRD'S EYE (UNILEVER 3) IMPERIAL GREEN ISLE
150	Pneumatiques de première monte pour voitures	1973	I	100	142	-	34	68	89	-	1) MICHELIN 2) PIRELLI 3) CEAT

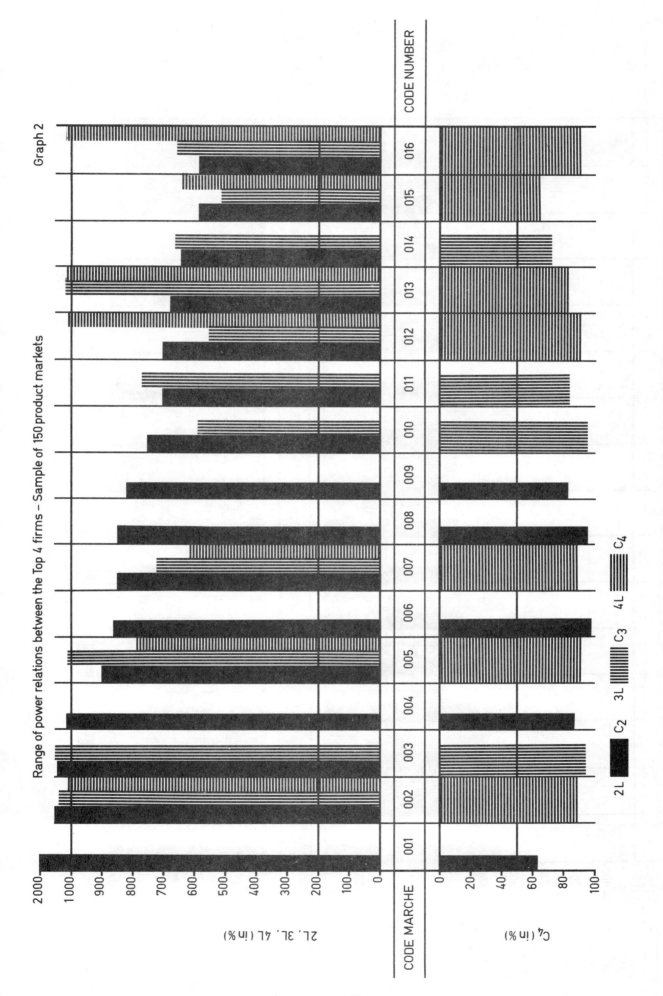

Graph 2

Range of power relations between the Top 4 firms – Sample of 150 product markets

231

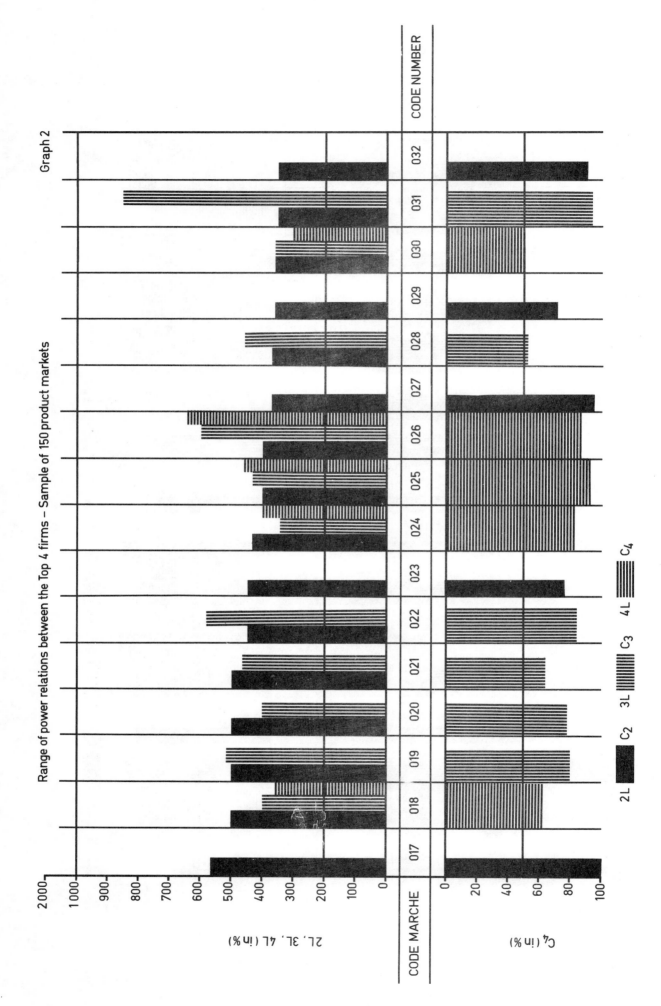

Graph 2

Range of power relations between the Top 4 firms – Sample of 150 product markets

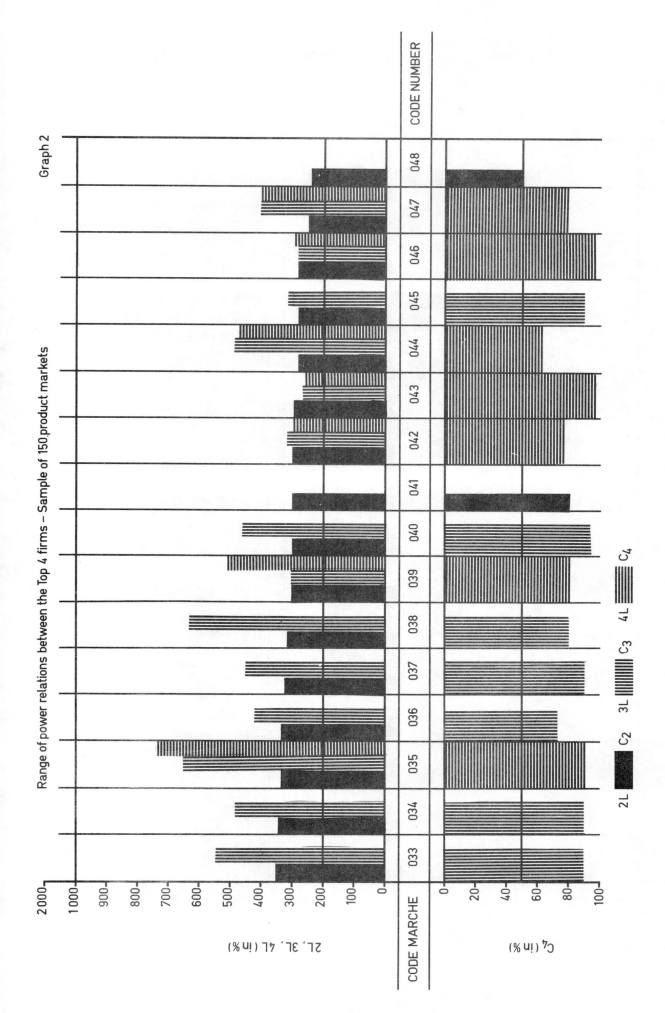

Graph 2

Range of power relations between the Top 4 firms – Sample of 150 product markets

233

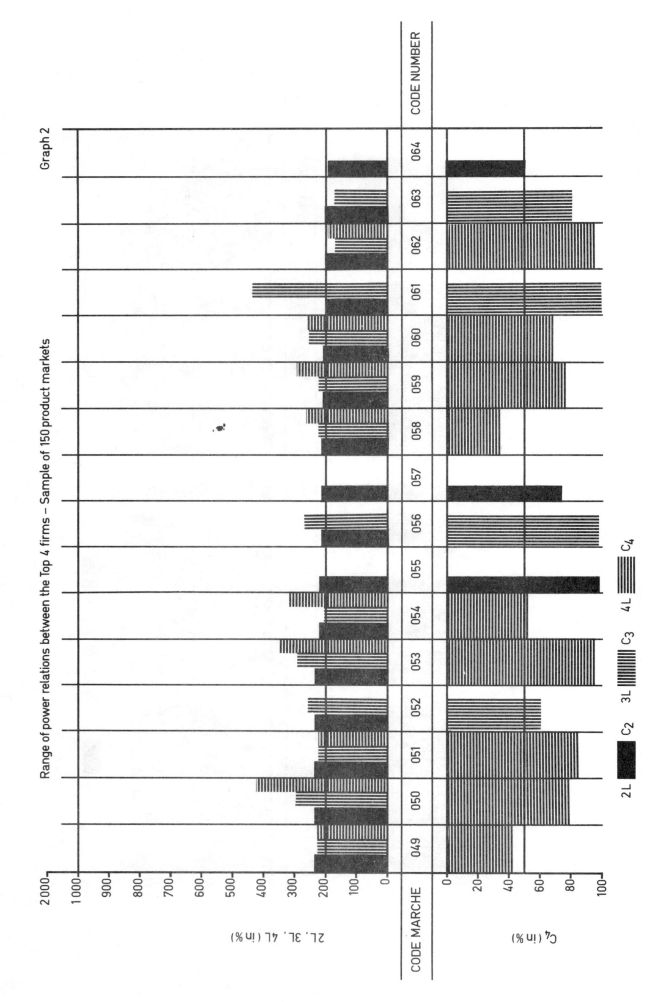

Graph 2

Range of power relations between the Top 4 firms – Sample of 150 product markets

CODE NUMBER

2L   3L   4L   C₄
C₂   C₃

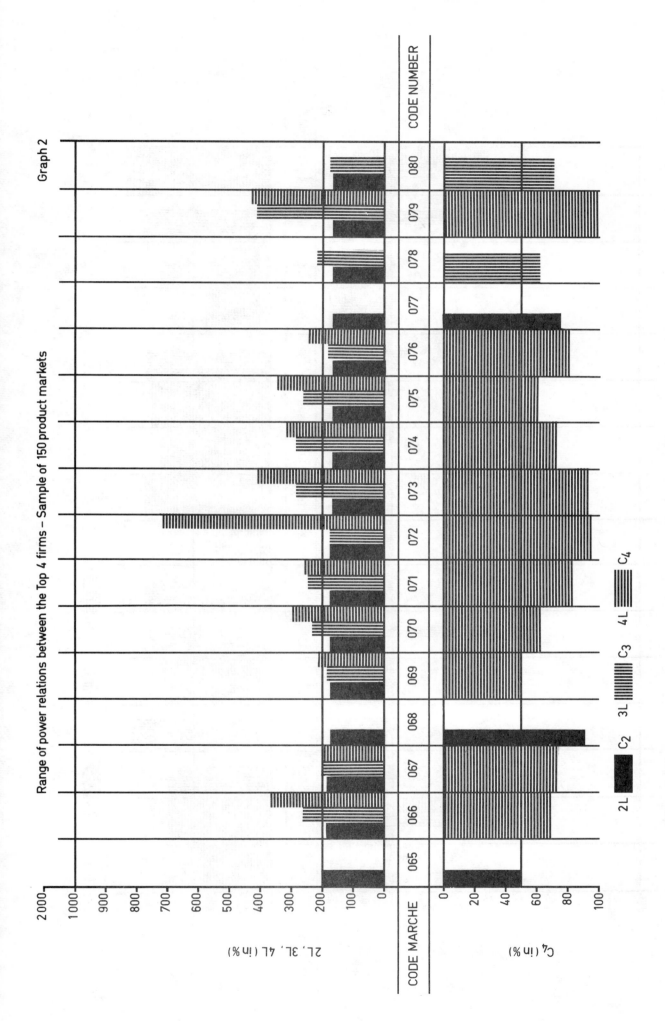

Graph 2

Range of power relations between the Top 4 firms – Sample of 150 product markets

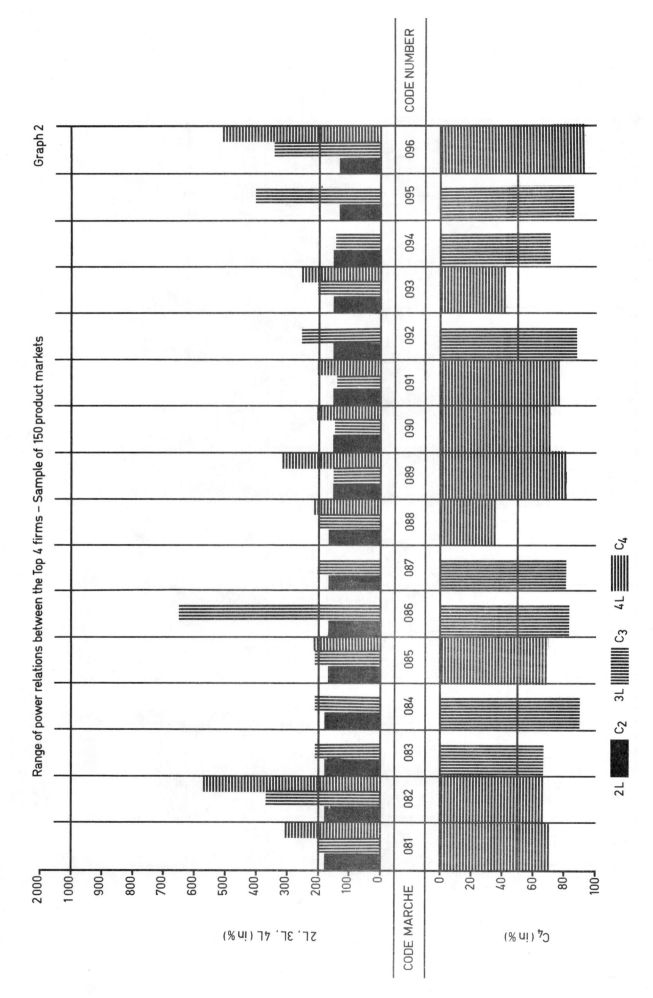

Graph 2

Range of power relations between the Top 4 firms – Sample of 150 product markets

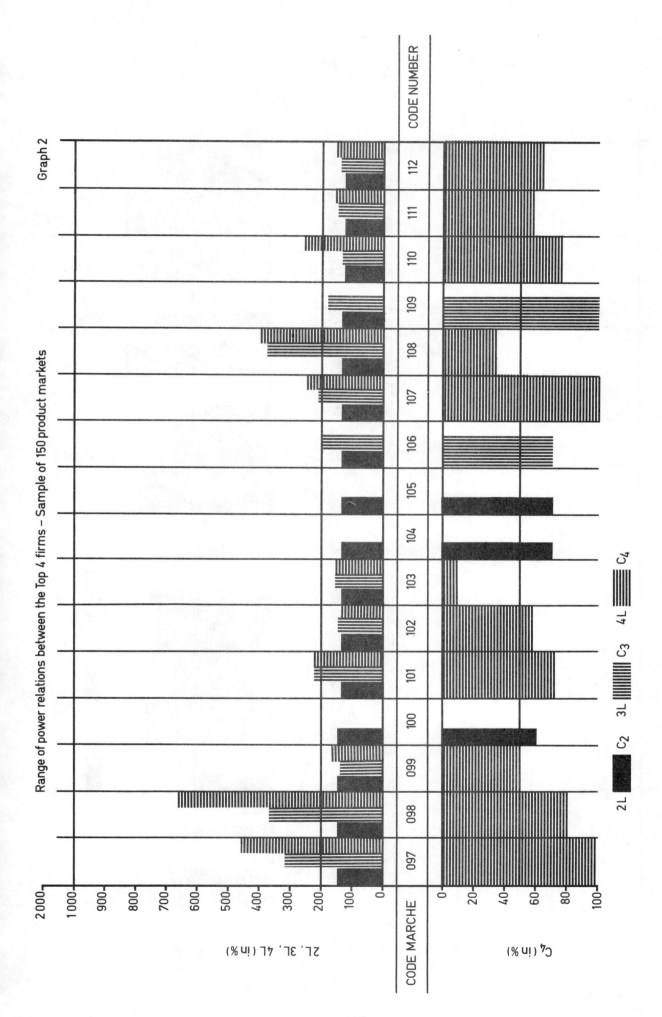

Graph 2

Range of power relations between the Top 4 firms – Sample of 150 product markets

237

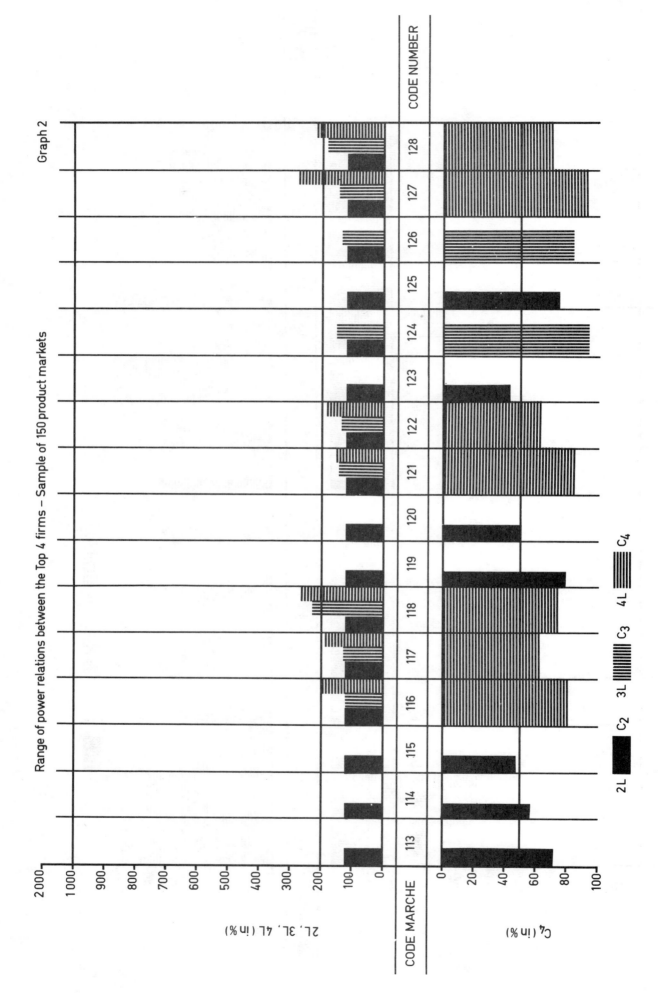

Graph 2

Range of power relations between the Top 4 firms – Sample of 150 product markets

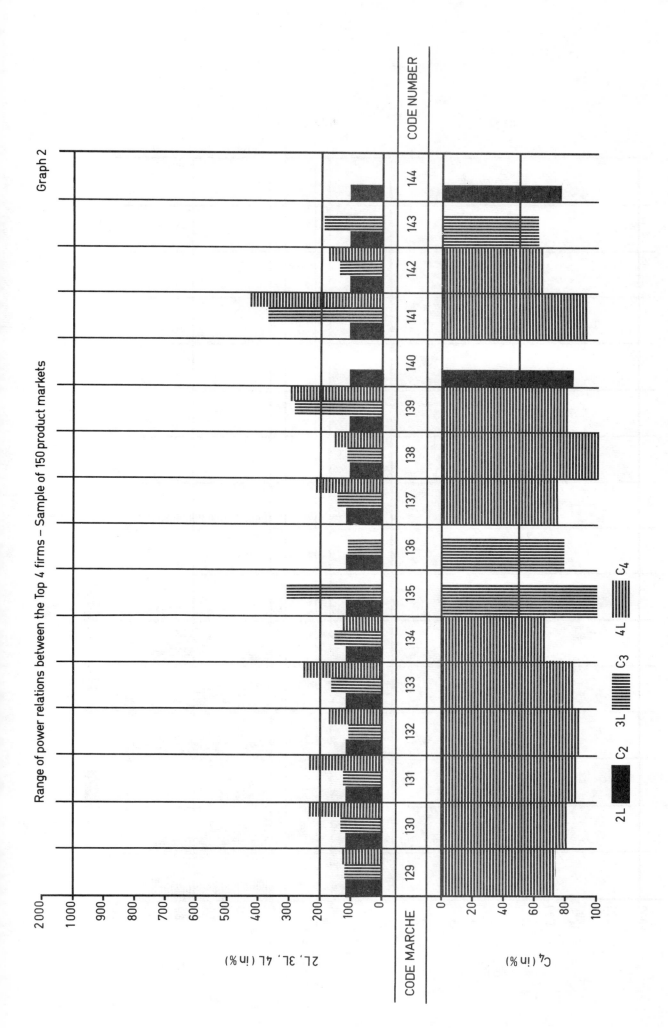

Graph 2

Range of power relations between the Top 4 firms – Sample of 150 product markets

CODE NUMBER

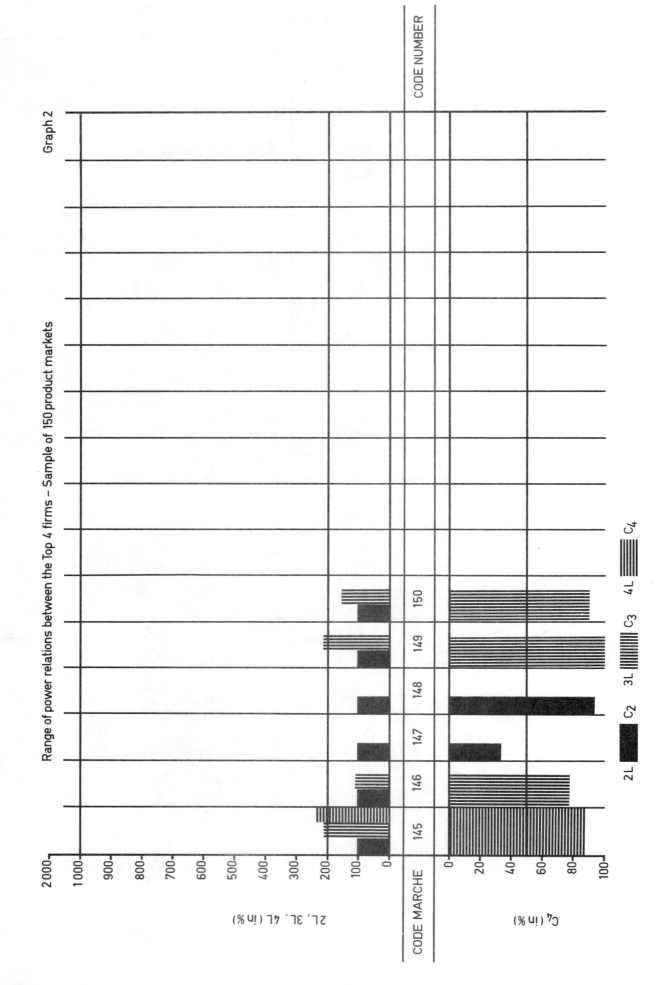

Graph 2

Range of power relations between the Top 4 firms – Sample of 150 product markets

CODE NUMBER

Product code number	Description	Year	Country	Product code number	Description	Year	Country
001	Margarine	1974	F	021	Frozen foods (in general)	1974	D
002	Biscuits	1974	IRL	022	Car batteries	1973	I
C03	Beer	1974	DK	C23	Preserved fish products	1974	GB
004	Coffee substitues (beverages)	1974	D	024	General purpose computers	1972	D
005	Frozen foods (in general)	1973	I	025	Preserved meat products	1973	I
006	Baby foods (rusks and cereals)	1973	GB	C26	Oils and fats in general	1974	D
007	Adhesives	1974	NL	027	Condensed milk	1972	F
008	Confectionery (chewing gum)	1972	F	028	Fresh cheeses	1972	F
009	Aniseed-based aperitifs (beverages)	1974	F	029	Mustard	1972	F
010	Sparkingplugs	1973	I	030	Oils and fats in general	1973	GR
011	Concentrated milk	1972	D	031	Instant coffee substitues (beverages)	1974	D
012	Soups (stock cubes)	1972	F	032	Milk-based baby foods	1972	F
013	Margarine	73/76	GB	033	Frozen fish	1973	GB
014	Processed cheese	1972	F	034	Frozen foods in general	1973	GB
015	Rusks	1972	F	035	Canned soups	1973	F
016	Milk powder	1973	GB	C36	Beer	1975	F
017	Sugar	1973	DK	037	Canned and bottled baby foods	1973	GB
018	Sedatives and hypnotic drugs	1973	NL	038	Edible oils	1972	F
019	Canned soups	1973	GB	039	Antirheumatic drugs	1972	NL
020	Fresh desserts	1972	F	040	Baby foods in general	1972	F

Product code number	Description	Year	Country	Product code number	Description	Year	Country
041	Yoghurt	1973	IRL	061	Baby foods in general	1974	DK
042	Biscuits	1973	NL	062	Instant coffee	1974	D
043	Black tea	1974	D	063	Dried soupes	1973	GB
044	Psychotherapeutic drugs	1973	NL	064	Alcoholic beverages (calvados)	1972	F
045	Potato-based products	1974	D	065	Pepper (condiments)	1972	F
046	Electric cookers	1973	DK	066	Washing machines	1974	GB
047	Alcoholic beverages (rum)	1972	F	067	Color T.V. sets	1974	GB
048	Fruit and vegetables (as condiments)	1972	F	068	Sugar	1977	GB
049	Hormones	1973	NL	069	Sound reprod.equipm. (other than radio, T.V. sets)	1974	GB
050	Frozen foods in general	1972	F	070	Refrigerators and freezers	1974	GB
051	Combine harvesters	1972	I	071	General purpose computers	1973	NL
052	Condensed milk	1974	D	072	Spa waters (beverages)	1976	F
053	Baby foods, dietary foods	1973	I	073	General purpose computers	1973	B
054	Non-alcoholic beverages in general	1974	F	074	Antidiabetic drugs	1973	NL
055	Soap powder	1972	GB	075	Soft drinks (lemonade etc.)	1976	DK
056	Milk powder	1972	F	076	Diuretic drugs	1973	NL
057	Biscuits	1973	GB	077	Washing machines	1973	DK
058	Milling industry	1973	GR	078	Sugar	1974	D
059	Yoghurt	1974	GB	079	General purpose computers	1973	I
060	Ice cream	1974	D	080	Baby foods in general	1973	GB

Product code number	Description	Year	Country	Product code number	Description	Year	Country
081	Black-and-white T.V. sets	1974	GB	101	Car batteries (replacement market)	1972	I
082	Antibiotics	1973	NL	102	Stationery	1974	NL
083	"Entremets"	1974	F	103	Preserved vegetable products	1973	GR
084	Ice cream	1974	DK	104	Car batteries	1974	D
085	Beer	1974	I	105	Sauces (condiments)	1974	F
086	Pasta (prepared meals)	1972	F	106	Sugar	1973	I
087	Mayonnaise (condiments)	1974	F	107	Baby foods in general	1974	D
088	Preserved fish products	1972	F	108	Milk products	1973	GR
089	Gynaecological drugs	1973	NL	109	Flour	1973	GB
090	Chocolate, confectionery and biscuits	1973	GR	110	Margarine	1974	DK
091	Tyres (replacement market)	1974	GB	111	Spasmolytics	1973	NL
092	Motor vehicles (lighting systems)	1974	D	112	Beer	1974	GB
093	Dermatological drugs	1973	NL	113	Dried soups	1972	F
094	Industrial cranes	1973	GB	114	Knitting garn (wool)	1974	F
095	Vacuum cleaners	1974	GB	115	Preserved meat products	1973	GB
096	General purpose computers	1973	F	116	Combine harvesters	1974	GB
097	Condensed and concentrated milk	1973	GB	117	Radiators	1974	GB
098	Pasta	1972	F	118	General purpose computers	1973	GB
099	Cardio-vascular drugs	1973	NL	119	Milling industry	1973	NL
100	Ladies' stockings	1973	GB	120	Liquid detergents	1974	GB

Product code number	Description	Year	Country	Product code number	Description	Year	Country
121	Electric cookers	1974	GB	136	Sugar	1972	F
122	Yoghurt	1972	F	137	Tyres (replacement market)	1974	I
123	Preserved meat products	1973	GR	138	Motorcycles	1974	D
124	Milk-based baby foods	1973	GB	139	Preserved meat products	1974	DK
125	Condensed milk	1973	GB	140	Ice cream	1973	GB
126	Alcoholic beve-rages (gin)	1974	F	141	Cereals (Flakes)	1972	GB
127	Newsprint paper	1972	I	142	Agricultural tractors	1972	D
128	Agricultural tractors	1974	GB	143	Preserved fruits in in syrup	1972	F
129	Corrugated cardboard and cardboard boxes	1974	NL	144	Threads for needle-work	1972	GB
130	Frozen foods in general	1974	DK	145	Ice cream	1972	F
131	Cardboard, sanitory and household paper	1974	NL	146	Preserved mushrooms	1972	F
132	Tyres (original fit)		GB	147	Biscuits	1973	GR
133	Newsprint and prin-ting paper	1972	I	148	Synthetic powders	1974	GB
134	Coffee in grains	1974	D	149	Frozen foods in general	1976	IRL
135	Frozen and deep-frozen foods	1973	IRL	150	Tyres (original fit - cars)	1973	I

244

TABLE 3

A MODEL OF ECONOMETRIC **X** - RAY OF DOMINANCE AND INEQUALITY STRUCTURE

HYPOTHESIS	2L		3L		4L	
	N° of cases	% of total cases	N° of cases	% of total cases	N° of cases	% of total cases
⩾ 600 %	14	9	12	10	11	14
⩾ 400 %	24	16	30	25	21	27
⩾ 200 %	60	40	70	60	61	78
< 200 %	90	60	48	40	17	22
Total number of cases	150	100	118	100	78	100

HYPOTHESIS	N° of cases	% of total cases
4L > 2L	68	87
4L < 2L	10	13
Total number of cases	78	100
4L > 3L	64	82
4L < 3L	14	18
Total number of cases	78	100
3L > 2L	93	80
3L < 2L	25	20
Total number of cases	118	100

The table 1 (150 product markets) of this Appendix has been carried out
by Mrs. M.A. HAFER, MMrs. M. LEVECQ and G. HOEBANCKX, belonging to the
Staff of the Division "Market Structures" of the Commission, on the
bases of data supplied by the national research Institutes, who carried
out the enquiries on industrial concentration.

APPENDIX TWO

INTERNATIONAL COMPARISONS OF RETAIL PRICES
FOR SOME LARGE CONSUMPTION PRODUCTS

TABLES : 1) INSTANT COFFEE (NESCAFE)

2) TEA

3) KELLOGG'S CORNFLAKES

4) SCHWEPPES, Indian Tonic Water

5) COLA BEVERAGES, small sizes

6) COLA BEVERAGES, large sizes

INTRODUCTORY AND EXPLANATORY REMARKS

This Appendix contains 18 tables, three for each product considered.
The first number indicates the product (1 : Instant coffee ; 2. Tea ;
and so on). The second number of each table refers to its more specific
contents, according to the following code :

1. Degree of local prices dispersion in national currency.

2. Degree of local prices dispersion in european units of account (EUA).

3. Degree of dispersion and international comparison of retail unit prices
   (minimum price recorded = 100).

All tables outline the top 4 maxima retail prices :

- the first maximum, i.e. the highest price registered for the given
  product in the local sample of shops considered for each country ;

- the second, the third and the fourth maximum, which follow the first one ;

- the average price, resulting from the arithmetic mean of all prices
  registerd for the given product in the local sample of shops ;

- the minimum price, that is the cheapest price registered therefore in
  the cheapest shop (within the local sample considered) as regards the
  given product.

By this way a concrete picture of the degree of dispersion existing in each
local sample considered, for each country, is outlined. The last column
outlines the ε_{Rp} (in %) : the coefficient of relative difference (see
n. 1.3.5. of this volume).

Table 1 shows the actual prices recorded by enquiries in national currency,
according to the country considered (new pence in United Kingdom, DM in
Germany, FF in France and so on), while table 2 shows the corresponding
prices in european units of account (E.U.A. = U.C.E. = Unités de comptes
européennes). The conversion rates being indicated, as regards years 1976
and 1977, in Annexe to table 9 of Chapter One.

Both, Tables 1 and 2 show also the sizes, weights and packages considered,
for any given product, and accordingly, the retail unit prices,
from one country to another there exist sometimes slight differences in
weights recorded, in relation to national customs and practices.

As regards Cola beverages, two different sizes have been considered as two different products :

- small sizes (0,25 l ; 0,27 l ; 0,35 l) : product n. 5 ;

- large sizes (1 liter) : product n. 6.

The purpose of Table 3 is to stress international differences in the unit prices for the same identical product. For this reason, the minimum price recorded for the given product is fixed equal to 100, all other prices being therefore related proportionally to this basis. The set of Tables 3 (each for each product considered) gives the series of unit retail selling prices observed at the various surveys in the various countries for the same product, the base (= 100 %) being the lowest price observed in the cheapest country on the date when that price was at its lowest. We thus have a sort of minimum minimorum equal to 100.

It is to be underlined that the differences between international prices are very considerable, especially for tea, which costs in other countries (especially Germany) even 7 times more than in the United Kingdom.

*

*   *

The tables of this Appendix have been carried out according to the methodology developped in the present volume (Chapter One) by Mr. Raphael BUYSE and Mr. Roger VAN HELMONT, belonging to the staff of the Division "Market Structures" of the Commission, on the basis of data collected and elaborated by the National Research Institutes, who carried out the prices enquiries.

RvH/jg

DEGREE OF LOCAL PRICES DISPERSION IN NATIONAL CURRENCY

(FF, DM, New pence, Lit.)

TABLE 1.1.a.

PRODUCT : INSTANT COFFEE   MANUFACTURER : NESTLE

Country	Date of Enquiry	Detailed description of product	Weight/contents Oz.	Gr.	Consumer maximum selling prices — Selling prices I	II	III	IV	Unit prices (Kg.) I	II	III	IV	Minimum Selling prices	Unit (Kg)	Average Selling prices	Unit (Kg)
F (FF)	1.1.76	Café soluble Nescafé lyophilisé Special phyltre		50	5,00	4,80	4,75	4,65	100	96	95	93	3,90	78	4,30	86
	1.7.76				6,85	6,35	6,15	6,13	137	127	123	122	5,10	102	5,82	116
	1.1.77				9,55	9,00	8,25	8,23	191	180	165	164	6,80	136	8,30	166
	1.7.77															
D (DM)	1.1.76	Nescafé gold		200	14,45	13,95	13,78	13,48	72	69	68	67	10,85	54	12,50	62
	1.7.76				18,98	15,98	15,48	14,90	95	80	77	74	10,85	54	13,90	69
	1.1.77				18,48	17,98	17,75	16,95	92	89	88	84	13,49	67	15,60	78
	1.7.77				25,50	22,99	22,95	21,75	127	114	114	108	15,98	79	19,41	97
GB (New pence)	1.1.76	Nescafé, Instant powder	4	113,4	54	47	46,5	42	476	414	410	370	37	326	40,94	361
	1.7.76				67	57,5	57	56	591	507	503	494	51	450	55	485
	1.1.77				86	77	75	73	758	679	661	644	68	600	71,4	630
	1.7.77				140				1234				93	820	119,1	1050

251

DEGREE OF LOCAL PRICES DISPERSION IN NATIONAL CURRENCY

(FF, DM, New pence, Lit.)

PRODUCT : INSTANT COFFEE   MANUFACTURER : NESTLE

Country	Date of Enquiry	Detailed description of product	Weight/contents Oz.	Weight/contents Gr.	Consumer maximum selling prices — Selling prices I	II	III	IV	Unit prices(Kg.) I	II	III	IV	PRICE IN NATIONAL CURRENCY Minimum Selling prices	Minimum Unit (Kg)	Average Selling prices	Average Unit (Kg)
GB (New pence)	1.1.76	Nescafé, Instant powder	8	226,8	85	78	73		375	344	322		73	322	77	339
	1.7.76				125	120	110	108	551	529	485	476	99	436	108	476
	1.1.77				192	150	148	140	846	661	652	617	132	582	141	622
	1.7.77				264				1164				193	851	237	1044
I (Lit)	1.1.76	Nescafé Nestlé (10 buste)		18	400	395	390	380	22220	21940	21660	21110	270	15000	359	19940
	1.7.76				580	510	500	490	32220	28330	27770	27220	390	21660	459	25550
	1.1.77				700	650	630	600	38880	36110	35000	33330	490	27220	561	31160
	1.7.77				850	750	700	680	47220	41660	38880	37770	508	28220	620	34440

RvH/jg

TABLE 1.2.ä.

DEGREE OF LOCAL PRICES DISPERSION IN EUROPEAN UNITS OF ACCOUNT (EUA)

PRODUCT : INSTANT COFFEE   MANUFACTURER : NESTLE   PRICE IN E.U.A.

Country	Date of Enquiry	Detailed description of product	Weight/contents Oz.	Weight/contents Gr.	Consumer maximum selling prices — Selling prices I	II	III	IV	Unit prices (Kg.) I	II	III	IV	Minimum Selling prices	Minimum Unit (Kg)	Average Selling prices	Average Unit (Kg)
F	1.1.76	Café soluble Nescafé lyophilisé Spécial phyltre		50	0,95	0,92	0,91	0,89	19,0	18,4	18,2	17,8	0,74	14,8	0,82	16,4
	1.7.76															
	1.1.77				1,31	1,13	1,10	1,10	26,2	22,6	22,0	22,0	0,91	18,2	1,04	20,8
	1.7.77				1,71	1,61	1,47	1,47	34,2	32,2	29,4	29,4	1,21	24,2	1,49	29,8
D	1.1.76	Nescafé Gold		200	4,76	4,60	4,54	4,44	23,8	23,0	22,7	22,2	3,57	17,8	4,12	20,6
	1.7.76				6,72	5,65	5,48	5,26	33,6	28,2	27,4	26,3	3,84	19,2	4,92	24,6
	1.1.77				7,03	6,70	6,62	6,32	35,1	33,5	33,1	31,6	5,03	25,2	5,81	29,1
	1.7.77				9,71	8,75	8,74	8,28	48,5	43,7	41,4		6,08	30,4	7,39	36,9
GB	1.1.76	Nescafé, Instant powder	4	113,4	0,940	0,820	0,810	0,730	8,2	7,2	7,1	6,4	0,640	5,6	0,712	6,3
	1.7.76				1,090	0,939	0,927	0,912	9,6	8,3	8,2	8,0	0,830	7,3	0,895	7,9
	1.1.77				1,314	1,176	1,146	1,112	11,0	10,3	10,1	9,8	1,040	9,1	1,091	9,6
	1.7.77				0,099				18,5				1,395	12,3	1,790	16,0

TABLE 1.2.b.

DEGREE OF LOCAL PRICES DISPERSION IN EUROPEAN UNITS OF ACCOUNT (EUA)

PRODUCT : INSTANT COFFEE   MANUFACTURER : NESTLE   PRICE IN E.U.A.

Country	Date of Enquiry	Detailed description of product	Weight/contents Oz.	Weight/contents Gr.	Consumer maximum selling prices — Selling prices I	II	III	IV	Unit prices(Kg.) I	II	III	IV	Minimum Selling prices	Minimum Unit (Kg)	Average Selling prices	Average Unit (Kg)
GB	1.1.76	Nescafé, Instant powder	8	226,8	1,48	1,36	1,27		6,5	6,0	5,6		1,27	5,6	1,34	5,9
	1.7.76				2,04	1,95	1,79	1,76	9,0	8,5	7,9	7,8	1,61	7,1	1,76	7,8
	1.1.77				2,93	2,29	2,26	2,14	12,9	10,1	10,0	9,4	2,01	8,9	2,15	9,4
	1.7.77				3,96				17,4				2,89	12,7	3,55	15,7
I	1.1.76	Nescafé Nestlé (10 buste)		18	0,488	0,482	0,476	0,465	27,1	26,7	26,4	25,8	0,330	18,3	0,439	24,3
	1.7.76				0,632	0,555	0,544	0,534	35,1	30,8	30,2	29,6	0,424	23,5	0,500	27,7
	1.1.77				0,710	0,660	0,639	0,609	39,4	39,4	35,5	33,8	0,497	27,6	0,569	31,6
	1.7.77				0,838	0,739	0,690	0,670	46,5	46,6	38,3	37,2	0,501	27,8	0,611	33,9

254

TABLE 1.3.

DEGREE OF DISPERSION AND INTERNATIONAL COMPARISON OF RETAIL UNIT PRICES
PRODUCT : NESCAFE, instant coffee : 100 gr.

Date of Enquiry	Detailed description of product	Country	CONSUMER UNIT PRICE (minimum price = 100 %) (*)						ε_{Rp} (en %) (**)
			Maximum				Average	Minimum	
			I	II	III	IV			
January 1976	Café soluble,Nescafé,50gr	F	343	329	326	319	295	268	28,1
	Nescafé Gold, 200 gr.	D	426	411	406	397	368	318	33,7
	Nescafé Instant powder	GB	148	129	128	115	113	102	45,7
	113,4 gr. et 226,8 gr.	GB	117	107	100	–	105	100 (x)	16,8
	Nescafé Nestlé,10.b.18 gr.	I	486	479	473	461	436	328	48,1
July 1976	Idem	F	n.a.	n.a.	n.a.	n.a.	n.a.	n.a.	74,9
		D	572	481	466	448	419	327	31,3
		GB	164	141	139	137	134	125	26,1
		GB	153	146	134	132	132	121	48,8
		I	597	525	514	504	472	401	
January 1977	Idem	F	395	366	355	354	336	294	34,4
		D	554	539	531	508	468	404	37,1
		GB	186	167	163	158	155	147	26,5
		GB	208	163	160	152	153	143	45,3
		I	634	589	571	544	509	441	42,8
July 1977	Idem	F	546	514	471	470	475	389	40,4
		D	774	698	696	660	589	485	59,5
		GB	295	n.a.	n.a.	n.a.	251	196	50,4
		GB	278	n.a.	n.a.	n.a.	250	203	36,7
		I	742	655	611	594	541	443	67,4

(*) Minimum price = 100. The minimum price corresponds to the lowest price found in any shop in any country among all the surveys carried out in the given period for the given product. As concerns NESCAFE, instant coffee, the lowest price has been registered in the United Kingdom in the enquiry of January 1976. This price represents the basis for the comparisons.

(**) ε_{Rp} is the difference between the maximum price (first maximum) and the minimum price, this difference being divided by the minimum price and expressed in %.
The formula is therefore: $\varepsilon_{Rp} \dfrac{\text{Maximum price} - \text{Minimum price}}{\text{minimum price}} \times 100.$

255

RvH/jg

TABLE 2.1.a.

DEGREE OF LOCAL PRICES DISPERSION IN NATIONAL CURRENCY

(FF, DM, New pence, Lit.)

PRODUCT : TEA MANUFACTURER :

Country	Date of Enquiry	Detailed description of product	Weight/contents Oz. | Gr.	Consumer maximum selling prices Selling prices				Unit prices (100 gr.)				PRICE IN NATIONAL CURRENCY Minimum		Average	
				I	II	III	IV	I	II	III	IV	Selling prices	Unit (100gr)	Selling prices	Unit (100gr)
GB (New pence)	1.1.76	TETLEY tea bags (36 bags)	4 | 113,4	17,5	16,5	15,0		15,43	14,55	13,23		15	13,23	16,4	14,46
	1.7.76			17	16,5	16		14,99	14,55	14,11		16	14,11	16,7	14,73
	1.1.77			27	25,5	25	24	23,80	22,48	22,04	21,16	21,5	18,96	24,5	21,60
	1.7.77			42,5				37,48				34	29,98	38,8	34,22
I (Lit.)	1.1.76	ATI-PILETTI (10 bustine)	17,5	270	255	200	180	1542	1457	1142	1028	170	971	204	1165
	1.7.76			220	200	180	170	1257	1142	1028	971	170	971	181	1034
	1.1.77			250	220	215	200	1428	1257	1228	1142	154	880	204	1165
	1.7.77			300	250	244	240	1714	1428	1394	1371	200	1142	204	1165
D (DM)	1.1.76	TEEFIX (25 Beutel)	43,75	2,68	2,50	2,48	2,45	6,12	5,71	5,67	5,60	190	4,34	2,26	5,16
	1.7.76			2,69	2,50	2,48	2,45	6,15	5,71	5,67	5,60	190	4,34	2,28	5,21
	1.1.77			2,60	2,50	2,48	2,45	5,94	5,71	5,67	5,60	190	4,34	2,24	5,12
	1.7.77			2,99	2,98	2,88	2,79	6,83	6,81	6,37	6,5	225	5,14	2,71	6,19

RvH/jg

TABLE 2.1.b.

DEGREE OF LOCAL PRICES DISPERSION IN NATIONAL CURRENCY

(FF, DM, New pence, Lit.)

PRODUCT : TEA   MANUFACTURER :   PRICE IN NATIONAL CURRENCY

Country	Date of Enquiry	Detailed description of product	Weight/contents Gr.	Consumer maximum selling prices								Minimum		Average	
				Selling prices				Unit prices (100 gr.)				Selling prices	Unit (100gr)	Selling prices	Unit (100gr)
				I	II	III	IV	I	II	III	IV				
DK (DKr)	1.1.76	THE MEDOVA (25 bags)	50	5,40	5,35	5,25	4,95	10,80	10,70	10,50	9,90	3,75	7,50	4,75	9,50
	1.7.76			5,50	5,48	5,45	5,35	11,0	10,96	10,90	10,70	3,75	7,50	4,75	9,50
	1.1.77			5,10	5,00	4,95	4,90	10,20	10,0	9,90	9,80	3,75	7,50	4,75	9,50
	1.7.77														

RvH/jg

TABLE 2.2.a.

DEGREE OF LOCAL PRICES DISPERSION IN EUROPEAN UNITS OF ACCOUNT (EUA)

PRODUCT : TEA   MANUFACTURER :   PRICE IN E.U.A.

Country	Date of Enquiry	Detailed description of product	Weight/contents Oz.	Gr.	Consumer maximum selling prices — Selling prices I	II	III	IV	Unit prices (100 gr.) I	II	III	IV	Minimum Selling prices	Minimum Unit (100gr)	Average Selling prices	Average Unit (100gr)
GB	1.1.76	TETLEY Tea bags (36 bags)	4	113,4	0,3047	0,2873	0,2612		0,2687	0,2533	0,2303		0,2612	0,2303	0,2856	0,2518
	1.7.76				0,2768	0,2686	0,2605		0,2441	0,2369	0,2297		0,2605	0,2297	0,2719	0,2397
	1.1.77				0,4125				0,3638				0,3285	0,2866	0,3744	0,3301
	1.7.77				0,6494				0,5727				0,5195	0,4581	0,5929	0,5228
I	1.1.76	ATI - PILETTI (10 bustine)		17,5	0,3300	0,3117	0,2445	0,2200	1,89	1,78	1,40	1,26	0,2078	1,19	0,2494	1,43
	1.7.76				0,2396	0,2178	0,1960	0,1851	1,37	1,24	1,12	1,06	0,1851	1,06	0,1971	1,13
	1.1.77				0,2538	0,2233	0,2182	0,2030	1,45	1,28	1,25	1,16	0,1563	0,89	0,2070	1,18
	1.7.77				0,2958	0,2465	0,2406	0,2366	1,69	1,41	1,37	1,35	0,1971	1,13	0,2011	1,15
D	1.1.76	TEEFIX (25 beutel)		43,75	0,8838	0,8245	0,8178	0,8080	2,02	1,88	1,87	1,85	0,6266	1,43	0,7453	1,70
	1.7.76				0,9524	0,8852	0,8780	0,8675	2,18	2,02	2,01	1,98	0,6727	1,54	0,8073	1,85
	1.1.77				0,9700	0,9327	0,9252	0,9140	2,22	2,13	2,11	2,09	0,7088	1,62	0,8357	1,91
	1.7.77				1,1389	1,1351	1,0970	1,0628	2,60	2,59	2,51	2,43	0,8571	1,95	1,0323	2,36

258

RvH/jg

TABLE 2.2.b.

DEGREE OF LOCAL PRICES DISPERSION UN EUROPEAN UNITS OF ACCOUNT (EUA)

PRODUCT : TEA   MANUFACTURER :   PRICE IN E.U.A.

Country	Date of Enquiry	Detailed description of product	Weight/contents Oz.	Weight/contents Gr.	Consumer maximum selling prices — Selling prices				Unit prices (100 gr.)				Minimum Selling prices	Minimum Unit Selling prices (100gr)	Average Selling prices	Average Unit Selling prices (100gr)
					I	II	III	IV	I	II	III	IV				
DK	1.1.76	THE MEDOVA (25 bags)		50	0,7526	0,7456	0,7317	0,6899	1,50	1,49	1,46	1,38	0,5226	1,04	0,6620	1,32
	1.7.76				0,8134	0,8104	0,8060	0,7912	1,63	1,62	1,61	1,58	0,5546	1,10	0,7024	1,40
	1.1.77				0,7726	0,7574	0,7499	0,7423	1,55	1,51	1,50	1,48	0,5763	1,15	0,6930	1,39
	1.7.77															

TABLE 2.3.

DEGREE OF DISPERSION AND INTERNATIONAL COMPARISON OF RETAIL UNIT PRICES
PRODUCT : TEA : 100 gr.

Date of Enquiry	Detailed description of product	Country	CONSUMER UNIT PRICE (minimum price = 100 %) (*)						ξR_p (en %) (**)
			Maximum				Average	Minimum	
			I	II	III	IV			
January 1976	TEEFIX, 25 bags, 43,75 gr.	D	925	862	855	851	779	655	41,0
	The Mendova, 25 bags, 50gr.	DK	688	682	670	631	606	478	44,0
	TETLEY, 36 bags, 113,4 gr.	GB	123	116	105	-	115	105	16,6
	ATI PILETTI, 10 bags, 17,5 gr.	I	863	815	639	575	652	543	58,8
July 1976	Idem	D	948	881	871	864	804	670	41,6
		DK	708	706	702	689	612	483	46,6
		GB	106	103	100	-	104	100 (x)	6,3
		I	596	542	488	461	490	461	29,4
January 1977	Idem	D	913	877	870	860	786	667	36,9
		DK	636	623	617	611	592	492	29,12
		GB	150	141	139	133	136	119	25,5
		I	597	525	513	477	487	367	62,4
July 1977	Idem	D	1062	1059	1023	991	963	799	32,9
		DK	n.a.	n.a.	n.a.	n.a.	n.a.	n.a.	
		GB	229				209	183	25,0
		I	690	575	561	552	469	460	49,9

(*) Minimum price = 100. The minimum price corresponds to the lowest price found in any shop in any country among all the surveys carried out in the given period for the given product. As concerns TEA, the lowest price has been registered in the United Kingdom in the enquiry of July 1976. This price represents the basis for the comparisons.

(**) ξR_p is the difference between the maximum price (first maximum) and the minimum price, this difference being divided by the minimum price and expressed in %.
The formula is therefore: $\xi R_p = \dfrac{\text{Maximum price} - \text{Minimum price}}{\text{minimum price}} \times 100.$

260

RvH/jg

TABLE 3.1.

DEGREE OF LOCAL PRICES DISPERSION IN NATIONAL CURRENCY

(FF, DM, New pence, Lit.)

PRODUCT : CORNFLAKES MANUFACTURER : KELLOGG

Country	Date of Enquiry	Detailed description of product	Weight/ contents Gr.	Consumer maximum selling prices								Minimum		Average	
				Selling prices				Unit prices(Kg.)				Selling prices	Unit (Kg)	Selling prices	Unit (Kg)
				I	II	III	IV	I	II	III	IV				
GB (New pence)	1.1.76	Kellogg Cornflakes	375	22,0	21,0	20,5	20,0	58,66	56,0	54,66	53,33	17,0	45,33	20,59	54,90
	1.7.76			25,5	23,5	23,0	22,5	68,00	62,66	61,33	60,00	21,0	56,0	22,20	59,20
	1.1.77			25,5	25,0	24,5	24,0	68,00	66,66	65,33	64,00	23,0	61,33	24,00	64,00
	1.7.77			30,0				80,00				26,0	69,33	28,00	74,00
D (DM)	1.1.76	Kornflakes	340	2,48	2,30	2,29	2,28	7,29	7,76	6,73	6,70	1,18	3,47	2,11	6,20
	1.7.76			2,99	2,88	2,58	2,30	8,79	8,47	7,59	6,76	1,68	4,94	2,20	6,47
	1.1.77			3,05	2,79	2,68	2,59	8,97	8,20	7,88	7,62	1,82	5,35	2,38	7,00
	1.7.77			2,79	2,40	2,39	2,38	8,20	7,05	7,02	7,00	1,39	4,08	2,06	6,06
DK (DKr)	1.1.76	Kellogg Corn- flakes	500	4,95	4,88	4,75	4,69	9,90	9,76	9,50	9,38	3,95	7,90	4,58	9,16
	1.7.76			5,15	4,95	4,88	4,78	10,30	9,90	9,76	9,56	4,25	8,50	4,70	9,40
	1.1.77			5,80	5,15	4,95	4,85	11,60	10,30	9,90	9,70	3,48	6,96	4,62	9,24
	1.7.77														

261

TABLE 3.2.

RvH/jg

DEGREE OF LOCAL PRICES DISPERSION IN EUROPEAN UNITS OF ACCOUNT (EUA)

PRODUCT : CORNFLAKES MANUFACTURER : KELLOGG PRICE IN E.U.A.

Country	Date of Enquiry	Detailed description of product	Weight/contents Gr.	Consumer maximum selling prices — Selling prices I	II	III	IV	Unit prices(Kg.) I	II	III	IV	Minimum Selling prices	Minimum Unit (Kg)	Average Selling prices	Average Unit (Kg)
GB	1.1.76	Kellogg Cornflakes	375	0,3830	0,3656	0,3569	0,3483	1,021	0,975	0,952	0,9288	0,2960	0,789	0,3585	0,956
	1.7.76			0,4151	0,3825	0,3744	0,3663	1,107	1,020	0,998	0,977	0,3419	0,912	0,3614	0,964
	1.1.77			0,3896	0,3820	0,3744	0,3667	1,038	1,018	0,998	0,978	0,3515	0,937	0,3667	0,978
	1.7.77			0,4499				1,200				0,3899	1,039	0,4199	1,120
D	1.1.76	Kornflakes	340	0,8178	0,7585	0,7552	0,7519	2,405	2,230	2,221	2,211	0,3891	1,144	0,6959	2,047
	1.7.76			1,0586	1,0197	0,9135	0,8143	3,114	2,999	2,686	2,395	0,5948	1,749	0,7789	2,290
	1.1.77			1,1379	1,0408	0,9998	0,9663	3,347	3,061	2,940	2,842	0,6790	1,997	0,8879	2,611
	1.7.77			1,0627	0,9142	0,9104	0,9066	3,125	2,689	2,678	2,841	0,5295	1,557	0,7847	2,304
DK	1.1.76	Kellogg Cornflakes	500	0,6890	0,6801	0,6620	0,6537	1,378	1,360	1,324	1,307	0,5505	1,101	0,6383	1,277
	1.7.76			0,7616	0,7320	0,7217	0,7069	1,523	1,464	1,443	1,414	0,6285	1,257	0,6950	1,390
	1.1.77			0,8786	0,7802	0,7499	0,7347	1,757	1,560	1,500	1,469	0,5272	1,054	0,6999	1,400
	1.7.77														

TABLE 3.3.

DEGREE OF DISPERSION AND INTERNATIONAL COMPARISON OF RETAIL UNIT PRICES
PRODUCT : KELLOGG'S CORNFLAKES : 1 kg.

Date of Enquiry	Detailed description of product	Country	CONSUMER UNIT PRICE (minimum price = 100 %) (*)						$\mathcal{E}_{Rp}$ (en %) (**)
			Maximum				Average	Minimum	
			I	II	III	IV			
January 1976	KELLOGG'S Cornflakes D 340 gr. DK 500 gr. GB 375 gr.	D	305	283	281	280	259	145	110,1
		DK	175	172	168	166	162	139	25,3
		GB	129	123	121	118	121	100 (x)	29,4
July 1976	Idem	D	375	361	324	289	276	211	78,0
		DK	184	176	174	170	168	152	21,2
		GB	133	123	120	118	116	110	21,4
January 1977	Idem	D	381	349	335	315	297	227	67,6
		DK	200	178	171	167	159	120	66,7
		GB	118	116	114	111	111	107	10,9
July 1977	Idem	D	353	304	302	301	261	176	100,7
		DK	n.a.	n.a.	n.a.	n.a.	n.a.	n.a.	
		GB	135	n.a.	n.a.	n.a.	126	117	15,4

(*) Minimum price = 100. The minimum price corresponds to the lowest price found in any shop in any country among all the surveys carried out in the given period for the given product. As concerns Kellogg's Cornflakes, the lowest price has been registered in the United Kingdom in the enquiry of January 1976. This price represents the basis for the comparisons.

(**) $\mathcal{E}_{Rp}$ is the difference between the maximum price (first maximum) and the minimum price, divided by the minimum price and expressed in %. The formula is therefore: $\mathcal{E}_{Rp} = \dfrac{\text{Maximum price} - \text{Minimum price}}{\text{minimum price}} \times 100.$

TABLE 4.1.

DEGREE OF LOCAL PRICES DISPERSION IN NATIONAL CURRENCY

(FF, Lit. DM)

PRODUCT : Indian tonic water MANUFACTURER : SCHWEPPES PRICE IN NATIONAL CURRENCY

Country	Date of Enquiry	Detailed description of product	Weight/contents L	Consumer maximum selling prices								Minimum		Average	
				Selling prices				Unit prices (liter)				Selling prices	Unit (liter)	Selling prices	Unit (liter)
				I	II	III	IV	I	II	III	IV				
F (FF)	1.1.76	Schweppes Indian tonic water	0,20	1,083	1,066	1,060	1,050	5,42	5,33	5,30	5,25	0,758	3,79	0,928	4,68
	1.7.76			1,250	1,150	1,083	0,975	6,25	5,75	5,40	4,88	0,792	3,97	0,927	4,63
	1.1.77			1,133	1,033	1,016	1,00	5,67	5,16	5,08	5,00	0,775	3,88	0,930	4,65
	1.7.77														
I (Lit)	1.1.76	Schweppes Indian tonic water	0,18	200	170	153	152	1110	943	849	844	125	694	145	805
	1.7.76			180	163	162	160	999	905	899	888	125	694	151	838
	1.1.77			200	185	180	160	1110	1026	999	888	110	611	154	855
	1.7.77			216	200	180	175	1199	1110	999	971	130	722	171	949
D (DM)	1.1.76	Schweppes Indian tonic water	0,70	1,79	1,70	1,68	1,66	2,56	2,43	2,40	2,37	1,38	1,97	1,53	2,19
	1.7.76			1,79	1,68	1,66	1,59	2,56	2,40	2,37	2,27	1,28	1,83	1,51	2,16
	1.1.77			1,99	1,70	1,69	1,68	2,84	2,43	2,41	2,40	1,38	1,97	1,56	2,23
	1.7.77			2,29	1,79	1,69	1,59	3,27	2,56	2,61	2,27	1,16	1,66	1,53	2,19

RvH/jg

TABLE 4.2.

DEGREE OF LOCAL PRICES DISPERSION IN EUROPEAN UNITS OF ACCOUNT (EUA)

PRODUCT : Indian tonic water   MANUFACTURER : SCHWEPPES   PRICE IN E.U.A.

Country	Date of Enquiry	Detailed description of product	Weight/contents L	Consumer maximum selling prices								Minimum		Average	
				Selling prices				Unit prices (liter)				Selling prices	Unit (liter)	Selling prices	Unit (liter)
				I	II	III	IV	I	II	III	IV				
F	1.1.76	Schweppes Indian tonic water	0,20	0,208	0,204	0,203	0,201	1,040	1,020	1,015	1,005	0,145	0,725	0,178	0,890
	1.7.76														
	1.1.77			0,224	0,206	0,194	0,175	1,120	1,030	0,970	0,875	0,142	0,710	0,166	0,830
	1.7.77			0,203	0,185	0,182	0,179	1,015	0,925	0,910	0,895	0,139	0,695	0,167	0,835
I	1.1.76	Schweppes Indian tonic water	0,18	0,244	0,208	0,187	0,186	1,355	1,155	1,038	1,033	0,153	0,850	0,177	0,983
	1.7.76			0,196	0,177	0,176	0,174	1,088	0,983	0,978	0,967	0,136	0,756	0,164	0,911
	1.1.77			0,203	0,188	0,183	0,162	1,127	1,044	1,017	0,900	0,112	0,622	0,156	0,867
	1.7.77			0,213	0,197	0,177	0,172	1,183	1,094	0,983	0,955	0,128	0,711	0,169	0,939
D	1.1.76	Schweppes Indian tonic water	0,70	0,590	0,561	0,554	0,547	0,842	0,801	0,791	0,781	0,455	0,650	0,504	0,720
	1.7.76			0,633	0,595	0,588	0,563	0,904	0,850	0,840	0,804	0,453	0,647	0,535	0,764
	1.1.77			0,742	0,634	0,630	0,627	1,060	0,905	0,900	0,895	0,515	0,735	0,582	0,831
	1.7.77			0,812	0,682	0,644	0,606	1,160	0,974	0,920	0,865	0,442	0,631	0,583	0,832

TABLE 4.3.

DEGREE OF DISPERSION AND INTERNATIONAL COMPARISON OF RETAIL UNIT PRICES

PRODUCT : SCHWEPPES, Indian Tonic Water : 1 Liter

Date of Enquiry	Detailed description of product	Country	CONSUMER UNIT PRICE (minimum price = 100 %) (*)						ξ_{Rp} (en %) (**)
			Maximum				Average	Minimum	
			I	II	III	IV			
January 1976	Schweppes, Indian tonic water D 0,70 L. F C,20 L. I 0,18 L.	D	151	144	142	140	129	117	29,6
		F	186	184	182	181	160	130	42,9
		I	244	207	187	185	177	152	60,1
July 1976	Idem	D	155	145	143	137	130	111	39,8
		F	n.a.	n.a.	n.a.	n.a.	n.a.	n.a.	
		I	186	168	167	165	156	129	44,0
January 1977	Idem	D	171	168	146	144	134	119	44,2
		F	181	166	157	141	134	115	57,8
		I	182	168	164	146	140	100 (x)	81,9
July 1977	Idem	D	199	156	147	138	133	101	97,4
		F	163	148	144	144	133	111	46,2
		I	170	175	158	153	150	114	49,6

(*) Minimum price = 100. The minimum price corresponds to the lowest price found in any shop in any country among all the surveys carried out in the given period for the given product. As concerns SCHWEPPES, the lowest price has been registered in Italy in the enquiry of January 1977. This price represents the basis for the comparisons.

(**) ξ_{Rp} is the difference between the maximum price (first maximum) and the minimum price, this difference being divided by the minimum price and expressed in %.

The formula is therefore: $\xi_{Rp} \dfrac{\text{Maximum price} - \text{Minimum price}}{\text{minimum price}} \times 100.$

266

RvH/jg

TABLE 5.1.

DEGREE OF LOCAL PRICES DISPERSION IN NATIONAL CURRENCY

(New pence, DM, DKr.)

PRODUCT : COLA (small sizes) MANUFACTURER : COCA-COLA PRICE IN NATIONAL CURRENCY

Country	Date of Enquiry	Detailed description of product	Weight/contents fl. oz	Weight/contents L	Consumer maximum selling prices								Minimum		Average	
					Selling prices				Unit prices (liter)				Selling prices	Unit (liter)	Selling prices	Unit (liter)
					I	II	III	IV	I	II	III	IV				
GB (New pence)	1.1.76	Coca-Cola (can)	11,5	0,27	10,5	9,5	9		38,88	35,18	33,33		9	33,33	9,4	34,81
	1.7.76				10,5	10	9,5	8,5	38,88	37,03	35,18	31,48	8,5	31,48	9,7	35,93
	1.1.77				15	14	13,5	13	55,55	51,85	50,00	48,15	10,5	38,88	12,43	46,04
	1.7.77				15				55,55				10	37,03	12,5	46,30
D (DM)	1.1.76	Coca-Cola (can)		0,35	0,99	0,79	0,70	0,69	2,82	2,26	2,00	1,97	0,39	1,11	0,58	1,66
	1.7.76				0,79	0,70	0,69	0,59	2,26	2,00	1,97	1,69	0,49	1,40	0,54	1,54
	1.1.77				0,79	0,70	0,69	0,59	2,26	2,00	1,97	1,69	0,49	1,40	0,57	1,63
	1.7.77				0,75	0,70	0,59	0,54	2,14	2,00	1,69	1,54	0,45	1,29	0,53	1,51
DK (DKr)	1.1.76	Coca-Cola (can and bottle)		0,25	1,23	1,20	1,18	1,15	4,92	4,80	4,72	4,60	1,04	4,16	1,17	4,68
	1.7.76				1,62	1,60	1,48	1,25	6,48	6,40	5,92	5,00	1,07	4,28	1,23	4,92
	1.1.77				1,60	1,53	1,30	1,29	6,40	6,12	5,20	5,16	1,09	4,36	1,24	4,96
	1.7.77															

267

RvH/jg

TABLE 5.2.

DEGREE OF LOCAL PRICES DISPERSION IN EUROPEAN UNITS OF ACCOUNT (EUA)

PRODUCT : COLA (small sizes)   MANUFACTURER : COCA-COLA   PRICE IN E.U.A.

Country	Date of Enquiry	Detailed description of product	Weight/contents Fl. Oz.	Weight/contents L	Consumer maximum selling prices — Selling prices I	II	III	IV	Unit prices (liter) I	II	III	IV	Minimum Selling prices	Minimum Unit (liter)	Average Selling prices	Average Unit (liter)
GB	1.1.76	Coca-Cola (can)	11,5	0,27	0,1828	0,1654	0,1567	0,1567	0,677	0,613	0,580		0,1567	0,580	0,1636	0,605
	1.7.76				0,1709	0,1628	0,1546	0,1383	0,633	0,603	0,573	0,512	0,1383	0,512	0,1579	0,585
	1.1.77				0,2292	0,2139	0,2062	0,1986	0,848	0,792	0,764	0,735	0,1604	0,594	0,1899	0,703
	1.7.77				0,2249				0,832				0,1499	0,555	0,1874	0,694
D	1.1.76	Coca-Cola (can)		0,35	0,3264	0,2605	0,2308	0,2275	0,932	0,744	0,659	0,650	0,1286	0,367	0,1912	0,546
	1.7.76				0,2797	0,2478	0,2443	0,2088	0,799	0,708	0,698	0,597	0,1734	0,495	0,1911	0,546
	1.1.77				0,2947	0,2611	0,2574	0,2201	0,842	0,746	0,735	0,629	0,1828	0,522	0,2126	0,607
	1.7.77				0,2856	0,2666	0,2247	0,2057	0,816	0,761	0,642	0,588	0,1714	0,490	0,2018	0,577
DK	1.1.76	Coca-Cola (can and bottle)		0,25	0,1714	0,1672	0,1644	0,1602	0,686	0,669	0,658	0,641	0,1449	0,580	0,1630	0,6520
	1.7.76				0,2395	0,2366	0,2188	0,1848	0,958	0,946	0,875	0,739	0,1582	0,6328	0,1818	0,7272
	1.1.77				0,2423	0,2317	0,1969	0,1954	0,969	0,927	0,788	0,782	0,1651	0,6604	0,1878	0,7512
	1.7.77															

TABLE 5.3.

DEGREE OF DISPERSION AND INTERNATIONAL COMPARISON OF RETAIL UNIT PRICES
PRODUCT : COCA COLA (small sizes) : 1 liter

Date of Enquiry	Detailed description of product	Country	CONSUMER UNIT PRICE (minimum price = 100 %) (*)						ε_{R_p} (en %) (**)
			Maximum				Average	Minimum	
			I	II	III	IV			
January 1976	COCA COLA D 0,35 l DK 0,25 l GB fl.oz.11,5 (0,27 l)	D DK GB	254 187 184	202 182 167	179 179 158	177 175 –	149 177 165	100 (x) 158 158	15,3 18,4 16,8
July 1976	Idem	D DK GB	207 248 164	183 245 156	181 227 148	155 191 133	141 188 151	128 164 133	61,1 51,5 23,6
January 1977	Idem	D DK GB	206 237 208	183 227 194	180 193 187	154 191 236	149 184 172	128 161 145	61,3 46,8 42,9
July 1977	Idem	D DK GB	198 n.a. 265	185 n.a.	156 n.a.	143 n.a.	140 n.a. 221	119 n.a. 177	66,8 50,0

(*) Minimum price = 100. The minimum price corresponds to the lowest price found in any shop in any country among all the surveys carried out in the given period for the given product. As concerns COCA COLA (small sizes) the lowest price has been registered in Germany in the enquiry of January 1976. This price represents the basis for the comparisons.

(**) ε_{Rp} is the difference between the maximum price (first maximum) and the minimum price, this difference being divided by the minimum price and expressed in %.

The formula is therefore: $\varepsilon_{R_p} \dfrac{\text{Maximum price} - \text{Minimum price}}{\text{minimum price}} \times 100.$

RvH/jg

TABLE 6.1.

DEGREE OF LOCAL PRICES DISPERSION IN NATIONAL CURRENCY

(FF, DM, Lit.)

PRODUCT : CCLA (large sizes)   MANUFACTURER : COCA-COLA

Country	Date of Enquiry	Detailed description of product	Weight/contents L	Consumer maximum selling prices								PRICE IN NATIONAL CURRENCY			
				Selling prices				Unit prices (liter)				Minimum		Average	
				I	II	III	IV	I	II	III	IV	Selling prices	Unit (liter)	Selling prices	Unit (liter)
F (FF)	1.1.76	Coca-Cola	1												
	1.7.76														
	1.1.77			2,35	1,80	1,75	1,70					1,30		1,56	
	1.7.77			2,50	2,00	1,75	1,70					1,42		1,73	
D (DM)	1.1.76	Coca-Cola	1	1,48	1,40	1,19	1,12					0,99		1,18	
	1.7.76			1,40	1,12	1,10	0,99					0,99		1,15	
	1.1.77			1,19	1,12	1,00	0,99					0,99		1,09	
	1.7.77			1,12	1,00	0,99	0,79					0,79		0,97	
I (Lit)	1.1.76	Coca-Cola	1	270	265	260	250					190		241	
	1.7.76			300	295	285	280					230		262	
	1.1.77			350	340	330	325					177		279	
	1.7.77			420	410	390	350					273		324	

RvH/jg

TABLE 6.2.

DEGREE OF LOCAL PRICES DISPERSION IN EUROPEAN UNITS OF ACCOUNT (EUA)

PRODUCT : COLA (Large sizes) MANUFACTURER : COCA-COLA

PRICE IN E.U.A.

Country	Date of Enquiry	Detailed description of product	Weight/contents L	Consumer maximum selling prices — Selling prices I	II	III	IV	Unit prices (liter) I	II	III	IV	Minimum Selling prices	Minimum Unit (liter)	Average Selling prices	Average Unit (liter)
F	1.1.76	Coca-Cola	1												
	1.7.76			0,422	0,323	0,314	0,305					0,233		0,280	
	1.1.77			0,448	0,359	0,314	0,305					0,255		0,310	
	1.7.77														
D	1.1.76	Coca-Cola	1	0,488	0,462	0,392	0,369					0,326		0,389	
	1.7.76			0,496	0,397	0,389	0,351					0,351		0,407	
	1.1.77			0,444	0,418	0,373	0,369					0,369		0,407	
	1.7.77			0,427	0,381	0,377	0,301					0,301		0,369	
I	1.1.76	Coca-Cola	1	0,330	0,324	0,318	0,306					0,232		0,295	
	1.7.76			0,326	0,321	0,310	0,305					0,250		0,285	
	1.1.77			0,355	0,345	0,335	0,330					0,180		0,283	
	1.7.77			0,414	0,404	0,385	0,345					0,269		0,319	

DEGREE OF DISPERSION AND INTERNATIONAL COMPARISON OF RETAIL UNIT PRICES

PRODUCT : COCA COLA (large sizes) : 1 liter

TABLE 6.3.

Date of Enquiry	Detailed description of product	Country	CONSUMER UNIT PRICE (minimum price = 100 %) (*)							$\mathcal{E}_{Rp}$ (en %) (**)
			Maximum				Average	Minimum		
			I	II	III	IV				
January 1976	CCCA COLA D 1 liter F 1 liter I 1 liter	D F I	302 n.a. 205	286 n.a. 201	243 n.a. 197	229 n.a. 189	241 n.a. 182	202 n.a. 144		49,5 42,6
July 1976	Idem	D F I	292 n.a. 193	234 n.a. 189	229 n.a. 183	207 n.a. 180	240 n.a. 168	207 n.a. 148		41,4 30,4
January 1977	Idem	D F I	247 235 198	233 180 192	208 175 186	206 170 184	226 156 158	206 130 100 (x)		20,2 80,7 97,8
July 1977	Idem	D F I	236 247 229	210 225 223	208 173 212	166 168 191	204 171 176	166 141 149		41,9 76,0 53,9

(*)   Minimum price = 100. The minimum price corresponds to the lowest price found in any shop in any country among all the surveys carried out in the given period for the given product. As concerns COCA COLA (large sizes), the lowest price has been registered in Italy in the enquiry of January 1977. This price represents the basis for the comparisons.

(**) $\mathcal{E}_{Rp}$ is the difference between the maximum price (first maximum) and the minimum price, this difference being divided by the minimum price and expressed in %.
The formula is therefore: $\mathcal{E}_{Rp} = \dfrac{\text{Maximum price} - \text{Minimum price}}{\text{minimum price}} \times 100.$

Conclusions

The tables reveal that in January 1976 a consumer who was willing to travel to whichever Community country sold a given product at the lowest price would have shopped around as follows:

(i) buying tea and instant coffee, and perhaps also Kellogg's Cornflakes in a British supermarket;

(ii) buying small bottles of Coca Cola and Schweppes Indian Tonic in a German supermarket;

(iii) buying large (1 litre) bottles of Coca Cola in an Italian supermarket.

But he should have been careful to avoid buying tea or instant coffee in Germany, where he would have paid seven times and four times the British prices respectively.

As for the trend of prices between January 1976 and July 1977, prices rose more quickly in the United Kingdom than elsewhere in the Community.

By July 1977, the prices of instant coffee and tea had almost tripled there in the course of no more than a year and a half.

But at the same time the pound declined in value, which cushioned the impact of these price increases for foreign buyers. In other Community countries, however, during the same eighteen-month period, prices were fairly stable as regards tea, Kellogg's Cornflakes, Coca Cola and Schweppes Indian Tonic (the latter even went down in Italy).

In the second half of 1977 the price gap between the United Kingdom and the other countries narrowed (for tea, coffee and Kellogg's Cornflakes).

Even so the use of free market exchange rates for international price comparisons still tends to show that, despite a general pattern of price alignment in the Community, the United Kingdom is still the cheapest country for buyers from other Community countries seeking the products we have analysed.

APPENDIX 3

COMMISSION SCHEME OF "TABLE BY PRODUCT"

It appears useful to conclude the present volume, by preparing a very concise General Scheme of "Table by Product", according to the guidelines set up in the methodology analysed above.

The scheme will be applied to each critical or "relevant" product to be taken into account by each Research Institute, namely :

- canned garden peas, (best quality) (Hero, Hak, Bonduelle, Cassegrain, ...)

- canned soups (Campbell, Unox, ...)

- chicken soup (dry) (Knorr, Royco, Maggi, ...)

- beef tea (tablets) (Maggi, Liebig, Knorr, ...)

- baby foods (strained desserts ; meat and vegetables) (Heinz, Nutricia, Gerber, Fali, Olvarit, ...)

- margarine (miscellaneous ; from plants) (Unilever,...)

- sunflower oil, arachide oil, etc. (Becel,...)

- chocolate bars (Nestlé, Verkade, Lindt, ...)

- breakfast foods (Cornflakes, ricecrisp, etc.)   (Kellogg's, ...)

- sugar

- instant coffee powder (Moccona, Nescafé, Maxwell, Jacobs, ...)

- tea-bags (Ceylon melange, Lipton, Pickwick, ...)

- ice creams (Iglo, Motta, Artic, ...)

- frozen fish fingers (Iglo, Findus, ...)

- frozen garden peas (Iglo,...)

- frozen fried potatces (Iglo, ...)

- other frozen vegetables and fruits

- pilsner beer and export beer(canned, bottled) (Tuborg, Carlsberg, DAB, Kronenbourg, Heineken, Amstel, Guinness,Skol, Stella Artois, ...)

- aperitifs(Ricard, Pernod, Pastis Duval, ...)

- cola drinks (Coca-Cola, Pepsi-Cola, ...)

- tonic waters (Schweppes, Tuborg - Carlsberg, ...)

- mineral waters (Apollinaris, Vittel, Badoit, Perrier, Evian, ...)

As concerns the data to be outlined in the scheme, it is worth noting that :

I) The second, the third and the fourth maxima prices are to be displayed only when their values differ from the first maximum as well as from one another. Thus, it is out of the question to list more than one maximum price at the same level, since one value applies even to the case where several shops apply the same price (or mark-up). So when, for instance, price referring to a given item are identical, only three prices are to be displayed (first maximum only, minimum and average) and obviously these three prices will coincide.

II) The average is the arithmetic mean of prices (or mark-ups), based on all observations available (n) for each given item and it is not therefore only the mean of the maxima values and minimum outlined in "the table".

III) In order to have a complete picture of the structure taken into account, the "tables by product" have to be published and analyzed jointly with table 1 of Chapter One in the present volume.

IV) This "Scheme" represents the final result of the Commission experience up to the end of 1978, based on the enquiries carried out until this date.

This general scheme aims to outline the main results emerging from these enquiries in order to stress the multiple aspects that are relevant for international comparisons of evolution of different prices (and possibly mark-ups).

In order to keep due account of objections formulated by "the professional", the "Scheme" does not specify the names (or the code numbers) of retailers and wholesalers. However the number of shops applying the same retail unit price (or mark-up) for an identical brand, is outlined in parentheses (points 3 and 5 of the Scheme), when this price (or mark-up) coincides with one of the 4 top maxima prices (or mark-ups) or with the minimum price (or mark-up) or with the "most frequent" identical unit price (or mark-up).

Thus, the Scheme represents the sharp "simplification", on the one hand, and the quantitative generall overview, on the other, of the several tables and patterns of analysis displayed in "Chapter Two" of the present methodology. These tables are therefore progressive steps and converging paths aiming to culminate - through a logical and empirical development - in this overall conclusive and dynamic "Scheme".

TABLE 1

COMMISSION SCHEME OF
"TABLE BY PRODUCT"

(according to the guidelines of the present
volume methodology)

PRODUCT : . . . _____

Code number :

Group   :

1. ITEMS CONSIDERED

- Brands and sizes (or weights) taken into account ;

- n = number of observations (number of shops where a given item has been found);

- Date of enquiry : for example :

  1. Jan/Feb.78 ; 2. July/Aug.78 ; 3. Jan/Feb.79 ; 4. July/Aug.79 ;

- List of items (in parentheses the number of observations in each enquiry) :

  - 01 = Brand-size ...   (1.n = ; 2.n = ; ...) ;
  - 02 = Brand-size ...   (1.n = ; 2.n = ; ...) ;

  and so on

  - Own Label (OL) of shop ...   size ...   ;
  - Own Label (OL) of shop ...   size ...   ;

  and so on ;

- Changes in items of the sample

  a) New items :

  The following brands (and/or sizes) have been found in following shops
  in more recent surveys :

  - item 01 in shops ...   since ...
  - item 02 in shops ...   since ...

  and so on ;

  b) Items no longer sold :

  The following brands (and/or sizes) have been dropped by the following
  shops during the period under survey :

  - item 01 in shops ...   since ...
  - item 02 in shops ...   since ...

  and so on.

2. LOCAL PRICE DISPERSION IN THE PERIOD UNDER SURVEY

(for instance : 1. Jan/Feb.78 ; 2.July/Aug.78 ; and so on)

Date of enqui-ry	Item (brand and size)	n	Measures of dispersion (1)			Item (brand and size)	n	Measures of dispersion (1)		
			εR_p	SD	V			εR_p	SD	V
1.	01					02				
2.	"					"				
3.	"					"				
.										
.										
.										

and so on.

3. EVOLUTION OF RETAIL UNIT PRICE (2)

(for instance : 1. Jan/Feb.78 ; 2. July/Aug.78 ; and so on)

Date of enqui-ry	Item (brand and size)	Maximum unit price				Minimum	average	Most frequent	n
		I	II	III	IV	Unit	price		
1.	01	( )	( )	( )	( )	( )		( )	
2.	"	( )	( )	( )	( )	( )		( )	
3.	"	( )	( )	( )	( )	( )		( )	
.									
.									
.									

4. EVOLUTION OF UNIT PRICE PAID BY RETAILER (BUYING UNIT PRICE)

See the Scheme under point 3.

5. EVOLUTION OF RETAILERS MARK-UPS (3)

(for instance : 1. Jan/Feb.78 ; 2. July/Aug. 78 ; and so on)

Date of enqui-ry	Item (brand and size)	Maximum mark-up				Minimum	Average	Most frequent	n
		I	II	III	IV	Mark - up			
1.	01	( )	( )	( )	( )	( )		( )	
2.	"	( )	( )	( )	( )	( )		( )	
3.	"	( )	( )	( )	( )	( )		( )	
.									
.									
.									

6. EVOLUTION OF MANUFACTURERS' UNIT PRICE (4)

Date consi-dered	Item (brand and size)	Name of Manufac-turer	Official or cata-logue price	Maxima Discounts	Minima Price	Product	
				Possible		Home prod.	Impor-ted
...	01						
...	"						
...	"						
...	"						
...	"						
...	"						

7. INCIDENCE OF TAXES AND DUTIES

The rates of value added tax (VAT), of customs duties and of all other taxes
- for a given product - will be displayed. The difference of tax burden between
home-produced products and imported ones will be outlined. A break-down of the
tax burden according to the stage of economic circuit (production, wholesaling,
retailing) might be very helpful.

8. ECONOMIC OBSERVATIONS COMMENTARIES AND OVERALL CONCLUSIONS

This aspect of the "SCHEME" will be developped as far as possible, in relation to :

- the set of 140 questions analysed in the "Methodology" of Chapter Two, as concerns more particularly the analysis by product ;

- the practices of price fixing carried out by manufacturers, wholesalers, retailers ;

- possible discriminations in pricing carried out by some manufacturers (or wholesalers) to take into account big retailers bargaining power (or "demand power") ;

- the "loss-leader" practices carried out by some retailers ;

- the differences (in retail prices as well as in actual manufacturers'prices) existing between the prices of branded products and the prices of unbranded ones (own labels : OL) ;

- the evolution of market shares, as concerns the more important brands and manufacturers (at the local level, at the national level), having recourse to reasonable criteria of estimation ;

- all other aspects both of conduct and of performances, as concerns the main retailers and manufacturers (and possibly, wholesalers, exporters or importers), in so far as they may be useful for appreciating the evolution :

  (a) of concentration, with reference to producing and distributive structures and systems ;

  (b) of power relations (between manufacturers and retailing enterprises, between big and small enterprises, industrial as well as commercial);

  (c) of competition mechanism (highlighting and qualifying "multiple competition")

(1) Measures of dispersion :

$$\xi Rp \ (in\ \%) = \frac{Maximum\ Price - Minimum\ Price}{Minimum\ Price} \times 100$$

SD = Standard Deviation.

V = Variation Coefficient, i. e. Standard Deviation divided by
average unit price.

(2) The top 4 maximum unit prices will be indicated in national currency by
decreasing order. By definition : 1st MAX > 2nd MAX > 3rd MAX > 4th MAX.
When unit prices are uniform, the 2nd, 3rd and 4th MAX will be not displayed.
In this case only 3 prices will be outlined : 1st MAX = MINIMUM = AVERAGE.
In parentheses will be displayed the number of shops applying the same identical
price for a same identical item, when this number is equal or superior to 2.
It is noteworthy that the AVERAGE PRICE is the arithmetic mean of all unit
prices observed for a given identical item in all shops where this item was
actually available (n prices, the n being the number of observations outlined
in last column of the table). (*)

(3) See note 2. Mark-up is defined as the percentage of the buying price added
by a retailer for fixing his retail (or selling) price.

(4) The scheme of this point may be changed by each Institute in order to take
into account the information actually available.
It is essential to try to stress the maximum difference that might exist
between official prices and actual prices allowed by manufacturers
(or wholesalers) to the big retailers.
Quantitative remarks to be inserted in point 8. of the "scheme", will help
in appreciating the role played by   manufacturers' pricing in the
evolution of the competition mechanism.

IMPORTANT REMARK

The present "Scheme" has to be published and analysed jointly with the basis Table 1
of Chapter One (of the present methodological volume), outlining all detailed
data by sales points (shops) and products. The latter one (Table 1, Chapter One)
reproduces therefore the data emerging directly from the surveys with the addition :

I) Of the type of pricing (1 : usual product price ; 2 : a special offer in the
context of an advertising campaign ; 3 : undefined pricing pattern).

II) Of the buying prices (paid by the retailer) and of the retailer mark-up,
the latter   being generally roughly estimated on the basis of several
sources of information.

III) Of the name and nationality of the actual manufacturer for any given item,
as well as of the origin of this item (home produced, imported, mixed,
undefinable).

(*) In some cases there will be displayed not only the 1st "most frequent price",
but also the 2nd and the 3rd "most frequent prices".

EXAMPLE OF A "TABLE BY PRODUCT"
AS PROPOSED BY THE EUROPEAN COMMISSION
FOR THE PRODUCT: CANNED GARDEN PEAS, VERY FINE

by Hugo Smies

Foundation for Economic Research
of the University of Amsterdam

1. ITEMS CONSIDERED

1.1 Item List

A number of 20 items was taken into account at the surveys which were carried out in Amsterdam in February and August 1978. Table 1.1 shows these items.

Table 1.1   Items Considered

Code number	Description			Number of observations	
				1.	2.
600101	Hero	tin can,	560 gr.	10	10
02	Hero	,, ,	270 gr.	9	14
03	Hak	glass,	470 gr.	10	17
04	Hak	,, ,	230 gr.	7	15
05	Veluco	tin can,	550 gr.	4	5
06	Bonduelle	,, ,	560 gr.	3	2
07	Bonduelle	,, ,	280 gr.	2	3
08	Maribel	,, ,	560 gr.	2	6
09	Maribel	,, ,	280 gr.	3	4
10	Daucy	,, ,	560 gr.	-	-
11	OL AH	,, ,	570 gr.	2	1
12	OL AH	,, ,	280 gr.	2	0
13	OL V&D	glass,	470 gr.	1	1
14	OL A&O	tin can,	650 gr.	0	1
15	OL Centra	,, ,	600 gr.	0	2
16	OL De Gruyter	,, ,	650 gr.	2	2
17	OL De Gruyter	,, ,	270 gr.	2	2
18	OL Végé	,, ,	530 gr.	1	1
19	OL 4=6	,, ,	560 gr.	1	1
20	OL Vivo	,, ,	530 gr.	1	1

1.: February 1978

2.: August 1978

Region: Amsterdam, the Netherlands

1.2 Brands/sizes appeared

The item list was made up in February 1978 as a result of the first survey which was a pilot enquiry.

The following observations, which were not in the first survey, appeared in August 1978.

Table 1.2 Items appeared between February and August 1978

Item	Shops
01	6, 20, 29
02	2, 6, 11, 14, 20, 26, 19
03	3, 6, 13, 20, 25, 26, 27, 28, 31, 32
04	6, 11, 13, 19, 20, 25, 28, 32
05	1
07	3
08	8, 17, 21, 28, 32
09	8, 11, 17
14	19
15	13, 22
19	20

1.3 Brands/sizes disappeared

The following observations from the first survey at February 1978 did not appear in the survey of August 1978.

Table 1.3 Items disappeared between February and August 1978

Item	Shops
01	2, 23, 27
02	21, 22
03	19, 23, 30
06	13
08	16
09	6, 22
11	4
12	3, 4
19	28

2. LOCAL PRICE DISPERSION

Table 2.1 shows some measures of price dispersion calculated for the observations of each item over all sales points. In the colum marked 'n' the number of shops in which the item has been found is shown.

The given figures under ER_p are calculated with the formula:

$$ER_p = \frac{\text{max. selling price} - \text{min. selling price}}{\text{min. selling price}} \times 100 \%$$

In the fourth colum the standard deviation is given of the observations of each item
and the last colum shows the variation coëfficient V being:

$$V = \frac{\text{standard deviation}}{\text{average selling price}} \times 100 \ \%$$

Finally all data are shown for the first survey in February 1978 (1.) and the second
survey in August 1978 (2.)

Table 2.1 Local Price Dispersion

Item	n		ER$_p$		σ		V	
	1.	2.	1.	2.	1.	2.	1.	2.
600101	10	10	54	27	70.12	15.30	28.50	6.27
02	9	14	14	32	7.38	9.92	5.13	6.75
03	10	17	56	12	35.19	12.73	13.96	5.05
04	7	15	14	10	7.00	5.27	4.83	3.49
05	4	5	37	43	15.69	16.68	11.37	11.91
06	3	2	40	13	22.88	9.50	14.57	6.01
07	2	3	12	12	6.00	5.66	5.77	5.55
08	2	6	23	39	15.00	22.51	10.42	15.31
09	3	4	11	29	4.50	8.66	4.74	10.31
11	2	1	0	–	–	–	–	–
12	2	0	0	–	–	–	–	–
13	1	1	–	–	–	–	–	–
14	0	1	–	–	–	–	–	–
15	0	2	–	15	–	12.00	–	7.02
16	2	2	0	6	–	5.00	–	3.13
17	2	2	0	0	–	–	–	–
18	1	1	–	–	–	–	–	–
19	1	1	–	–	–	–	–	–
20	1	1	–	–	–	–	–	–

1. = February 1978

2. = August 1978

3. *EVOLUTION OF THE RETAIL UNIT-PRICES*

To get a picture of the retail unit prices and their evolution, table 3.1 has been
made up.
In this table is shown: the date of the enquiry, 1.: February 1978 and 2.: August 1978,
the item number, the four highest retail selling prices, the minimum unit price found,
the average, the price which was most frequently found in shops and the number of
observations n.

289

Between the parentheses the number of shops in which the price that is shown has been found, if equal or more than two. The unit prices have been calculated by:

$$U.P. = \frac{\text{selling price}}{\text{quantity}} \times 1000$$

which gives a price in Dfl. 0,01 per kilogram.

Table 3.1 Evolution of the retail unit prices

Date	Item No.	Maximum				Min.	Average	Most Freq.	n
		I	II	III	IV				
1.	600101	601	455	442	426(4)	391	439	426(4)	10
2.	01	498	462	455	426(6)	391	436	426(6)	10
1.	02	581	574	548(2)	514	511(4)	534	511(4)	9
2.	02	625	603	574	548(6)	511(2)	546	548(6)	14
1.	03	744	563(2)	506(5)	478(2)	478(2)	535	506(5)	10
2.	03	591(4)	527(13)	-	-	527(13)	542	527(13)	17
1.	04	686	643(3)	599(3)	-	599(3)	630	(643(3) 599(3)	7
2.	04	686(6)	647	643(7)	621	621	659	643(7)	15
1.	05	294	252	245	214	214	251	-	4
2.	05	307	261	245	214	214	254	245(2)	5
1.	06	337	266	241	-	241	281	-	3
2.	06	299	266	-	-	266	282	-	2
1.	07	392	349	-	-	349	370	-	2
2.	07	392	349(2)	-	-	349	363	349(2)	3
1.	08	283	230	-	-	230	256	-	2
2.	08	319	299	283	230(2)	212	262	230(2)	6
1.	09	353	349	317	-	317	339	-	3
2.	09	317(3)	246	-		246	299	317(3)	4
1.	11	226(2)	-	-	-	226	266	226(2)	2
2.	11	236	-	-	-	236	236	-	1
1.	12	349(2)	-	-	-	349	349	349(2)	2
2.	12	-	-	-	-	-	-	-	0
1.	13	421	-	-	-	421	421	-	1
2.	13	421	-	-	-	421	421	-	1
1.	14	-	-	-	-	-	-	-	0
2.	14	259	-	-	-	259	259	-	1
1.	15	-	-	-	-	-	-	-	-
2.	15	304	264	-	-	264	284	-	2
1.	16	253(2)	-	-	-	253(2)	253	253(2)	2
2.	16	253	238	-	-	238	245	-	2
1.	17	366(2)	-	-	-	366(2)	366	366(2)	2
2.	17	366(2)	-	-	-	366(2)	366	366(2)	2
1.	18	318	-	-	-	318	318	-	1

Table 3.1 Evolution of the retail unit prices (continued)

Date	Item No.	Maximum				Min.	Average	Most Freq.	n
		I	II	III	IV				
2.	600118	299	–	–	–	299	299	–	1
1.	19	266	–	–	–	266	266	–	1
2.	19	299	–	–	–	299	299	–	1
1.	20	273	–	–	–	273	273	–	1
2.	20	292	–	–	–	292	292	–	1

4. EVOLUTION OF THE BUYING UNIT PRICES

Unfortunately not much can be said or shown about buying prices. Retailers don't give their buying prices, and the prices shown are advised prices by the manufacturers. For 'own labels' no buying prices are available at all. Prices are taken to be the same for every retailer which is not realistic.

As always date 1. is February 1978 and date 2. is August 1978.

Table 4.1 Buying unit prices

Date	Item No.	Buying unit Price	n
1.	600101	320	10
2.	01	298	10
1.	02	430	9
2.	02	396	14
1.	03	409	10
2.	03	409	17
1.	04	487	7
2.	04	500	15
2.	08	223	6
1.	09	204	3

5. EVOLUTION OF MARK-UPS

What has been said about buying prices in paragraph 4. has of course its impact on the structure of mark-ups as shown in table 5.1.

Care has to be taken if conclusions are drawn, the table is far from complete and the picture unrealistic as a result of the assumption of equal buying prices.

The table shows the top four ranking of mark-ups, the minimum mark-up, the average, the most frequently registered one and the total number of observations.

Date 1. is February 1978, date 2. is August 1978.

The mark-ups are calculated as: $\dfrac{\text{selling price} - \text{buying price}}{\text{buying price}} \times 100 \%$

291

Table 5.1 Evolution of mark-ups

Date	Item No.	Maximum				Min.	Average	Most Freq.	n
		I	II	III	IV				
1.	600101	88	42	38	33(4)	22	37	33(4)	10
2.	01	67	55	52	43(6)	31	46	43(6)	10
1.	02	36	34	28	20	19(4)	24	19(4)	9
2.	02	57	52	44	39	19	37	38(6)	14
1.	03	82	38(2)	23(5)	17(2)	17(2)	30	23(5)	10
2.	03	44(4)	29(13)	–	–	29(13)	32	29(13)	17
1.	04	41	32(3)	23(3)	–	23(3)	29	(32(3) 23(3)	7
2.	04	37(6)	29	28(7)	24	24	31	28	15
2.	08	43	34	27	3(2)	‾/– 4	17	3(2)	6
1.	09	73	71	56	–	56	66	–	3

6. ECONOMIC REMARKS, COMMENTARIES AND OVERALL CONCLUSIONS

6.1 Price Level

The average unit price of Canned Garden Peas in February 1978 (all items considered) was Dfl. 4.32 per kilogram and in August 1978 Dfl. 4.59. The total number of observations (n) was 62 in February and 88 in August 1978.

The average unit price of the items, however, varies widely as indicated by the standard-deviation (σ) which was 134.48 in February and 145.79 in August[1])

Another indication for the wide pricing gap between brands is the difference between maximum and minimum average unit price which is 151% in February and 180% in August.

Which are the causes of this non-uniform price-pattern?

A look at table 6.1.1 shows that the large price differences are mainly caused by the

Table 6.1.1 Average unit prices by producers

Manufacturer	Code No.	Average unit price		σ		n	
		Febr. '78	Aug. '78	Febr.	Aug.	Febr.	Aug.
Hero	01 – 02	484	500	65.57	63.76	19	24
Hak	03 – 04	575	597	76.46	63.65	17	32
Other producers	05 – 10	294	285	53.38	48.39	14	20
Own labels	11 – 20	306	300	61.49	55.20	12	12

items of the manufacturers HERO and HAK which have a considerably higher price level than all other items. The strong brand policy of these producers leads to a high price level.

[1]) Standard deviation of the average of all unit prices.

Little price difference can be found between 'other producers' and 'own labels o
distributors', although both in February and August 1978 the price level of
'own labels' is higher than of the 'other producers'.

To take a further look in the structure of prices we will examine items Hero, 560 gr.
(600101) and Hak, 470 gr. (600103) which both have a large number of observations
(see table 1.1, Items considered).

We will consider three types of sales points:

- mutiples (warehouse, supermarket chains),

- buying combines + voluntary chains,

- independents.

Table 6.1.2 Average unit prices of Hak and Hero

Shops	Hero				Hak			
	Febr.		Aug.		Febr.		Aug.	
	Unit price	n	Unit price	n	Unit price	n	Unit price	n
Multiples, wareh.	482	3	426	3	513	4	527	7
Buying comb. etc.	429	5	432	5	566	4	540	5
Independents	401	2	462	2	521	2	522	5
Total	439	10	416	10	535	10	542	17

Taken into account that HERO and HAK are similar brandtypes (strong advertising,
strong brand-policy) it is remarkable that no uniform pricing pattern can be derived
from the table. It might be possible that once we have more surveys done, general
statements can be made.

A comparison of the unit prices of 'own labels' can not be made for the individual
items, because every shop has its own 'own label'. The average unit price of own labels
registered in 'multiples' and 'buying combines etc.' is almost equal, both in
February and August.

6.2 Price Trends

The average price of all items of the product green peas rose with 1,7% in the
period between February and August 1978.

Four items decreased in price:

Hero   560 gr.: -0,7%

Bonduelle 280 gr.: -1,9%

Maribel   280 gr.: -11,8%

Two items didn't change:

OL V&D   470 gr.

OL De Gruyter 270 gr.

Do differences in price variations occur between different types of labels?
It appears that the average price of all manufacturers labels decreased by
-1,1% and the average price of own labels rose by +12%.
However as a result of the higher number of observations of producers labels
the total average is +1,7%.